A Bibliography of
Doctoral Research on the Negro
1933 - 1966

A Bibliography of
Doctoral Research on the Negro
1933 - 1966

Compiled by Earle H. West
Associate Professor of Education
Howard University

XEROX

University Microfilms
A Xerox Company

1969

TABLE OF CONTENTS

INTRODUCTION

This bibliography is intended to serve as a guide to dissertations accepted in American universities during the period 1933-1966. It lists 1,452 dissertations arranged in seven major categories covering every aspect of study relating to the Negro in the United States. It also includes dissertations which deal primarily with the problem of race, as well as those in which race is a variable and not the focus of research. Dissertations concerned primarily with the Negro outside the United States were excluded.

Two major sources have been used in compiling the bibliography: *American Doctoral Dissertations* and *Dissertation Abstracts*. It is believed that these two sources provide virtually definitive coverage of doctoral dissertations accepted by colleges and universities in the United States.

Each entry includes the name of the author, full title of the dissertation, the name of the accepting institution, and the date of completion. This is the only information provided for those dissertations which were found in *American Doctoral Dissertations*. Additional information has been provided for dissertations found in *Dissertation Abstracts*, including a brief annotation and the University Microfilms' order number. The order number appears at the right margin of the last line of each citation. Dissertations cited without an order number are not listed in *Dissertation Abstracts* and presumably are available only from the accepting institution. The author index at the end of this volume also provides references to *Dissertation Abstracts* (volume/issue) and price information for dissertations available from University Microfilms.

The seven major categories and forty sub-categories of the bibliography have been devised to facilitate the search for relevant materials, while avoiding undue narrowness and specialization. Where a dissertation might have been placed in two or more categories, a judgment was made based upon an evaluation of the main thrust of the dissertation.

The compiler expresses appreciation to the administration of Howard University for a university sponsored research grant during 1967-68 which made development of this bibliography possible.

Earle H. West
June 1969

SOCIAL INSTITUTIONS AND CONDITIONS

1. Demography

Beall, John W. *A study of population and capital movements involving the South.* University of Illinois, 1954. Includes analysis of Negro migration.   **9035**

Jahn, Julius A. *Principles and methods of area sampling applied to a survey of employment, housing, and place of residence of white and non-white ethnic groups in Seattle, Washington, from July to October, 1947.* University of Washington, 1949.

Malone, Erwin L. *The phenomenon of increasing uniformity in unrelated areas of the United States: an investigation into industrial and sociological patterns and trends in certain states of the United States, 1870 to 1950.* Columbia University, 1957. Includes racial data.   **20587**

Mayhew, Bruce H., Jr. *Religion and fertility in a Negro ghetto: a study in micro demography.* University of Kentucky, 1966.

Reid, Ira DeA. *The Negro immigrant, his background, characteristics and social adjustment, 1899-1937.* Columbia University, 1939.

Richards, Eugene S. *The effects of the Negro's migration to Southern California since 1920 upon his sociocultural patterns.* University of Southern California, 1941.

Valien, Preston. *Southern Negro internal migration between 1935 and 1940: its direction, distance and demographic effects.* University of Wisconsin, 1947.

Watson, Ora V. *A comparative demographic analysis of two Louisiana cities: Baton Rouge and Shreveport.* Louisiana State University, 1956. Includes racial data.   **17456**

Williams, Dorothy S. *Ecology of Negro communities in Los Angeles County: 1940-1959.* University of Southern California, 1961. Tested hypotheses related to proportion of Negroes in the population and existence of a spatial gradient in Negro distribution outward from central city.   **61-2541**

Willie, Charles V. *Socio-economic and ethnic areas of Syracuse, New York.* Syracuse University, 1957. Data on areas occupied by six ethnic groups analyzed in terms of three major theories of urban organization.   **24139**

2. Religion

Carter, Luther C., Jr. *Negro churches in a southern community.* Yale University, 1955.

Coan, Josephus R. *The expansion of missions of the African Methodist Episcopal Church in South Africa, 1896-1908.* Hartford Seminary Foundation, 1961. An historical study.   **61-5212**

Coleman, John W. *Criteria for evaluating a program of education for professional workers in Oklahoma metropolitan Negro Baptist churches.* Oklahoma A & M University, 1956.

Crawford, Evans E., Jr. *The leadership role of the urban Negro minister.* Boston University Graduate School, 1957. The characteristics, role conceptions and expectations of Chicago Negro Baptist ministers and laymen interpreted by ideal-type sociological theory.   **21938**

Culver, Dwight W. *Negro segregation in the contemporary Methodist church.* Yale University, 1948.

Daniel, Vattel E. *Ritual in Chicago's south side churches for Negroes*. University of Chicago, 1941.

Dillard, James A. *Developing music activities in the Negro church with emphasis especially on the Concord Baptist Church of Christ, Brooklyn, New York*. Columbia University, Teachers College, 1951.

Dorey, Frank D. *The church and segregation in Washington, D.C. and Chicago, Illinois*. University of Chicago, 1951.

Eubanks, John B. *Modern trends in the religion of the American Negro*. University of Chicago, 1948.

Fahey, Frank J. *The sociological analysis of a Negro Catholic parish*. University of Notre Dame, 1959.

Foley, Albert S. *The Catholic Church and the Washington Negro*. University of North Carolina, 1950.

Garman, Harold W. *A theory of responsible action for Boston clergymen in relation to the 1963 march on Washington*. Boston University Graduate School, 1965. Eight criteria for responsible action developed and employed as norms for judging the actions of Boston clergymen.   **65-11244**

Gelman, Martin. *Adat Boyt Moshe – the colored house of Moses: a study of a contemporary Negro religious community and its leader*. University of Pennsylvania, 1965. Study of first colored Jewish community in America.   **66-4614**

Glass, Victor T. *An analysis of the sociological and psychological factors related to the call to Christian service of the Negro Baptist ministers*. Southern Baptist Theological Seminary, 1952.

Harlow, Harold C., Jr. *Racial integration of the YMCA: a study of the closing of certain Negro YMCA's with special reference to the role of religious factors*. Hartford Seminary Foundation, 1961. Case study of 5 YMCA's in which Negro branch had been closed, with emphasis on leaders and the religious factors involved.   **61-4570**

Harr, Wilber C. *The Negro as an American Protestant missionary in Africa*. University of Chicago, 1945.

Harrison, Walter R. *The attitudes of the Negro towards the church*. Cornell University, 1945.

Harte, Thomas J. *Catholic organizations promoting Negro-white relations in the United States*. Catholic University of America, 1947.

Haynes, Leonard L., Jr. *The Negro community in American Protestantism: 1619-1844*. Boston University, 1949.

Hodges, Ruth H. *Materials for a program of creative art activities in the Christian education of children*. New York University, 1965. A handbook for teachers' use in the African Methodist Episcopal Church schools of Atlanta, Georgia.   **66-9480**

Howard, John R. *Becoming a Black Muslim: a study of commitment processes in a deviant political organization*. Stanford University, 1965. The process by which persons first question conventional modes of conduct, then attribute legitimacy to norms found among Black Muslims, the John Birch Society and the American Communist Party.   **66-2569**

Howell, Hazel W. *Black Muslim affiliation as reflected in attitudes and behavior of Negro adolescents with its effect on policies and administrative procedures in schools of two eastern cities, 1961-64.* Columbia University, 1966. Attitudes of Black Muslim students and their effect on school achievement and behavior.   **66-10295**

Jenkins, John J. *The structure and function of the American Negro church in race integration.* Boston University, 1952.

Johnstone, Ronald L. *Militant and conservative community leadership among Negro clergymen.* University of Michigan, 1963. Differentiation between militant, moderate, and conservative types of leadership among clergy.   **64-8178**

Jowers, Joseph B. *Negro Baptists and Methodists in American Protestantism: aspects and trends.* New School for Social Research, 1957.

Kramer, Alfred S. *Patterns of racial inclusion among selected congregations of three Protestant denominations: an analysis of the processes through which congregations of Protestant denominations have included persons of racial and cultural minority groups.* New York University, 1955. Dynamics of social change in churches considering Christian theology, prevailing community patterns, and empirical power relationships.   **13621**

Lawton, Samuel M. *The religious life of South Carolina coastal and Sea Island Negroes.* George Peabody College for Teachers, 1939.

Leonard, Joseph T. *Theology and race relations.* Catholic University of America, 1963. The theological implications of racial discrimination according to Catholic moral theology.   **63-7566**

Lincoln, Charles E. *The Black Muslims in the United States.* Boston University Graduate School, 1960. Examines Muslims as a form of response to prejudice, and reaction of other Negro organizations toward Muslims.   **60-3466**

Loescher, Frank S. *The Protestant church and the Negro.* University of Pennsylvania, 1946.

Mathews, Donald G. *Antislavery, piety, and institutionalism: the slavery controversies in the Methodist Episcopal church, 1780-1844.* Duke University, 1962. A detailed account of attitudes in the Methodist church which led to a split over slavery in 1844.   **64-13179**

Morrow, Ralph E. *The Methodist Episcopal church, the South, and Reconstruction, 1865-1880.* Indiana University, 1954. Discusses efforts to educate Negroes and to make the church racially inclusive. **7535**

Newborn, Captolia D. *Proposals for developing a program of Christian education at William Institutional C.M.E. church.* Columbia University, Teachers College, 1955.

Ohsberg, Harry O. *The race problem and religious education among Baptists in the U.S.A.* University of Pittsburgh, 1964. Official church documents and educational materials expressed commitment to racial justice, giving theological reasons and constitutional and legal reasons.   **65-7939**

Onwuachi, Patrick C. *Religious concepts and socio-cultural dynamics of Afro-American religious cults of St. Louis, Missouri.* St. Louis University, 1963. Study of Fahmme Temple of Islam and Culture and Muhammed's Nation of Islam.   **64-4264**

Osborne, William A. *The race problem in the Catholic church in the United States between the time of the second plenary council (1866) and the founding of the Catholic Interracial Council of New York (1934).* Columbia University, 1954. A study of Catholic treatment of the Negro in mission, parish and educational work.   **10273**

Pearson, Colbert H. *A non-denominational program of Christian education for a group of Negro churches serving the Negro community of Englewood, New Jersey.* New York University, 1948. Survey of community factors influencing well-being of Negroes in Englewood, N.J., with recommended ways for churches to render greater service.   **983**

Penetar, Michael P. *The social thought of the Catholic worker on the Negro.* Catholic University of America, 1953.

Perez, Joseph A. *Some effects of the central jurisdiction upon the movement to make the Methodist church an inclusive church.* Boston University Graduate School, 1964. The Negro in Methodism, with emphasis on the role of the Central Jurisdiction, a structure within Methodism that has practiced segregation.   **64-11646**

Pool, Frank K. *The southern Negro in the Methodist Episcopal church.* Duke University, 1939.

Prestwood, Charles M. *Social ideas of Methodist ministers in Alabama since unification.* Boston University Graduate School, 1960. Social ideas of Methodist ministers in the Birmingham area, 1939-60; includes ideology of race relations.   **60-3477**

Richardson, Harry Van B. *The rural Negro church; a study of the rural Negro church in four representative southern counties to determine ministerial adequacy.* Drew Theological Seminary, 1945.

Shockley, Grant S. *Development of the status and in-service education of Negro Methodist accepted supply pastors.* Columbia University, Teachers College, 1953.

Sinclair, George H. *The religious attitudes of forty institutionalized Protestant girls with implications for Christian education: a comparative study.* Hartford Seminary Foundation, 1964. Racial differences were included in this comparative study.   **65-2679**

Thomas, James S. *A study of the social role of the Negro rural pastor in four selected southern areas.* Cornell University, 1954.

Whiting, Albert N. *The United House of Prayer for all people. A case study of a charismatic sect.* American University, 1952.

Wilson, Robert L. *The association of urban social areas in four cities and the institutional characteristics of local churches in five denominations.* Northwestern University, 1958. Criteria for social area classification included social rank, urbanization and segregation.   **58-5794**

Wingeier, Douglas E. *The treatment of Negro-white relations in the curriculum materials of the Methodist church for intermediate youth, 1941-1960.* Boston University Graduate School, 1962. Content analysis to determine the extent to which curriculum materials reflect historical trend of society and church toward racial problems.   **62-4559**

Wogaman, John P. *A strategy for racial desegregation in the Methodist church.* Boston University Graduate School, 1960. Proposes a strategy for achieving racial desegregation in the Methodist church.   **60-3493**

3. Marriage, Family, Child Rearing

Anderson, Mable B. *Child-rearing practices of Negro migrant mothers in three Pennsylvania counties.* Pennsylvania State University, 1965. **65-14731**

Bieber, Toby B. *A comparison study of Negro wed and unwed mothers.* Columbia University, 1963. Personality characteristics rather than maternal dominance found to be indicators of marital resistance. **64-3254**

Blue, John T., Jr. *An empirical study of parent-child relations: matricentrism in the southern family.* American University, 1958. Effects of sex, race and social status on parent who has closer relationship with child. **58-3028**

Borlick, Martha M. *The effects of a parent group discussion program on parental learnings of unwed, expectant Negro adolescent girls from low-income families.* University of Maryland, 1966. Areas assessed include factual knowledge, attitude of self-assurance in parental role, performance during labor and in management of infant at home. **66-9275**

Cash, Eugene, Jr. *A study of Negro-white marriages in the Philadelphia area.* Temple University, 1956. Investigation of nature of social and interpersonal adjustment required in racially mixed marriages. **16371**

Charlton, Huey E. *Stability of the Negro family in a southern community.* Temple University, 1958. Extent of stability of Negro families in Richland County, South Carolina. **58-1976.**

Cox, Oliver C. *Factors affecting the marital status of Negroes in the United States.* University of Chicago, 1939.

Doherty, Rev. Joseph F. *Moral problems of interracial marriage.* Catholic University, 1950.

Farley, Reynolds. *Negro cohort fertility.* University of Chicago, 1965.

Finley, Jarvis M. *Fertility trends and differentials in Seattle.* University of Washington, 1958. Fertility trends, 1940-1950, analyzed by various economic and educational categories and by race. **58-3272.**

Fortune, Hilda O. *A study of the power position of mothers in contemporary Negro family life in New York City.* New York University, 1963. Data on home division of labor and significant decision-making failed to disclose significant differences in the role of the mother of white and Negro families in comparable social classes. **63-6689**

Gillette, Thomas L. *The working mother: a study of the relationship between maternal employment and family structure as influenced by social class and race.* University of North Carolina, 1961. Effects of working mother upon parental division of labor; motives for working or not working differentiated according to social class and race. **61-6108**

Golden, Joseph. *Negro-white marriage in Philadelphia.* University of Pennsylvania, 1951.

Gordon, Joan L. *Some socio-economic aspects of selected Negro families in Savannah, Georgia: with special reference to the effects of occupational stratification on child rearing.* University of Pennsylvania, 1955. Relationships between child-rearing patterns and occupation, home ownership, income, age at marriage, educational attitudes, church affiliation. **11409**

Jacobson, Paul H. *Some statistical patterns of marriage in the U.S.* Columbia University, 1952. Includes racial data. **3894**

Kamii, Constance K. *Socio-economic class differences in the preschool socialization practices of Negro mothers.* University of Michigan, 1965. Concluded that socialization practices rather than value differences are the significant factors underlying inability of lower class children to conform to middle class standards of behavior.   **66-5089**

Karashkevych, Boris. *The postwar fertility of the American Negro.* New York University, 1964. Increased Negro fertility due to higher fertility of married women, shorter birth intervals and great increase in illegitimate births.   **65-6639**

Kean, George G. *A comparative study of Negro and white homeless men.* Yeshiva University, 1965. Social and psychological factors which cause Negro and white men to choose homelessness as a way of life; racial differences included but were of little effect.   **65-8827**

King, Charles E. *Factors making for success or failure in marriage among 466 Negro couples in a southern city.* University of Chicago, 1951.

King, Karl B., Jr. *Comparison of the power structure of the Negro and white family by socioeconomic class.* Florida State University, 1964. Significant racial differences disappeared when socio-economic correlates were applied to comparison.   **64-10587**

Kittrell, Flemmie P. *A study of Negro infant feeding practices in a selected community of North Carolina.* Cornell University, 1936.

Korn, Shirley. *Family dynamics and childhood schizophrenia: a comparison of the family background of the two low socioeconomic minority groups, one with schizophrenic children, the other with rheumatic fever children.* Yeshiva University, 1963. Reported that families with a higher rate of family disorganization had higher proportion of schizophrenic children.   **64-10009**

Lynn, Sister Annella. *Interracial marriages in Washington, D.C., 1940-47.* Catholic University of America, 1954.

McIntyre, Jennie J. *Illegitimacy: a case of stretched values?* Florida State University, 1966. Assessment of marriage by 107 Negro women who had borne illegitimate children.   **66-9075**

Misra, Bhaskar D. *Correlates of males' attitudes towards family planning: a study of the low socio-economic status Negro males of Chicago.* University of Chicago, 1965.

Rydman, Edward J., Jr. *Factors related to family planning among lower-class Negroes.* Ohio State University, 1965. A study of patients in Planned Parenthood clinics who were successful and unsuccessful in avoiding unplanned pregnancy.   **65-13277**

Stodolsky, Susan B. S. *Maternal behavior and language concept formation in Negro pre-school children: an inquiry into process.* University of Chicago, 1966.

Thomas, Paula J. *Sub-cultural differences in sex role preference patterns.* Western Reserve University, 1965. The learning of sex roles in the deprived Negro subculture as distinguished from the white culture and the non-deprived Negro subculture.   **66-3046**

Winslow, Samuel W. *The stability of a selected sample of Negro families in North-Central Philadelphia, Pennsylvania.* Temple University, 1963. A study of factors associated with differences in family stability.   **64-1120**

4. Community Life, Leaders, Organizations

Anderson, Floydelh. *The function of social process in recruiting, training and upgrading volunteer indigenous leadership.* New York University, 1955. A study of the operation of a community workshop program concerned with recruiting and training indigenous leadership for Negro welfare work.   **13643**

Bouquet, Susana. *Acculturation of Puerto Rican children in New York and their attitudes toward Negroes and whites.* Columbia University, 1961. A projective technique used to study differences in attitudes due to race and degree of acculturation.   **62-2037**

Burgess, Margaret E. *The role of the minority community in desegregation: a study of leadership and power in a biracial setting.* University of North Carolina, 1960. A study of power and decision making related to desegregation issues in a minority community.   **60-6977**

Byuarm, Samuel W. *Community action: a case study in racial cleavage.* University of Illinois, 1962. Effectiveness of a community development program in improving community life in a border state community with traditional patterns of racial segregation.   **62-6113**

Caplan, Eleanor K. *Attitude and behavior in a middle class biracial neighborhood: a situational approach to relationship and prediction.* Western Reserve University, 1962.

Carter, Wilmoth. *The Negro main street of a contemporary urban community.* University of Chicago, 1960.

Cartwright, Walter J. *Minority without ethnicity.* University of Texas, 1964.

Claster, Daniel S. *Friendship formation in two adjacent interracial housing projects.* Columbia University, 1961. Effect of group (Negro, white, Puerto Rican), religion and economic status on friendships.   **61-2202**

Douglass, Joseph H. *A sociocultural study of the cape coloured people of South Africa and the American Negro.* Harvard University, 1946.

Gardner, Burleigh B. *Race relationships in a Mississippi community.* Harvard University, 1936.

Gardner, Mary E. B. *The Negro woman: her role as participant in volunteer community activities in Westchester communities.* New York University, 1961. Interracial health, educational and welfare activities; conflicts existed between activities for ethnic groups and activities for the wider community; no interracial social activities.   **62-1397**

Gomillion, Charles G. *Civic democracy in the South.* Ohio State University, 1959. Analysis of status and opportunities of Negroes; emphasis on South, but northern comparisons included.   **60-741**

Gulley, William H. *Relative effectiveness of voluntary associations.* University of North Carolina, 1961. Develops analysis designed to explain difference in effectiveness of Negro and white voluntary associations.   **61-6111**

Hardman, Dale G. *Small town gangs.* University of Illinois, 1964. Comparative study of two white and two Negro gangs.   **65-828**

Hesslink, George K. *Stability and change in a bi-racial northern rural community*. University of Chicago, 1966.

Hill, Mozell C. *The all-Negro society in Oklahoma*. University of Chicago, 1946.

Jay, Florence E. *Those who stay: a sociological study of the stability of a community*. University of Pittsburgh, 1956. A study of the solid core of persons who remain in a community over a period of years; Negroes included in this population.   **18239**

Johnson, Robert B. *The Nature of the minority community: internal structure, reactions, leadership, and action*. Cornell University, 1955. Intensive study of a Negro community in respect to differentiation and stratification; suggests ways to modify social isolation of a minority community.

15018

Kirk, James H. *Kinloch, Missouri: a study of an all-Negro community*. St. Louis University, 1951.

Lee, Carleton L. *Patterns of leadership in race relations: a study of leadership among Negro Americans*. University of Chicago, 1951.

Lewis, Edward S. *The Urban League, a dynamic instrument in social change: a study of the changing role of the New York Urban League, 1910-1960*. New York University, 1961. Historical study using hypothesis that an agency is dynamic to the extent that it is free to evaluate and continually alter its program.   **61-2556**

Lorenzini, August P. *A study of the patterns of communication used by fifty Negro and fifty Spanish-named residents of Phoenix, Arizona*. University of Denver, 1962. Differences in the channels of communication within a group and between groups.   **63-1168**

Milam, Albert T. *Ego-involved judgments and socio-defined sex roles*. University of Oklahoma, 1959. Data reported confirming hypothesis that group norms permit more freedom for feminine role of Negro woman than masculine role of Negro man.   **59-5496**

Morrison, Marshall L., Jr. *Issues vital to Negroes in Tennessee*. University of Tennessee, 1962. Ten Negro leaders ranked issues considered vital to Negroes.   **63-2180**

Mugrauer, Bertha M. M. *A cultural study of ten Negro girls in an alley*. Catholic University, 1951.

Parrish, Charles H., Jr. *The significance of color in the Negro community*. University of Chicago, 1944.

Pitts, Nathan A. *The cooperative movement in Negro communities of North Carolina*. Catholic University of America, 1950.

Sayler, Edward. *Negro minority group strategy as a social movement*. Ohio State University, 1948.

Smith, Charles V. *Social change in certain aspects of adjustment of the Negro in Seattle, Washington*. Washington State University, 1951.

Smothers, Robert L. *Perceptions of social forces influencing the Negro's quest for equality of opportunity*. State University of Iowa, 1964. Differences in perceptions of the role of education in the quest for equality among leadership groups and adult citizens.   **64-11047**

Stephens, Louise C. *The Urban League of Oklahoma City, Oklahoma.* University of Oklahoma, 1957. Historical account of the origin, development and activities of the Oklahoma City Urban League, 1946 to 1957. **24427**

Stone, Edith V. *Personal adjustment in aging in relation to community environment. A study of persons sixty years and over in Carrboro and Chapel Hill, N.C.* University of North Carolina, 1960. Racial variations in effects of social institutions (family, religion, education, economics) on adjustment in aging. **60-4871**

Strickland, Arverh E. *The Chicago Urban League, 1915-1956.* University of Illinois, 1962. Historical analysis of the Chicago branch showing adjustments to economic and social changes. **62-6236**

Strong, Samuel M. *Social types in the Negro community of Chicago: an example of social type method.* University of Chicago, 1941.

Strong, Willa A. *The origin, development, and current status of the Oklahoma Federation of Colored Women's Clubs.* University of Oklahoma, 1957. **24429**

Sudnow, David N. *Passing on: the social organization of dying in the county hospital.* University of California, Berkeley, 1966. Analysis of varying meanings of dying depending on age, race and class status. **66-8405**

Tewell, Fred. *A study of the channels of communication used by one hundred Negroes in Baton Rouge, Louisiana.* Louisiana State University, 1956. Various media by which persons obtain information; frequency and variations of use by educational level. **17454**

Walker, Harry J. *Changes in race accomodation in a southern community.* University of Chicago, 1946.

Walker, Jack L., Jr. *Protest and negotiation: a study of Negro political leaders in a southern city.* State University of Iowa, 1963. Motives and political tactics of Negro civic leaders in Atlanta during April-May, 1962. **63-8045**

Wilson, James Q. *Negro leaders in Chicago.* University of Chicago, 1960.

5. Urban Problems

Bahr, Howard M. *Racial differentiation in American metropolitan areas.* University of Texas, 1965. 1960 census data used to test the theory that racial differentiation as to residence, education, occupation, and income are linked in causal sequence. **66-1888**

Brunson, Rose T. *Socialization experiences and socio-economic characteristics of urban Negroes as related to use of selected southern foods and medical remedies.* Michigan State University, 1962. Found that urban Negroes retain many of their southern ways concerning medical remedies, but retention declines as Negroes rise on the socio-economic scale. **62-4424**

Cherry, Frank T. *Southern in-migrant Negroes in North Lawndale, Chicago, 1949-59: a study of internal migration and adjustment.* University of Chicago, 1966.

Gallagher, Eugene F. *Provision for education practices and facilities in an era of urban renewal.* St. Louis University, 1963. Strengths, weaknesses, and gaps in the educational provisions of areas affected by urban renewal. **64-4246**

McQueen, Albert J. *A study of anomie among lower class Negro migrants.* University of Michigan, 1959. Analysis of the adjustments of Negro men who migrated to Ypsilanti, Michigan, between 1940 and 1957.   **59-4953**

Minor, Richard C. *The Negro in Columbus, Ohio.* Ohio State University, 1937.

Moore, William F., Jr. *Status of the Negro in Cleveland.* Ohio State University, 1953. Status of the Negro in Cleveland compared to Negroes in Cincinnati and Columbus in regard to Langston Hughes' seven "wants of Negroes."   **58-729**

Moses, Earl R. *Migrant Negro youth: a study of culture conflict and patterns of accommodation among Negro youth.* University of Pennsylvania, 1948. Impact of urban culture upon migrant Negro youth from rural South especially in terms of family life.   **2055**

Mugge, Robert H. *Negro migrants in Atlanta.* University of Chicago, 1957.

Omari, Thompson P. *Urban adjustment of rural southern Negro migrants in Beloit, Wisconsin.* University of Wisconsin, 1955.

Robinson, Leonard H. *Negro street society: a study of racial adjustment in two southern urban communities.* Ohio State University, 1950.

Watts, Lewis G. *Attitudes toward moving of middle-income Negro families facing urban renewal.* Brandeis University, 1964. Both economic and racial factors influence housing intentions.   **64-12876**

Williams, William J. *Attacking poverty in the Watts area: small business development under the Economic Opportunity Act of 1964.* University of Southern California, 1966. Analysis of concepts involved in Federal programs to combat poverty.   **66-11597**

Wolf, Eleanor P. *Changing neighborhood: a study of racial transition.* Wayne State University, 1959. The racial invasion-succession sequence in private housing in urban neighborhoods.   **60-2334**

6.   Rural Problems

Adams, Samuel C., Jr. *The changing organization of a rural Negro community and its implications for race accommodation.* University of Chicago, 1953.

Edwards, Otis B. *An economic history of the Negro in agriculture in Dallas, Macon and Madison Counties, Alabama, 1910-1950.* University of Nebraska, 1955. Investigation of the activities of Negro farm owners to determine opportunities for greater security.   **14354**

Holland, John B. *Attitudes toward minority groups in relation to rural social structure.* Michigan State College, 1950. Attitudes toward Negroes, Jews, and Mexicans in the rural Midwest.   **2206**

Hooker, Emile N. *An economic study of farms operated by Negro farmers in Dallas County, Alabama.* Cornell University, 1943.

King, Louis E. *Negro life in a rural community.* Columbia University, 1951. Describes differences between Negroes and whites in a rural West Virginia community, 1927-31. **65-4575**

Taylor, Grady W. *An analysis of certain factors differentiating successful from unsuccessful farm families in two counties in Alabama.* University of Wisconsin, 1958. A study of Negro farm families in Alabama. **58-2579**

Thomasson, Maurice E. *A study of special kinds of education for rural Negroes.* Columbia University, 1936.

Yarbrough, Dean S. *Racial adjustment in small communities.* University of Pittsburgh, 1935.

7. Recreation and Leisure

Bell, John A. *A study of the relationship between recreation interest and participation and intelligence, scholastic achievement, vocational interest, and socio-economic status of Negro students enrolled in the secondary public schools of Eastern Tennessee.* Indiana University, 1966. **66-9247**

Davitz, Lois J. *The high school student's perception of most-liked and least-liked television figures.* Columbia University, 1959. Variables included sex, race, age, socio-economic status. **59-3095**

Fox, Grace I. *Ring games and other games of the Florida Negro.* Indiana University, 1951.

Gerson, Walter M. *Social structure and mass media utilization.* University of Washington, 1963. Negro adolescents use mass media as a social agency to a greater extent than do white youth. **64-4504**

Harvey, John A. *The role of American Negroes in organized baseball.* Columbia University, Teachers College, 1961.

Jung, Raymond K. *Leisure activities of children of different socio-economic status and from different ethnic groups.* University of California, Berkeley, 1963. Differences in leisure time activities were not pronounced, but such differences were along ethnic lines more than socio-economic divisions. Orientals, Negroes, and Caucasians were the ethnic groups studied. **64-5327**

Young, Marechal-Neil E. *Some sociological aspects of the recreational guidance of Negro children.* University of Pennsylvania, 1944.

8. Intergroup Relations

Amerman, Helen E. *The impact of intergroup relations on non-segregated urban public education.* University of Chicago, 1954.

Baker, Paul E. *Negro-white adjustment: an investigation and analysis of methods in the interracial movement in the United States.* Columbia University, 1934.

Barnett, Suzanne E. *Persuasion and prejudice: an experimental study of the effects upon listener attitudes of the addition of extreme and moderate ideas to persuasive speeches.* Indiana University, 1962. Compares effects on listener attitudes of extreme and moderate ideas, racial and non-racial topics, interactions of speech treatment and initial opinion. **62-5007**

Berg, Kenneth R. *Ethnic attitudes and agreement of white persons with a Negro in the autokinetic situation.* University of Pennsylvania, 1961. Attraction to Negroes unrelated to agreement with a Negro confederate. **62-2820**

Carroll, James W. *Flatheads and whites: a study of conflict.* University of California, Berkeley, 1959.

Brewer, David L. *Utah elites and Utah racial norms.* University of Utah, 1966. Origin, status and probable future of Utah's unique racial norms.   **66-13548**

Boynton, John O. *A theory of the poor white: a study in race relations.* Duke University, 1953.

Culbertson, Frances J. *The modification of emotionally-held attitudes through role playing.* University of Michigan, 1955. Differential effect of role playing on attitudes toward allowing Negroes to move into white neighborhoods in persons of varying personality characteristics.   **12561**

Davis, Jerry B. *Attitude changes on fallout and race associated with special instruction in biology.* Columbia University, Teachers College, 1961.

De-Levie, Ari. *Attitudes of laymen and professionals toward physical and social disability.* Columbia University, 1966. Variables include sex and race.   **66-10286**

Dunn, Theodore F. *Assumed racial similarity as related to attitudes toward integration.* American University, 1958. Amount of assumed racial similarity covaries with attitude toward integrated schools for whites but not for Negroes.   **58-2809**

Epley, Dean G. *Adolescent role relationships in the dynamics of prejudice.* Michigan State College, 1953. Description of attitudes toward Jews and Negroes and attitude changes of adolescents in a rural midwestern community.   **7160**

Facen, Geneva Z. *The determination of the degree of tensions produced in selected white students when presented with certain beliefs and factual materials pertaining to Negroes.* University of Arkansas, 1959. No relationship was found between attitudes and tension in students at the University of Arkansas.   **59-3039**

Ford, Leon I. *The relationship between prejudice and dogmatism in opinion change.* Purdue University, 1956. Study of factors involved in opinion change.   **18847**

Ford, Robert N. *Techniques for scaling experiences: a study of white-Negro contacts.* University of Pittsburgh, 1940.

Freedman, Philip I. *Commonalities as a factor in cross-racial acceptance.* Columbia University, 1963. Personal interest variables were more effective than socio-economic status in eliciting choices of Negroes for partners in a work situation.   **63-7419**

Freeman, Felton D. *Theoretical bases for action programs in race relations.* University of North Carolina, 1950.

Goldstein, Naomi. *The roots of prejudice against the Negro in the United States.* Boston University, 1945.

Golovensky, David I. *Ingroup and outgroup attitudes of young pupils in a Jewish day school compared with an equivalent sample of pupils in public (mixed) schools.* New York University, 1954. Comparative effect of public and private schools on hostility to outgroups such as Negroes and Christians.   **22949**

Gordon, John E., Jr. *The effects on white student teachers of value clarification interviews with Negro pupils.* New York University, 1965. Comparative effects on student teacher attitudes toward Negro students in three types of contact with Negro pupils. **66-5778**

Green, Meredith W. *Interrelationships of attitude and information: a study based on the responses of southern white high school students to questions about the Negro.* Columbia University, 1953. Concluded that information is associated with increases in favorable attitudes. **8670**

Haney, Eleanor H. *A study of conscience as it is expressed in race relations.* Yale University, 1965. A description of conscience was developed, then tested in case studies of persons engaged in civil rights activities. **65-15051**

Hansen, Burrell F. *A critical evaluation of a documentary series of radio programs on racial and religious prejudice.* University of Minnesota, 1953. A series of 6 weekly programs reduced racial and religious group tensions in a group of college students during summer, 1947. **5535**

Hart, Thomas A. *The establishment of principles of human relations that may be used in the transition of all-white or all-Negro camps to interracial camps.* New York University, 1958. Develops principles which were then tested in a selected group of interracial camps. **59-1045**

Hennessey, Sister Mary A. *A study of the attitudes of college women toward selected intergroup problems and their relation to certain background factors.* St. Louis University, 1958. Explores attitudes among students in Catholic colleges for women toward intergroup problems, including interracial problems. **59-898**

Hertz, Hilda. *Language and the social situation: a study in race relations.* Duke University, 1950.

Hildebrandt, Charles A. *The relationship of some personal and social variables of school children to preferences for mixed schools.* Ohio State University, 1962. Examined relationship of 8 variables to feelings of racial hostility among Negro and white children in middle school grades, and also perceptions of racial feelings of in-groups and out-groups. **63-2503**

Hodges, Louis W. *A Christian analysis of selected contemporary theories of racial prejudice.* Duke University, 1960. Analysis of views of prejudice according to Allport, Myrdal, and principles of liberal Protestantism and realistic theology. **60-6032**

Holland, Ira H. *A study of interracial relationships and practices in selected YMCA's.* Columbia University, Teachers College, 1953.

Hong, Sung C. *Majority perception of minority behavior and its relationship to hostility toward ethnic minorities: a test of George A. Lundberg's hypotheses.* University of Washington, 1959. Negroes included among 18 groups studied. **60-858**

Hornseth, Richard A. *An index of Negro-white discrimination: a critique.* University of Wisconsin, 1949.

Horowitz, Eugene L. *The development of attitude toward the Negro.* Columbia University, 1936.

Houser, Leah S. *A sociometric test of aspects of reference group theory in a study of prejudice among youth.* Michigan State University, 1956. Analysis of verbalized prejudice toward Jews, Negroes and Mexicans expressed by 9th and 12th graders in a midwestern community, 1949. **24250**

Itzhoff, Seymour W. *Cultural pluralism and American education: a reinterpretation of the philosophy of Ernst Cassirer.* Columbia University, 1965. A social philosophy based upon the symbolic philosophy of Ernst Cassirer was applied to the dilemma of the Negro.   **65-8845**

Jenkins, Shirley. *Intergroup empathy: an exploratory study of Negro and Puerto Rican groups in New York City.* New York University, 1957. Attitudes of American Negro and Puerto Rican people toward each other in neighborhoods of intergroup contact.   **58-633**

Jones, Roy J. *The effects of inter-ethnic group contact in a desegregated hospital community.* American University, 1961. Findings supported previous studies on interracial contact and attitude.   **61-3714**

Jones, Thomas B. *An analysis of the interracial policies and practices of the group work agencies in Columbus, Ohio.* Ohio State University, 1947.

Kahn, Lessing A. *The scalability and factorial composition of a universe of content as functions of the level of formal education of the respondents.* University of Pennsylvania, 1950. A study of attitudes toward Negroes by educated and uneducated respondents.   **1730**

Kapos, Andrew. *Some individual and group determinants of fraternity attitudes toward the admission of members of certain minority groups.* University of Michigan, 1953. Exploration of dynamics of membership attitudes toward admitting Jews, Negroes and Orientals to white, gentile fraternities.
                        5053

Khoshboo, Yousef D. *A new approach to the problems of civil rights in the U.S.A.: an inquiry into the causes of American resentments in associating with Negroes.* Southern Illinois University, 1964. Argues that the civil rights problems persist because the American educational system has not attacked the general American feeling of superiority.   **64-7355**

Kraus, Sidney. *An experimental study of the relative effectiveness of Negroes and whites in achieving racial attitude change via kinescope recordings.* State University of Iowa, 1959. The effectiveness of Negro and white actors in films used to change attitudes of white secondary school children toward Negroes.   **59-5720**

Landau, Claire. *Interracial group work and social adjustment.* Columbia University, 1957. Exploration of the possibilities in interracial group work for achieving individual and social adjustment.   **21800**

Lawner, Rhoda L. *Social conflict as a subject of investigation in American research from 1919 to 1953.* New York University, 1956. Includes bibliography of 1,417 books and papers relating to social conflicts.   **16597**

Lent, Richard A. *Prejudice and the perception of race.* Harvard University, 1959-60.

Lewis, Dorothy G. *A study of the motivational base of anti-Negro prejudice in a southern sample.* Syracuse University, 1961. Results indicate that anti-Negro prejudice does not develop independently of ego-defensive needs to any greater degree in the South than in the North.   **62-1109**

Lombardi, Donald. *Factors affecting changes in attitudes toward Negroes among high school students.* Fordham University, 1962. Attitudes before and after school integration were the same for group as a whole, but individual and subgroup attitude changes were significant.   **623769**

Long, Herman H. *Sensitivity response patterns of Negro and white groups to anger-producing social stimuli.* University of Michigan, 1949. No racial types of response were found although there were racial differences of a highly specific nature. **1349**

MacKenzie, Barbara K. *The importance of contact in determining attitudes toward Negroes.* Columbia University, 1949.

Maliver, Bruce L. *Anti-Negro bias among Negro college students.* Yeshiva University, 1964. Subjects high in anti-Negro bias were more likely to have a negative view of the father, a generalized fear of rejection by adult figures, and were unlikely to participate in anti-segregation activities. **64-10006**

Mann, John H. *The influence of racial prejudice on sociometric choices and perceptions.* Columbia University, 1956. Concludes that prejudice influences sociometric choices in small interracial groups of Negro and white graduate students. **16905**

Martin, James G. *Differential personal and social characteristics of tolerant and prejudiced persons.* Indiana University, 1957. A comparison of 25 selected personal and social characteristics in persons strongly prejudiced and tolerant toward Negroes. **22697**

Mayo, George E. *A comparison of the "racial" attitudes of white and Negro high school students in 1940 and 1948.* Ohio State University, 1950.

McDonald, Franklin R. *The effect of differential cultural pressures on projective test performances of Negroes.* University of Southern California, 1952.

Muhyi, Ibrahim A. *Certain content of prejudices against Negroes among white children at different ages.* Columbia University, 1952. Study of age at which prejudice is manifested in white children and the changing content of that prejudice. **3908**

Mussen, Paul H. *Some personality and social factors related to changes in children's attitude toward Negroes.* Yale University, 1949.

Nielson, Alfred M. *Awareness of in-group attitudes.* Ohio State University, 1955. Amount of prejudice toward 3 groups (including Negroes) constitutes the data of this research. **16091**

Noel, Donald L. *Correlates of anti-white prejudice: attitudes of Negroes in four American cities.* Cornell University, 1961. The Guttman scale measured prejudice in Negroes and in whites; data interpreted as supporting both the competition and the personality theories of prejudice. **62-956**

O'Reilly, Charles T. *Race prejudice among Catholic college students in the United States and Italy: a comparative study of the role of religion and personality in inter-group relations.* University of Notre Dame, 1954. A study of anti-Jewish and anti-Negro attitudes in relation to personality and religion. **15676**

Park, Lawrence. *An investigation of some relationships between emotional needs and prejudice toward minority groups of intermediate grade children in selected Worcester County schools.* New York University, 1950. Evidence found to suggest that prejudice toward Negro, Jewish and Catholic persons may be an emotional disorder related to unmet emotional needs. **2194**

Pettigrew, Thomas F. *Regional differences in anti-Negro prejudice.* Harvard University, 1956.

Picher, Oliver L. *Attraction toward Negroes as a function of prejudice, emotional arousal, and the sex of the Negro.* University of Texas, 1966. Attempt to verify existence of a Southern taboo against white women interacting with Negro men; study reports that females do not take the taboo into consideration, but that males do. **66-7367**

Pinkney, Alphonso. *The anatomy of prejudice: majority group attitudes toward minorities in selected American cities.* Cornell University, 1961. Sociological and psychological correlates of prejudice.

61-6758

Pisani, Lawrence F. *Theories of ethnic and race prejudice.* Yale University, 1951.

Powell, Alice M. *Racial awareness and social behavior in an interracial four-year-old group.* University of Maryland, 1958. Effect of social learning about race at the beginning of attitude formation upon behavior in an interracial peer group. **59-2535**

Psaltis, Betty. *Children's views of their social environment: a comparative study.* Columbia University, 1963. Though little variation in attitude was found by type of community, differences did emerge in relation to the factors of race, religion and parental occupation. **64-1496**

Ragan, Roger L. *Attitudes of white Methodist church members in selected Los Angeles metropolitan area churches toward residential segregation of the Negro.* Southern California School of Theology, 1963. About one fourth of the subjects were tolerant of Negro residential proximity, about half were definitely intolerant. Several factors related to a tolerant attitude were identified. **63-7237**

Rasmussen, Donald E. *Social factors in southern white equalitarianism.* University of Illinois, 1952. The causes of equalitarian racial views in a southern social setting. **3597**

Rast, Robert. *The effects of group pressure on the modification and distortion of judgments in tolerant and prejudiced individuals.* American University, 1963. The more tolerant subjects were less influenced by group pressure and thus perceived more accurately and responded more correctly than the prejudiced subjects. **64-2851**

Redekop, Calvin. *The sectarian black and white world.* University of Chicago, 1960.

Rosner, Joseph. *Group dominance as a factor in intergroup relations.* New York University, 1954. Attitudes of white children toward self, color and racial role in majority and minority racial settings. **8010**

Ross, Bernard. *The local public Intergroup Relations Agency: a study of a new structure of local government.* University of Michigan, 1958. Rise and development (1943-56) of agencies formed in urban areas with large concentrations of non-whites. **58-3727**

Samelson, Babette F. *The patterning of attitude and beliefs regarding the American Negro: an analysis of public opinion.* Radcliffe College, 1945.

Scott, Woodrow W. *Interpersonal relations in ethnically mixed small work groups.* University of Southern California, 1959. Ethnically mixed factory work groups under benevolent management reduce conflict attitudes and increase cooperative attitudes. **59-6400**

Sharp, Evelyn W. *A study of the effects of a permissive classroom atmosphere on growth in social relationships in the classroom.* New York University, 1958. Negro pupils in grades 4, 5 and 6 were studied; social relationships were improved with permissive atmosphere.   **59-1021**

Shenfeld, Nathan. *Tolerant and intolerant attitudes and logical thinking.* University of Buffalo, 1958. Effect of a strong commitment (such as attitudes toward Jews or Negroes) upon syllogistic reasoning ability in the area of this commitment.   **58-1950**

Shepard, Loraine V. *A test of attitudes toward social intermingling of Negro and white boys in the upper elementary grades.* University of Michigan, 1954. Construction of a test to determine attitudes of white boys in grades 4, 5 and 6 toward social intermingling with Negroes.   **7723**

Singer, Lester C. *A comparative analysis of selected approaches to Negro-white relations in the U.S. for convergence and divergence.* Columbia University, 1958. Examination of existing views on Negro-white relations (Myrdal, Cox, Davis, Gardner) in search of an underlying theory of race relations.   **58-2603**

Smith, Fred T. *An experiment in modifying attitudes toward the Negro.* Columbia University, 1944.

Smith, Robert G. *A factorial study of attitudes toward the Negro.* University of Illinois, 1950.

Spurling, John J. *Social relationships between American Negroes and West Indian Negroes in a Long Island community. An exploratory examination of intergroup relationships in the Addisleigh Park neighborhood of St. Albans, Long Island, N.Y.* New York University, 1962. Nature and quality of social interrelationships with implications for theory of intergroup contact.   **62-5353**

Star, Shirley A. *Interracial tension in two areas of Chicago: an exploratory approach to the measurement of interracial tension.* University of Chicago, 1951.

Thomas, Charles H. *The opinion of Negro children toward whites.* University of Oklahoma, 1959. Whites were thought to be more mercenary and deceitful; Negroes were thought to be more physically powerful, musical and religious.   **59-5500**

Tiedemann, John G. *An investigation of the influence of group standards and deviate member behavior on the exhibited racial prejudice of an individual.* American University, 1961. Conditions presented in which group majority and deviant members influence overt prejudicial behavior.   **61-3725**

Vader, Anthony J. *Racial segregation within Catholic institutions in Chicago: a study in behavior and attitudes.* University of Chicago, 1963.

Valdes, Donald M. *The rank order of discriminations toward Negroes by white persons in Newark, Ohio.* Ohio State University, 1958. Results support Myrdal's hypothesis as to rank order of discriminations but with some differences in order below the first three.   **58-3468**

Wendel, Egon O. *Parent and student attitudes toward school in a predominantly Negro community.* New York University, 1961. Attitudes of parents and students toward Prospect Elementary School, Hempstead, N.Y.   **62-1458**

Williams, Robert E. *The relationship of racial valuations to interracial experiences.* University of Chicago, 1957.

Winder, Alvin E. *White attitudes toward Negro-white interaction in an area of changing racial composition.* University of Chicago, 1952.

Woodmansee, John J., Jr. *An evaluation of pupil response as a measure of attitude toward Negroes.* University of Colorado, 1965. A study of pupillary dilatation as an indicator of attitudes.   **66-3299**

Works, Ernest. *The prejudice-interaction hypothesis from the point of view of the Negro minority group.* University of Illinois, 1959. Data suggest that improvement of self-concept is related to diminished prejudice.   **59-2068**

Young, William L. *A study of the attitudes of high school students toward groups that are different in race, religion, and nationality.* University of Pittsburgh, 1947.

9. Delinquency, Crime, Riots

Amir, Menachem. *Patterns in forcible rape: with special reference to Philadelphia, Pennsylvania, 1958 and 1960.* University of Pennsylvania, 1965. Patterns sought regarding race, age, marital status, employment, season of year and time of day.   **66-4597**

Amos, William E. *A study of self-concept: delinquent boys' accuracy in selected self-evaluations.* University of Maryland, 1960. Differences in self-estimates between Negro delinquents and non-delinquents.   **61-876**

Brown, Paula M. *A comparative study of three therapy techniques used to effect behavioral and social status changes in a group of institutionalized delinquent Negro boys.* New York University, 1956. Therapy techniques used were immediate group therapy, delayed group therapy and attention, as applied to institutionalized children.   **17637**

Bugansky, Alex. *Certain factors in prejudice among inmates of three ethnic groups within a short-term penal institution. An analysis of prejudice: the determination of certain factors in prejudice and attitudes among ethnic groups in a prison population.* New York University, 1958. Prejudice in whites, Negroes and Puerto Ricans as related to Xenophobia Scale, Trait Attribution Scale, F-Scale and House-Tree-Person Test.   **59-1012**

Cameron, Mary B. *Department store shoplifting.* Indiana University, 1953. Race was one variable considered in analysis of shoplifting in Chicago.   **6434**

Diggs, Mary H. *A comparative study of delinquent behavior manifestations of 100 delinquent and 100 non-delinquent Negro boys.* Bryn Mawr College, 1945. Two groups of Negro boys were compared, using ideal-type methodology.   **814**

Epps, Edgar G. *Socio-economic status, level of aspiration, and juvenile delinquency.* Washington State University, 1959. Investigation of Merton's theory of delinquent behavior; included race as a variable.   **60-1513**

Forslund, Morris A. *Race and crime.* Yale University, 1966.

Grimshaw, Allen D. *A study in social violence: urban race riots in the United States.* University of Pennsylvania, 1959. Social violence in situations of social tension is determined by presence or absence of strong and non-partisan external forces of constraint.   **59-4624**

Hardy, John G. *A comparative study of institutions for Negro juvenile delinquents in southern states.* University of Wisconsin, 1947.

Himes, Joseph S., Jr. *The Negro delinquent in Columbus, 1935.* Ohio State University, 1938.

Justice, David B. *An inquiry into Negro identity and a methodology for investigating potential racial violence.* Rice University, 1966. A methodology was developed to measure racial tension using factors of mobility, anomie and complexity. **66-10352**

Konietzko, Kurt O. *An investigation of the concept of "behavioral rigidity" as applied to a penal population.* Temple University, 1959. Includes differences between white and Negro inmates. **59-2657**

Kramer, Samuel A. *Predicting juvenile delinquency among Negroes.* Ohio State University, 1961. Study of Negro delinquency in a lower-class area of Washington, D.C. **61-5097**

Lively, Edwin L. *A study of teen-age socialization and delinquency insulation by grade levels.* Ohio State University, 1959. Effect of differential socialization on differential self-concepts, changes with advancing age and relationship to delinquency vulnerability. Includes racial analysis of data. **60-1198**

Mauney, Jack E. *Race prejudice among Negro male delinquents.* Oklahoma A & M University, 1954.

Meese, Billie G. *An experimental program for juvenile delinquent boys.* University of Maryland, 1961. Effect of an experimental program on a group of delinquent Negro boys. **61-6868**

Morello, Michael. *A study of the adjustive behavior of prison inmates to incarceration.* Temple University, 1958. Population sample stratified in terms of race and length of incarceration. **58-1980**

O'Brien, William J. *An experimental use of modified group therapy in a public school setting with delinquent adolescent males.* University of California, Berkeley, 1963. Based on results from a specially devised group therapy program using Negro and Caucasian delinquent boys, this study concluded that it is possible to modify the regular school program to treat the severely delinquent. **64-5330**

Pecilunas, Leonard P. *Adolescent misconduct and attitudes toward certain family relationships.* Florida State University, 1965. Examined family relationships of Negro and white adolescents for their significance in adolescent misconduct and rejected the view that Negro adolescents judge fathers more unfavorably than whites. **66-2098**

Reeves, Earl Y. *A comparative study of the success or failure of Negro and white offenders on probation.* University of Pennsylvania, 1962. Reports significant differences between Negro and white successes and failures. **63-4169**

Roebuck, Julian B. *A tentative criminal typology of four-hundred Negro felons at the District of Columbia Reformatory, Lorton, Virginia.* University of Maryland, 1958. Developed a criminal typology to be used in tentative delineation of functional, etiological types of offender groups. **59-2798**

Rosengarten, Leonard. *Post-probation adjustment of 200 official cases of juvenile delinquency in Philadelphia.* Temple University, 1959. Evaluation of effectiveness of probation and nature of variables associated with subsequent behavior in both Negro and white subjects. **59-2344**

Walker, Lewis. *Matricentricity and delinquency: a study of the relation of female-based households to delinquency and non-delinquency among Negro and white boys.* Ohio State University, 1964. No significant differences in matricentricity were found between racial groups, but differences were seen between the delinquent and nondelinquent groups, leading to the conclusion that matricentricity is a general lower class rather than racial pattern. **64-9596**

Waskow, Arthur I. *The 1919 race riots: a study in the connection between conflict and violence.* University of Wisconsin, 1963. Generalizations as to how violence may be prevented were developed from study of seven race riots in 1919.   **64-621**

Wilson, John M. *A sociological investigation and comparative analysis of patterns of beliefs of Negro and white male alcoholic offenders regarding the use of alcoholic beverages.* University of Maryland, 1965. Hypothesized differences in beliefs were found, such as that Negro offenders express beliefs more broadly permissive.   **65-4480**

Watts, Frederick P. *A comparative clinical study of delinquent and non-delinquent Negro boys.* University of Pennsylvania, 1941.

10. Social Class

Blumenfeld, Ruth. *Children of integration.* University of Pennsylvania, 1965. Social structure and socialization patterns of the elite Negro community in Baltimore, Maryland, 1890-1962.   **66-251**

Brozovich, Richard W. *Group norms in sixth grade classrooms of contrasting socio-economic status and differing racial composition.* George Peabody College for Teachers, 1966. Race and sex found related to the social value of certain traits.   **66-11238**

Garrett, Romeo B. *Social aspects of the aging process among a selected older population in Peoria, Illinois.* New York University, 1963. Class differences were greater than racial differences, but Negroes tend to think of themselves as older for their age and to become more religious as they grow older than whites.   **64-247**

Glenn, Norval D. *The Negro population in the American system of social stratification: an analysis of recent trends.* University of Texas, 1962. Traces changes in the status of the American Negro population with respect to education, income and occupation.   **62-2544**

Hill, Adelaide C. *The Negro upper class in Boston – its development and present social structure.* Radcliffe College, 1952.

Jones, Clifton R. *Social stratification in the Negro population: a study of social classes in South Boston, Virginia.* University of Iowa, 1944.

Meeks, Donald E. *Race, social class, and level of aspiration: the effects of race and social class on the goal-striving behavior of white and Negro boys.* Smith College for Social Work, 1965. Social class but not race affected aspirations. Race of experimenter affected scores, with lower class Negroes and whites scoring lower with Negro experimenter.   **66-907**

Mitchell, Howard E. *Social class and race as factors affecting the role of the family in thematic apperception test stories of males.* University of Pennsylvania, 1951. Differences in projective expressions about role of the family as a function of race and social class.   **2370**

Platter, Allen A. *Educational, social, and economic characteristics of the plantation culture of Brazoria County, Texas.* University of Houston, 1961. Includes discussion of treatment of slaves and educational opportunity for Negroes.   **61-5678**

Porch, Marvin E. *The Main Line Negro: a social, economic and educational survey.* Temple University, 1935.

Rosenblum, Abraham L. *Social class membership and ethnic prejudice in Cedar City.* University of Southern California, 1959. Prejudice varies with social class standing.   **59-4399**

Seagull, Arthur A. *The ability to delay gratification: social class versus situational variables.* Syracuse University, 1964. Ability to delay gratification is related to the specific situation rather than to social class affiliation.   **65-3437**

Weddington, Rachel T. *The relative influence of social class and color in the stereotypes of young children.* University of Chicago, 1959.

INDIVIDUAL CHARACTERISTICS

1. Intelligence

Adler, Manfred. *A study of the identification and development of giftedness in two ethnic groups.* Kentucky State University, 1965. Comparisons were drawn between Negroes and Jews.   **66-4366**

Beck, Elizabeth J. *Relationships between social impact and selected intellectual traits in preadolescent boys.* Fordham University, 1964. Using Negro elementary children and a peer perception instrument, well socialized persons were found to be more intelligent than the poorly socialized.   **64-8571**

Blanks, Augustus C. *A comparative study of mentally bright and mentally dull Negro high school seniors (with reference to personality, background, school achievement, interest, ambition, and school marks).* New York University, 1954. School achievement and grades differentiate bright and dull Negro high school seniors in the South, while social and personality factors do not.   **12199**

Bruce, Myrtle H. *Factors affecting intelligence test performance of whites and Negroes in the rural South.* Columbia University, 1942.

Daniel, Mariel M. *Influence of selected occupational, racial and residence factors upon intelligence: a cultural-intellectual study of North Carolina.* University of North Carolina, 1950.

Fowler, William L. *A comparative analysis of pupil performance on conventional and culture-controlled mental tests.* University of Michigan, 1956. Comparison of pupil performance with sex, race, ethnicity, socioeconomic status and teacher opinion of pupil intelligence.   **18603**

Franzblau, Rose N. *Race differences in mental and physical traits: studied in different environments.* Columbia University, 1936.

Ilardi, Robert L. *Family disorganization and intelligence in Negro pre-school children.* University of Tennessee, 1966. Mean IQ in stable family group of children found to be significantly higher than in unstable family group.   **66-12609**

Katzenmeyer, William G. *Social interaction and differences in intelligence test performance of Negro and white elementary school pupils.* Duke University, 1962. Concluded that performance on intelligence tests is related to communality of experience and that increases follow greater social interaction.   **63-2227**

Lindner, Ronald S. *The Goodenough Draw-a-Man Test: its relationship to intelligence, achievement, and cultural variables of Negro elementary school children in the Southeast United States.* Florida State University, 1962. Norms developed for intellectual performance of Negro children in the Southeast.   **62-3512**

Lusienski, Dean R. *An analysis of the scores of urban Negro boys on the Wechsler Intelligence Scale for Children.* University of Nebraska, 1964. No significant differences on subscale scores found between matched groups of Negro and white boys. **64-11936**

Machover, Solomon. *Cultural and racial variations in patterns of intellect; performance of Negro and white criminals on the Bellevue Adult Intelligence Scale.* Columbia University, 1943.

Mitchell, Chloe H. *An experimental study using pictorial paired associates to compare learning rates of normal Negro and white children.* University of Oklahoma, 1963. The rates of learning for a group of Negro children and a group of white children equated on IQ were compared by using a Pictorial Paired Associate Test. The null hypothesis was rejected. **64-213**

Murray, Walter I. *The intelligence-test performance of Negro children of different social classes.* University of Chicago, 1948.

Rachiele, Leo D. *A comparative analysis of ten year old Negro and white performance on the Wechsler Intelligence Scale for Children.* University of Denver, 1953.

Saunders, Mauderie H. *An analysis of cultural differences on certain projective techniques.* University of Oklahoma, 1961. From House-Tree-Person and Draw-a-Person techniques, judges could evaluate mental ability, reading achievement and emotional adjustment, but not race. **61-2905**

Schaefer, Dorothy F. *Prejudice in mentally retarded, average, and bright Negro and Puerto Rican adolescents.* Columbia University, 1965. No interactions determined between prejudice and intelligence in populations of Negro and Puerto Rican adolescents. **65-14987**

Scruggs, Sherman D. *Effect of improvement in reading upon the intelligence of Negro children.* University of Kansas, 1935.

Tiber, Norman. *The effects of incentives on intelligence test performance.* Florida State University, 1963. No significant difference was found in intelligence test performance under various reinforcing conditions of second- and third-grade children divided into middle-class white, lower-class white and lower-class Negro groups. **63-6366**

Tomlinson, Helen. *An analysis of the performance of Negro children on the revised Stanford-Binet Tests.* University of Texas, 1942.

Tuttle, Lester E., Jr. *The comparative effect on intelligence test scores of Negro and white children when certain verbal and time factors are varied.* University of Florida, 1964. The Wechsler Intelligence Scale, Peabody Picture Vocabulary Test and the Columbia Mental Maturity Scale gave wide variations in test results. **65-6012**

Van de Riet, Vernon. *The standardization of the third revision of the Stanford-Binet Intelligence Scale on Negro elementary-school children in grades one, two, and three in the Southeastern United States.* Florida State University, 1962. Reports mean, standard deviation and other analyses. **63-1832**

Vega, Manuel. *The performance of Negro children on an oddity discrimination task as a function of the race of the examiner and the type of verbal incentive used by the examiner.* Florida State University, 1964. Found that white examiners of Negro children elicited increased mean reaction time as compared to Negro examiners. **64-10590**

White, James C., Jr. *The standardization of the third revision of the Stanford-Binet Intelligence Scale on Negro elementary school children in grades four, five and six in the Southeastern United States.* Florida State University, 1962. Reports mean, standard deviation and other analyses.   **63-1834**

Wilson, John L. *Changes in brightness of children, age three to eleven, living in a low socioeconomic environment.* Indiana University, 1967. Using Goodenough Draw-a-Man Test, decrease in brightness was interpreted as result of environment.   **22993**

Zimbelman, Ernest A. *The influences in the intellectual development of Negro American students.* University of Oregon, 1965. Considers such categories as the socialization processes, religion, socio-economic status, work opportunity, self and racial attitudes.   **65-12253**

2. Personality

Amos, Robert T. *Comparative accuracy with which Negro and white children can predict teachers' attitudes toward Negro students.* University of Michigan, 1951. White pupils predicted teacher attitudes more correctly than Negroes, but social class more important than race.   **2373**

Baehr, Rufus F. *Need achievement and dialect in lower class adolescent Negroes.* University of Chicago, 1965.

Barban, Arnold M. *Measurement of the differences in the perception of advertising by whites and Negroes through use of the semantic differential.* University of Texas, 1964. Concluded that responses were more similar than dissimilar and that an advertiser could reach both groups effectively through a common appeal.   **64-7162**

Benjamin, Lawrence H. *Authoritarianism and the expression of overt hostility in a biracial situation.* New York University, 1964. Results of an experimental situation failed to support the hypothesis that high authoritarians would express more hostility toward Negroes than authoritarians.   **65-1606**

Blake, Dudley A. *Racial and social-class differences as perceived by seventh-grade children through binocular rivalry.* University of Southern California, 1965. Devised a binocular presentation of disparate pairs of slides depicting racial and class difference as a means of determining the influence of race and social class upon children's perceptions.   **65-9967**

Blake, Elias, Jr. *A comparison of intraracial and interracial levels of aspiration.* University of Illinois, 1960. Compared levels of aspiration of Negro and white students in segregated and integrated public high schools.   **60-1616**

Bloom, Wallace. *Attitudes of mentally retarded students identified by educational level, ethnic group, sex, and socio-economic class.* University of Texas, 1964. Use of the Gordon Personal Profile, Peck Sentence Completion Test and the Brown Self-Report Inventory determined no significant difference between ethnic groups.   **65-4294**

Breen, Michael D. *Culture and schizophrenia: a study of Negro and Jewish schizophrenics.* Brandeis University, 1965. Shows that the dissimilar symptoms of Negro and Jewish male schizophrenics can be predicted from what is known about American Jewish and Negro culture.   **65-14413**

Brewer, June H. *An ecological study of the psychological environment of a Negro college and the personality needs of its students.* University of Texas, 1963. Data did not support the hypothesis that student success depends on compatibility of his needs and pressures of the environment.   **64-45**

Bryan, Laurence L. *A comparative study of moral discrimination in adult male mental patients and adult male federal prisoners.* Indiana University, 1956. A study of capacity for moral judgment; includes race as a variable.   **19458**

Caliman, Alvis W. *Personality adjustment of aging women.* Michigan State College, 1952. Personality study of 45 Negro women 50 to 83 years of age.   **5914**

Campion, Donald R. *Patterns of suicide in Philadelphia: 1948-1952.* University of Pennsylvania, 1960. Analysis of 894 cases of suicide; sex and race included in variables examined.   **60-3568**

Claye, Clifton M. *A study of the relationship between self-concepts and attitudes toward the Negro among secondary school pupils in three schools of Arkansas.* University of Arkansas, 1958. Found widespread prejudice which was unrelated to number of Negroes, schools' efforts to change attitudes, contact with Negroes or self-concept.   **58-2751**

Cohen, Melvin. *White students' reactions to the test performance of Negroes.* New York University, 1965. The response of white subjects to results of tests administered to either white or Negro confederates under two different conditions of potential threat to self-esteem.   **66-5652**

Copeland, Lewis C. *The function of racial ideologies with special reference to the beliefs about the Negro.* Duke University, 1939.

Corke, Patricia P. *A comparison of frustration-aggression patterns of Negro and white southern males and females.* University of Houston, 1961. Changes in aggressive reaction to frustration in Negro and white males and females from 1947 to 1961.   **61-5780**

Cothran, Tilman C. *Negro stereotyped conceptions of white people.* University of Chicago, 1949.

Cottrell, Ted B. *A physiological correlate of the effect of blame and examiner race on performance.* Florida State University, 1964. Negro students display greater change in heart rate when blamed by a white examiner than by a Negro examiner.   **65-312**

Davidson, Alene J. *Cultural differences in personality structure as expressed in drawings of the human figure.* New York University, 1953. Subjects were Negro and white children in St. Thomas, Virgin Islands, and in New York City.   **7092**

Davis, Alonzo J. *Status factors in personality characteristics of Negro college students.* University of Minnesota, 1948.

Driscoll, Willis C. *A study of judgment of time intervals in mixed-racial groups.* University of Florida, 1958. No racial differences found.   **58-3489**

Drumright, Russel G. *Some factors influencing remembering of pictorial and prose materials.* University of Oklahoma, 1956. Includes analysis of racial attitudes as one factor in remembering pictorial material.   **19488**

Drusine, Leon. *Some factors in anti-Negro prejudice among Puerto Rican boys in New York City.* New York University, 1955. Examination of relationship between prejudice and authoritarianism, intolerance of ambiguity, alienation, skin color, and other factors.   **16588**

Eagleson, Oran W. *Comparative studies of white and Negro subjects in learning to discriminate visual magnitude.* Indiana University, 1936.

Fendrich, James Max. *A study of whites' attitudes, commitment and overt behavior toward members of a minority group.* Michigan State University, 1965. The relationship between authoritarianism, past contact with Negroes, and perceived support from others for engaging in interaction with Negroes.
66-375

Gasser, Edith S. *An investigation of the body image of boys as expressed in self drawings: an inter-cultural study.* New York University, 1961. No ethnic differences found in a sample of Negro, white and Italian boys.
62-1464

Gay, Cleveland J. *Academic achievement and intelligence among Negro eighth grade students as a function of self concept.* North Texas State University, 1966. No difference found between the self-concepts of boys and girls; relationship between self-concept and achievement greater than between self-concept and intelligence.
66-6409

Ginott, Haim G. *The effects of psychotherapy on the race prejudice of disturbed children; an experimental study.* Columbia University, Teachers College, 1953.

Goff, Regina M. *Problems and emotional difficulties of Negro children as studied in selected communities and attributed by parents and children to the fact that they are Negro.* Columbia University, Teachers College, 1949.

Goldenberg, Herbert. *The role of the group identification in the personality organization of schizophrenic and normal Negroes.* University of California, Berkeley, 1953.

Gordon, Edmund W. *Toward meeting the mental health needs of underprivileged minority group children in the Harlem community of New York City.* Columbia University, Teachers College, 1958.

Gordon, Robert A. *The generality of semantic differential factors and scales in six American sub-cultures.* University of Chicago, 1963.

Green, Jerome. *The use of an information test about the Negro as an indirect technique for measuring attitudes, beliefs, and self-perceptions.* University of Southern California, 1955.

Green, Robert L. *The predictive efficiency and factored dimensions of the Michigan M-Scales for eleventh grade Negro students – an exploratory study.* Michigan State University, 1963. A significant difference was found between Negro and white males and females on the GSCI portion of the M-Scales, but no difference on the remaining subtests.
63-6152

Greenberg, Harold I. *Attitudes toward minority status among Negro adolescents as related to literacy level.* Columbia University, 1965. Concluded that attitude change depends on modification of slum life rather than changes in reading ability.
65-10037

Haggstrom, Warren C. *Self-esteem and other characteristics of residentially desegregated Negroes.* University of Michigan, 1962. Members of desegregated households tend to have higher self-esteem than matched members of segregated households.
63-359

Hatton, John M. *Reactions of Negroes in a biracial bargaining situation.* Stanford University, 1965. Confirmed hypothesis that Negro subjects would exploit yielding whites as opposed to yielding Negroes, but would yield to demanding whites and retaliate against demanding Negroes.
65-12792

Henderson, George. *Aspirations and social class in pockets of poverty: a study of educational obsolescence.* Wayne State University, 1965. Low-motivated students were found to be skeptical of early success and to maintain low aspirations after early failures.   **66-1235**

Howard, David H. *The American Negro's dilemma: attitudes of Negro professionals toward competition with whites.* Indiana University, 1963. Negro professionals exhibit a considerable amount of ethnocentricity and only reluctantly accept the idea of open competition with whites.   **64-5458**

Howell, William H. *The rank order of sensitivity to discriminations of Negroes in Orangeburg, South Carolina.* Ohio State University, 1957. Concludes that resentment against types of discrimination can be quantified and ranked; age and occupation are significant variables.   **58-2078**

Isler, Stanley M. *The expressed moral beliefs of adolescent boys of different socioeconomic status and race.* Columbia University, 1963. Boys of differing socioeconomic status and race also differ in their expressed moral beliefs.   **64-5684**

Jenkins, Martin D. *A socio-psychological study of Negro children of superior intelligence.* Northwestern University, 1935.

Johnson, George L. *Certain psychological characteristics of retarded readers and reading achievers.* Temple University, 1956. The relation between memory span and associative learning patterns of retarded and achieving readers in 4th and 5th grades of Negro public schools.   **18098**

Jones, Richard M. *The effect of experimentally increased self-acceptance on ethnic attitudes: an experiment in education.* Harvard University, 1956.

Karon, Bertram P. *A comparative study of the personality structures and problems of northern and southern Negroes in terms of differential caste sanctions.* Princeton University, 1957. Demonstrates that the effect of caste sanctions on humans is destructive and that effect varies with severity of sanctions.   **58-7852**

Kirkhart, Robert O. *Psychological and social-psychological correlates of marginality in Negroes.* Ohio State University, 1959. Relation between reaction to minority status and variables such as prejudice, music preferences, religious affiliation and skin color.   **60-1190**

Koontz, Miriam E. *A comparison of false nonauthoritarians in two ethnic groups.* George Peabody College for Teachers, 1955. Hypothesis not supported that a Negro group would have higher proportion of authoritarians not identified by the F Scale than a similar white group.   **15468**

Lefcourt, Herbert M. *Some empirical correlates of Negro identity.* Ohio State University, 1963. Reported findings similar to the "psychology of poverty" in which those with few success experiences tend to develop perceptions which overdetermine further failure.   **64-6926**

Levin, Hannah A. *A psycholinguistic investigation: do words carve up the world differently for Negro and white boys and girls from city and suburban junior high schools?* Rutgers— The State University, 1964. Hypothesized differences based upon the prevalent "self-hate" theory were unsupported, leading to the suggestion that previous estimates of Negro attitudes should be re-examined and that attention should be given to the democratizing influences creating more shared cultural meanings.
                                                                                                                        64-10931

Louie, James W. *Ethnic group differences in ability, temperament, and vocational aspiration.* University of Southern California, 1958.

Luke, Orral S. *Differences in musical aptitude in school children of different national and racial origin.* University of California, 1939.

Mahar, Pauline M. *Dimensions of personality as related to dimensions of prejudice in a survey of a northeastern city.* Cornell University, 1955. Dimensions of the authoritarian personality related to facets of prejudice toward Jews and Negroes. **12370**

Merbaum, Ann D. *Need for achievement in Negro and white children.* University of North Carolina, 1961. Higher achievement scores recorded for whites over Negroes, older over younger, Negro girls over Negro boys. **62-3140**

Mondlane, Edwardo C. *Role conflict, reference group and race.* Northwestern University, 1960. The influence of reference groups on attitudes toward cheating using regional origin and race as variables. **60-4780**

Needham, Walter E. *Intellectual, personality and biographical characteristics of southern Negro and white college students.* University of Utah, 1966. Similarities and differences in southern Negro and white college students with emphasis on creativity. **66-11849**

Norris, Clarence W. *A comparative study of selected white and Negro youth of San Antonio, Texas, with special reference to certain basic social attitudes.* University of Southern California, 1951.

Pace, Walter T. *Profiles of personal needs and college press of Negro teacher trainees.* Wayne State University, 1961. Need-press patterns moved from congruence to dissonance as the subjects moved from freshman to senior class. **62-915**

Parmee, Leila K. *Perception of personal-social problems by students of different ethnic backgrounds.* University of Arizona, 1965. More areas of the Mooney Problem Check List reflected general adolescent concerns than ethnic differences, but the most apparent differences were in personality and self-concept. **66-6897**

Partridge, Gaines R. *The effect on Negro youth in Nebraska high schools of their practices of identification.* University of Nebraska Teachers College, 1961. An examination of factors influencing formation of the "ideal-concept" of Negro youth in certain Nebraska high schools. **62-136**

Pitman, Dorothy E. *Reactions to desegregation: a study of Negro mothers.* University of North Carolina, 1960. Perception by minority group of itself using Negro mothers; indicated development of an image of the Negro as equal to whites. **60-4855**

Pogue, Betty C. *An exploration of the interrelationship among creativity, self-esteem and race.* Ball State Teachers College, 1964. Using a half-white and half-Negro population of children in grades 4, 5 and 6, significant relationships found between creativity and IQ, self-esteem and IQ and creativity and socio-economic level. **64-10468**

Powell, Edward C. *Retreatism and occupational status aspirations: a study of the socio-cultural system and anomie among Negro and white high school seniors.* University of Kentucky, 1966.

Price, Arthur C. *A Rorschach study of the development of personality structure in white and Negro children in a southeastern community.* University of Florida, 1953. Reported age-race differences in intellectual and emotional development. **14338**

Roberts, Shearley O. *The measurement of adjustment of Negro college youth: personality scales for whites versus criteria intrinsic to Negro groups.* University of Minnesota, 1944.

Roseman, Tena M. *Relationship between northern-born and reared Negro children and southern-born and reared Negro children in terms of self-concept, aspiration level, and achievement performance.* New York University, 1962. No regional differences found; negative perceptions indicate need for incentive-building efforts.   **62-3287**

Rousseve, Ronald J. *An analysis of the personality stresses of Negro Americans and their implications for education.* University of Notre Dame, 1958. Personality consequences drawn from existing literature; uniqueness of this study consists in drawing pedagogical implications.   **58-3082**

Shapiro, Deborah. *Social distance and illegitimacy: a comparative study of attitudes and values.* Columbia University, 1966. Race and social class differences found in values and attitudes related to illegitimacy expressed by unmarried mothers.   **66-12592**

Shapiro, Elliott S. *The effect of educational philosophies on the personalities of socio-economically deprived Negro children.* New York University, 1959. Effect of educational philosophies differing in willingness to encourage criticism on two matched 6th-grade groups.   **59-6252**

Sicha, Mary H. *A study of the Rorschach "Erlebniss-Typus" of comparable white and Negro subjects.* Columbia University, 1939.

Singer, Benjamin D. *Racial factors in psychiatric intervention.* University of Pennsylvania, 1965. Describes symptomatic and treatment differences in the psychiatric careers of Negro and white schizophrenics; interpreted as reflecting differing definitions of "normal" by psychiatrists.   **66-4651**

Smith, Paul M., Jr. *Personality characteristics of rural and urban Southern Negro children.* Indiana University, 1958. Urban children had higher intelligence scores, lower GPA and more problems; no difference in personal and social adjustment in relation to rural children.   **58-5216**

Spiaggia, Martin. *Self-group devaluation and prejudice in minority-group boys.* New York University, 1958. Self-group attitudes in Negroes and Puerto Ricans found to correlate with attitudes toward outgroups; not true of Jewish groups.   **59-1039**

Steckler, George A. *A study of authoritarian ideology in Negro college students.* Western Reserve University, 1954.

Stinson, Harold N. *The effect of desegregation on the adjustment and values of Negro and white students.* George Peabody College for Teachers, 1963. Scores on the Index of Adjustment and Values and the F Scale of students in a newly-segregated school situation indicate that desegregation had no damaging effects.   **64-5089**

Tabachnick, Benjamin R. *Some correlates of prejudice toward Negroes in elementary age children: satisfaction with self and academic achievement.* Stanford University, 1959. Found that satisfaction with self in 8 categories of Self-Concept Inventory is related to prejudice.   **59-1430**

Titus, Walter F. *Relationship of need for achievement, dependency, and locus of control in boys of middle and low socioeconomic status.* Indiana University, 1966. Racial variables as well as socio-economic variables included in study.   **66-12690**

Tolleson, Sherwell K. *A study of the interrelationships between race, socioeconomic status, and sex variables in the perception of needs and presses of high school seniors in segregated schools.* University of Alabama, 1964. Wide differences found between white and Negro high school seniors in their perceptions of personality needs and environmental presses.   **65-4070**

Touchstone, Frank V. *A comparative study of Negro and white college students' aggressiveness by means of sentence completion.* Purdue University, 1957. No significant ethnic differences were found in aggression and hostility. **21317**

Trent, Richard D. *An analysis of expressed self-acceptance among Negro children.* Columbia University, Teachers College, 1954.

Vittenson, Lillian K. *The sources of identification and choice of role models by selected white and non-white college students.* Northwestern University, 1965. Marked difference found between Negro female freshmen and other groups in identification with rebellious females. **65-12175**

Walton, Donald F. *Selected mental health factors significant to the early identification of potential school dropouts.* Baylor University, 1965. Reports differences in mental health characteristics of white, Mexican-American and Negro dropouts. **65-4757**

Washington, Justine W. *Self-concepts and socio-economic status of Negroes enrolled in grade six in public schools of Richmond County, Georgia.* University of Oklahoma, 1965. Reported a significant relationship between self-concepts and socio-economic status. **65-11694**

Webster, Elizabeth J. *Fears and worst happenings as reported by southern children.* Columbia University, 1961. Comparison between 1933 and 1961 reports by Negro and white children on the "worst thing that ever happened." **61-5486**

Yokley, Ratha L. *The development of racial concepts in Negro children.* Indiana University, 1953.

Young, Ulysses S. *The relation of social factors to mental syndromes: a case analysis of thirty seven Negro mental patients and their families.* University of Maryland, 1965. Investigated the relations of social factors, such as heavy drinking and illegitimacy, to mental syndromes, such as schizophrenia and psychoneurosis. **66-1370**

3.   Physical Health and Characteristics

Carlson, Robert O. *The influence of the community and the primary group on the reaction of southern Negroes to syphilis.* Columbia University, 1952. A study of factors which cause some persons with early syphilis to secure medical care and others to refrain from seeking care. **4164**

Codwell, John E. *A study of the kind and amount of change in motor function as the amount of Negro increases or decreases in the Negro-white hybrid.* University of Michigan, 1948.

Curry, Marion M. *Somatotype and its relationships to certain selected physical abilities in college Negro men.* University of Texas, 1960. Races equal, except whites superior to Negroes on Sargent Jump Test. **60-2004**

Dunston, Beverly N. *Pica, hemoglobin, and prematurity and perinatal mortality: an experimental investigation of the relationships between pica, hemoglobin levels, and prematurity and perinatal mortality among a clinic population of married Negro pregnant women.* New York University, 1961. Reported a significant relationship between frequency and duration of pica practice, hemoglobin levels and perinatal casualties. **62-1393**

Durham, Elizabeth. *A study of the dietary habits and nutritional status of five hundred Negro children.* Pennsylvania State University, 1949.

Eckhardt, Rudolph A. *Foveal luminosity functions of five Negroes in relation to macular and skin pigmentation.* Fordham University, 1966. No significant differences in foveal luminosity functions found between Negroes and whites. **66-7091**

Ferguson, Ira L. *Health education in tuberculosis with particular reference to the Negro population.* Columbia University, 1950. Investigation of factors contributing to the problem of tuberculosis among Negroes, and proposals for health education programs aimed at this problem. **1647**

Fitts, Howard M., Jr. *Problems reported by private medical practitioners of significance to health education for Negro groups in North Carolina.* Columbia University, Teachers College, 1961.

Fraley, Lester M. *A comparison of the general athletic ability of white and Negro men of college age.* George Peabody College for Teachers, 1940.

Franzblau, Rose N. *Race differences in mental and physical traits: studied in different environments.* Columbia University, 1936.

Gist, Annie L. *Health misconceptions subscribed to by freshmen in selected Negro colleges: a study of the relative prevalence of health misconceptions subscribed to by freshmen in selected Negro colleges.* New York University, 1956. Reported unfounded beliefs prevalent among freshmen in selected Negro colleges of the middle-Atlantic area. **17645**

Harper, Laura J. *Dietary practices of three samples of women: a longitudinal and cross-sectional study.* Michigan State University, 1956. Dietary intakes and food practices of three groups of women, one group composed of Negro women. **58-5712**

Houser, Paul M. *Mortality differentials in Michigan.* Michigan State College, 1948. Analysis of mortality characteristics of Michigan's population in 1940, with changes noted for the period 1910-1940; racial differences included. **1151**

Johnson, Kenneth L. *A study of the health problems of Negro senior-high-school youth in Arkansas.* Boston University, School of Education, 1959. Suggested modifications in school program in the light of problems checked. **59-5537**

Neumann, Holm W. *The American Negro – his origins and his present status as a hybrid or secondary race.* Indiana University, 1962. Detailed morphological description and analysis of a sample of 100 adult Negro skulls. **62-5066**

Phansomboom, Somsak. *The distributions of the Duffy, Kell, Kidd, Lewis and S (MN) blood factors of the American Negroes, with family study and statistical analysis.* Northwestern University, 1953. Gene frequency distributions of the above-named systems are determined for American Negroes.**7059**

Piscopo, John. *Skinfold and other anthropometrical measurements of preadolescent boys from selected ethnic groups.* Boston University, School of Education, 1960. Develops norms for skinfold and other measurements of Italian, Jewish and Negro boys. **60-6430**

Stamler, Rose S. *Racial differences in heart disease risk factors: some social-psychological aspects.* University of Chicago, 1962.

Stone, William J. *The influence of race and socio-economic status on physical performance.* University of California, Berkeley, 1966. Significant difference in performance favoring Negro boys found on 5 out of 7 items of the test. **66-8253**

Tomasson, Richard F. *Patterns in Negro-white differential mortality, 1930-1956.* University of Pennsylvania, 1960. Comparative mortality trends for 22 causes of death.   **60-3618**

Watkins, Elizabeth L. *The decision by Negro mothers to seek prenatal care.* Harvard University, 1966.

Webber, Irving L. *A sociological analysis of the health status of older people in selected counties of Peninsular Florida.* Louisiana State University, 1956. Relationships of certain sociological characteristics, including race, to the morbidity of older persons.   **17457**

ECONOMIC STATUS AND PROBLEMS

1. The Negro as Consumer

Alexis, Marcus. *Racial differences in consumption and automobile ownership.* University of Minnesota, 1959. Includes history of interest in the Negro as a consumer; reports variables on which Negroes and whites differ as consumers.   **60-906**

Dowdy, George T. *An economic analysis of consumer food buying habits of Negro households in Columbus, Ohio.* Ohio State University, 1952. Effect of such factors as income, education and buying days on buying habits.   **58-783**

Hurst, Robert L. *Consumer buying habits in selected areas of St. Louis, Missouri.* University of Missouri, 1954. Analysis of Negro families in terms of various food-buying habits.   **9181**

Kittles, Emma L. *The importance of clothing as a status symbol among college students.* Ohio State University, 1961. Negro-white differences respecting clothing importance, use of clothing as status symbol, factors affecting clothing choice.   **62-2145**

Mock, Wayne L. *Negro-white differences in the purchase of automobiles and household durable goods.* University of Michigan, 1965. Suggests possible existence of a separate Negro market for automobiles, but none for household durable goods.   **65-11001**

Mooney, Horace W. *Some factors associated with Negro-white savings differentials.* University of Michigan, 1953. Regional-racial differences in savings practices; rejects single-factor explanation. **5075**

Williams, Thomas T. *An economic analysis of Negro food habits in Tuskegee, Alabama.* Ohio State University, 1955. Food patterns of Negro professional and semi-professional workers as related to income, family size and regional background.   **14505**

Wilson, Norman. *Meat consumption patterns among Columbia Negroes.* University of Missouri, 1960. Patterns among Negro families in Columbia, Missouri, during summer, 1956, in relation to size of family, income and education.   **60-6828**

2. The Negro as Entrepreneur

Bryson, Winfred O., Jr. *Negro life insurance companies; a comparative analysis of the operating and financial experience of Negro legal reserve life insurance companies.* University of Pennsylvania, 1947.

Crump, Cecille E. *Problems encountered by Negro managers in the operation of business establishments in Nashville, Tennessee.* Indiana University, 1959. Problems in physical facilities, personnel, finance, record keeping and merchandising.   **59-4275**

Fulbright, Stewart B., Jr. *Training programs in Negro life insurance companies.* Ohio State University, 1953. Description of training programs of selected companies in the National Negro Insurance Association, with recommendations for improved training of agents.   **58-7202**

Gloster, Jesse E. *North Carolina Mutual Life Insurance Company: its historical development and current operations.* University of Pittsburgh, 1955. Interprets the success of the company as showing business ability of the Negro as well as the general economic and health progress of Negroes.   **13865**

Henderson, Vivian W. *A study of personnel relations in Negro businesses.* State University of Iowa, 1952. Findings show a general lack of operational efficiency in Negro businesses, which was traced in part to unsound personnel relations programs.   **4068**

Hypps, Irene C. *Changes in business attitudes and activities of the Negro in the United States since 1619.* New York University, 1944.

Livingston, Omeda F. *A study of women executives in life insurance companies owned and operated by Negroes with implications for business education.* New York University, 1964. Presents a curriculum for training women for work in life insurance companies based on an analysis of jobs and the women occupying those jobs in Negro life insurance companies.   **65-973**

Manners, George E. *History of Life Insurance Company of Georgia, 1891-1955.* Emory University, 1959. Analysis of policies and development of company which served only Negroes until 1931.**60-133**

3. Housing

Favor, Homer E. *The effects of racial changes in occupancy patterns upon property values in Baltimore.* University of Pittsburgh, 1960. Analysis of sales of residential properties from 1955-58; attributes other than racial composition cited as influencing property value.   **60-6178**

Fishbein, Annette. *The expansion of Negro residential areas in Chicago, 1950-1960.* University of Chicago, 1963.

Fulton, Robert L. *Russell Woods: a study of a neighborhood's initial response to Negro invasion.* Wayne State University, 1960. Differences between movers and non-movers were interpreted in terms of status prejudice rather than race prejudice.   **60-2322**

Gamberg, Herbert B. *White perceptions of Negro race and class as factors in the racial residential process.* Princeton University, 1964. Concluded that whites may be more prone to translate prejudice into action in choosing new neighborhoods than in leaving old ones and that residential integration is a concrete possibility, particularly at the middle-class level.   **64-12123**

Helper, Rose. *The racial practices of real estate institutions in selected areas of Chicago.* University of Chicago, 1959.

Kelley, Joseph B. *Racial integration policies of the New York City Housing Authority.* Columbia University, 1963. An analysis of policies and procedures of the NYC Housing Authority for the years 1958 to 1961 disclosed six policy approaches which improved racial balance.   **64-2763**

Roberts, Richard J. *The emergence of a civil right: anti-discrimination legislation in private housing in the United States.* St. Louis University, 1961. A study of the development, issues involved in and status of fair housing legislation.   **61-6488**

Schietinger, Egbert F. *Racial succession and changing property values in residential Chicago.* University of Chicago, 1953.

Taeuber, Alma F. A. *A comparative urban analysis of Negro residential succession.* University of Chicago, 1962.

Taeuber, Karl E. *Residential segregation by color in the United States cities, 1940 and 1950: a comparative analysis.* Harvard University, 1960.

Wallace, David A. *Residential concentration of Negroes in Chicago.* Harvard University, 1953.

Wheeler, Raymond H. *The relationship between Negro invasion and property prices in Grand Rapids, Michigan.* University of Michigan, 1962. Data for period 1952 to 1956.   **62-2805**

4. Employment and Income

Abrahamson, Mark J. *The integration of industrial scientists.* Washington University, 1963.

Bailer, Lloyd H. *Negro labor in the automobile industry.* University of Michigan, 1943.

Bechtol, Paul T., Jr. *Migration and economic opportunity in Tennessee counties, 1940-50.* Vanderbilt University, 1962. Describes the migration of labor that accompanies regional economic development; includes data for non-whites.   **62-4505**

Better, Norman M. *Discrimination in educational employment.* University of California at Los Angeles, 1966. Race and age differentiated successful and unsuccessful applicants for secondary school positions.   **66-4944**

Bloch, Herman D. *Socio-economic discrimination against the New York City Negro.* New School for Social Research, 1950.

Bradbury, William C., Jr. *Racial discrimination in the Federal service: a study of the sociology of administration.* Columbia University, 1952. Racial discrimination in Washington, D.C., 1940 to 1947.   **4557**

Brazeal, Brailsford R. *The Brotherhood of Sleeping Car Porters; its origin and development.* Columbia University, 1942.

Cahill, Edward E. *Occupational mobility in a tri-racial isolate.* Catholic University of America, 1965. The effects of biological inbreeding on the maintenance of a socio-cultural system, measured by occupational and geographical mobility.   **66-313.**

Champagne, Joseph E. *The attitudes and motivation of southern underprivileged workers.* Purdue University, 1966. Demonstrates that within the population of disadvantaged workers there is a job-motivation hierarchy which changes within subsamples of the population on basis of race, sex and age.   **66-7400**

Cook, Culbreth B., Jr. *Vocational guidance activities of the National Urban League.* Western Reserve University, 1955.

Crump, William L. *A study of the employment problems of Negro office workers in integrated work programs with implications for business education.* Northwest University, 1949.

Daniels, Virginia R. M. *Attitudes affecting the occupational affiliation of Negroes.* University of Pittsburgh, 1939.

Davis, N.F. *Trade union's practices and the Negro worker – the establishment and implementation of AFL–CIO anti-discrimination policy.* Indiana University, 1960. Analyzes effect of formation of AFL–CIO on racial discrimination by unions.   **60-6285**

Eberhart, E. K. *Discrimination against selected American minorities in the labor market.* University of Wisconsin, 1949.

Edwards, Gilbert F. *Occupational mobility of a selected group of Negro male professionals.* University of Chicago, 1952.

Franklin, Charles L. *The Negro labor unionist of New York; problems and conditions among Negroes in the labor unions in Manhattan with special reference to the N.R.A. and post-N.R.A. situations.* Columbia University, 1937.

Gaston, Edward A., Jr. *A history of the Negro wage earner in Georgia, 1890-1940.* Emory University, 1957. Study of major fields and trends of Negro employment.   **58-5143**

Gershenfeld, Walter J. *The Negro labor market in Lancaster, Pennsylvania.* University of Pennsylvania, 1964. Hiring standards were found to be often in excess of the actual requirements of open positions with a view to upgrading employees, which served to disqualify large numbers of Negroes.   **65-5762**

Hale, William H. *The career development of the Negro lawyer in Chicago.* University of Chicago, 1950.

Hall, Egerton E. *The Negro wage earner of New Jersey.* Rutgers– The State University, 1951.

Hare, Nathaniel. *The changing occupational status of the Negro in the United States: an intracohort analysis.* University of Chicago, 1963.

Hartshorn, Herbert H. *Vocational interest patterns of Negro professional men.* University of Minnesota, 1949.

Hiestand, Dale L. *Economic growth and the opportunities of minorities: an analysis of changes in the employment of Negro men and women.* Columbia University, 1963. From 1910 to 1960 the number of Negro men increased more rapidly than the number of white men in rapidly growing fields and decreased more rapidly in rapidly declining fields.   **64-2759**

Holland, Jerome H. *A study of Negroes employed by the Sun Shipbuilding and Dry Dock Company during World War II and their problems in the post war period.* University of Pennsylvania, 1950. Origin, types of jobs entered, work record, lay-off and re-employment problems of 772 Negroes. **6317**

Jackson, Thomas A. *Technical job opportunities for Negroes in the Atlanta metropolitan area.* University of Tennessee, 1962. Presents job opportunities for Negroes in the Atlanta area together with the educational requirements and implications for curriculum planning.   **63-2175**

Johnson, Keith W. *Racial division of labor and the American Negro. A statistical study of the occupational distribution of the four major race and nativity groups in the United States, with particular discussion of the Negro.* Duke University, 1944.

Kiehl, Robert E. *Preparation of the Negro for his professional engineering opportunities.* Rutgers– The State University, 1957. Explores engineering employment opportunities open to Negroes as well as training opportunities available.   **22571**

Lloyd, Kent M. *Solving an American dilemma. The role of the FEPC official: comparative study of state Civil Rights Commissions.* Stanford University, 1964. The role of the FEPC in four widely separated states.   **64-7665**

Loop, Anne S. *The nature of the relationship between education and careers of Negroes living in Manhattan covering the years 1929-1937.* New York University, 1940.

Martin, Ralph H. *A biracial study of entry job facts found among selected manufacturing and research industries located in metropolitan Knoxville, Tennessee, and their implications for selected secondary schools and colleges.* University of Tennessee, 1961. Presents new work opportunities for Negroes and analyzes vocational programs available.   **61-2874**

Morrison, Alexander H. *The impact of industry on a rural area in northern Virginia: a case study of development in Warren and surrounding counties, 1930-1954.* University of Virginia, 1959. Treats effects of industry on both Negro and white population.   **59-4240**

Morrison, Richard D. *Occupational opportunities in agricultural and related fields and their implications for agricultural education of Negro students.* Michigan State College, 1954. Prevalence of occupational opportunities for Negroes in agriculture and related fields in Alabama, Arkansas, Mississippi and Tennessee; educational implications.   **8506**

Mundy, Paul W. *The Negro boy-worker in Washington, D.C.* Catholic University of America, 1951.

Northrup, Herbert R. *Negro labor and union policies in the South.* Harvard University, 1943.

Oliver, Leavy W. *An historical survey and analysis of the progress of Negroes in public service (1932-52).* Indiana University, 1956. Description and evaluation of data on Negro appointments to public office.   **17972**

Palmer, Edward N. *Factors associated with Negro unemployment in urban United States.* University of Michigan, 1946.

Phillips, William M., Jr. *Labor force and demographic factors affecting the changing relative status of the American Negro, 1940-1950.* University of Chicago, 1958.

Raymond, Richard D. *Interaction between discrimination, inter-regional migration and regional economic development.* Brown University, 1963. From an analysis of 1940 census data it was shown that about half the relative economic progress registered by the Negro was due to changes in population distribution. Techniques are suggested to improve measurement of relative economic status.   **64-1996**

Ruchames, Louis. *The F.E.P.C.: history and accomplishment.* Columbia University, 1951. Description and analysis of origin and achievements of FEPC from 1941 to 1946.   **2856**

EDUCATION

1. Patterns and Conditions

Almond, John F. *The responsiveness of selected state aid programs for education in relation to changes caused by socio-economic factors in selected New Jersey school districts.* Rutgers— The State University, 1963. Comparison of responsiveness to change in New Jersey with Maryland, Pennsylvania, Rhode Island, New York and Massachusetts.   **64-1219**

Biggers, John T. *The Negro women in American life and education: a mural presentation.* Pennsylvania State University, 1954.

Blanding, James D. *The public schools of Sumter, South Carolina.* George Peabody College for Teachers, 1957. School survey; includes data on Negro schools. **24461**

Bottosto, Samuel S. *Relationships between county-wide measures of certain socio-economic factors, intelligence, and academic achievement of high school seniors in Florida.* University of Florida, 1959. Includes racial differences. **59-3538**

Bowen, Irwin W., Jr. *An appraisal of the present status of the Negro in the state of Georgia.* Southern Baptist Theological Seminary, 1952.

Brooks, Lyman B. *A socio-economic and educational study of Negro high-school and junior-college training.* University of Michigan, 1943.

Davids, Robert B. *A comparative study of white and Negro education in Maryland.* Johns Hopkins University, 1936.

Frazier, Gordon E. *A conceptual paradigm of the culturally disadvantaged: an inquiry into interrelationships and consequences with implications for education.* Southern Illinois University, 1965. Study of selected hard core population to identify the ways in which a person may be disadvantaged and the traits emerging from such disadvantagement. **66-1071**

Good, Warren. *Procedures and factors in school site selection in Delaware.* Temple University, 1964. Factors emphasized were community size and the tradition of racial segregation. **64-13687**

Greenberg, Herbert M. *Some effects of segregated education on various aspects of the personality of those members of disadvantaged groups experiencing this form of education: a study designed to determine some effects of segregated education on various aspects of the personality of those members of three disadvantaged groups experiencing this form of education.* New York University, 1955. Concluded that for blind persons and Negroes, integrated education had a more beneficial effect on personality than segregated education. **13609**

Griffin, John A. *Biracial education in the South: a study in social change.* University of Wisconsin, 1956. Description and sociological analysis of changing patterns of biracial education in the South; trend lines of indices of change were developed. **16168**

Henderson, Thomas H. *Some correlates of progress in equalizing educational opportunity for Negroes in southeastern states.* University of Chicago, 1947.

Hurd, Merrill F. *The education of the children of agricultural migrants in the public schools of New York State.* Syracuse University, 1960. Normative survey of 3,000 Negro children of migrant agricultural workers; includes case studies and extensive bibliography to 1957. **61-511**

Jerrems, Raymond L. *A sociological-educational study of a public school in a Negro lower-class area of a big city.* University of Chicago, 1966.

Lyles, Joseph H. *A study of selected phases of school district reorganization as carried out in South Carolina from July 1, 1951 through June 30, 1954.* University of North Carolina, 1958. Includes analysis of effects on Negro education of general changes in school district organization. **58-5956**

Meador, Bruce S. *Minority groups and their education in Hays County, Texas.* University of Texas, 1959. Detailed description of educational situation for Latin Americans and Negroes.   **59-4729**

Meyers, Alfred V. *The financial crisis in urban schools: patterns of support and non-support among organized groups in an urban community.* Wayne State University, 1964. The racial revolution, with its atmosphere of suspicion and distrust, has been a factor contributing to lack of financial support for schools.   **65-1840**

Riggs, Sidney N. *Descriptive study of behavior problems in a mixed race school.* New York University, 1939.

Saunders, Socrates W. *Legal aspects of the education of Negroes with special emphasis on the equalization principle.* University of Pittsburgh, 1943.

Shelley, Herman W. *An analysis of the relationships between eight factors and three measures of quality in thirty-nine South Carolina secondary schools.* University of Florida, 1957. Schools examined included 29 white and 10 Negro schools.   **20779**

Simpson, William B. *A proposed plan for Negro education in Delaware.* Temple University, 1951.

Smart, Alice M. *Geographic factors in the education of Negroes in six selected areas of Missouri.* Washington University, 1952.

Smith, Elizabeth C. *A study of system-wide evaluation in selected schools for Negroes in Georgia, 1956-1960.* New York University, 1961. An analysis of the nature and purview of improvements influenced by system-wide evaluation activities from 1956 to 1960.   **62-1454**

Walker, John E. *The costs of education: an empirical inquiry.* University of Virginia, 1963. Includes data on racial differences in the cost of education at elementary and secondary levels in Virginia.
          64-730

Wilkerson, Doxey A. *Some correlates of recent progress toward equalizing white and Negro schools in Virginia.* New York University, 1958. Examines relevance of certain social factors to progress in equalization between 1940-41 and 1956-57.   **59-1026**

2.   The Law and the Courts

Badger, William V. *A systematic analysis of the U.S. Supreme Court cases dealing with education: 1790-1951.* Florida State University, 1953. Includes cases involving race.   **5391**

Dauterive, Verna B. *Historical legal development of integration in public schools.* University of Southern California, 1966. Narrative summary of judicial decisions and educational developments relative to integration and segregation in the public schools of the U.S.   **66-10538**

Grier, Boyce M. *Legal bases for salary differentials of white and Negro teachers.* George Peabody College for Teachers, 1948.

Hearn, Edell M. *Public educational changes through legislation in Tennessee, 1935-1959.* University of Tennessee, 1959. Includes development of schools for Negro children.   **59-6283**

Jones, Butler A. *Law and social change: a study of the impact of new legal requirements affecting equality of educational opportunities for Negroes upon certain customary official behaviors in the South, 1938-1952.* New York University, 1955. Examines effectiveness of law as an instrument of social change, with special reference to unequal distribution of school funds and discriminatory pay scales.   **24441**

McKee, Jay W. *State exclusion laws: the conflict between state law prohibiting the entrance of free Negroes and the privileges and immunities clause of the Federal Constitution in the period, 1789-1860.* Ohio State University, 1935.

O'Brien, Kenneth B., Jr. *The Supreme Court and education.* Stanford University, 1956. Traces influence of court decisions on educational leaders.   **17732**

Perpener, John O., Jr. *The effects of the Gilmer-Aikin laws upon fifteen schools in Texas that have Negro superintendents or supervising principals.* University of Colorado, 1953.

Rice, Pamela H. *Racial discrimination in education under the United States Constitution.* University of Wisconsin, 1953.

Risen, Maurice L. *The courts and the separation of races in the public schools.* Temple University, 1935.

Romanoli, Peter J. *School attendance areas and the courts relative to de facto segregation.* University of Pittsburgh, 1964. Appellate court decisions defining the authority of boards of education in respect to school attendance areas.   **65-8314**

Strother, David B. *Evidence, argument and decision in Brown vs. Board of Education.* University of Illinois, 1958. Analysis of materials from lower courts and Supreme Court for arguments and responses.   **59-587**

Tyer, Harold L. *The legal status of pupil placement in the public schools of the United States.* Duke University, 1965. Found pupil placement laws valid only where Negro students have absolute freedom between segregated and nonsegregated schools.   **66-92**

Walker, Paul. *Court decisions dealing with legal relationships between American colleges and universities and their students.* University of Southern California, 1961. Most frequently litigated question was attempted discrimination against Negroes.   **61-406**

Wiley, Walter E. *The influence of the state and the United States Supreme Court decisions on the education of the Negro.* Ohio State University, 1951.

Winstead, Elton D. *The development of law pertaining to desegregation of public schools in North Carolina.* Duke University, 1966. Analysis of constitutional, statutory and judicial law relating to racial segregation within its social context.   **66-13693**

3.   Adult and Extension Education

Bradford, Joseph. *Factors related to the use of press and radio by Negro extension personnel in Alabama.* University of Wisconsin, 1962. Training in, attitudes toward and use of mass media by Negro county and home demonstration agents.   **62-1955**

Buckman, Gabe. *A comparison of instruction in vocational agriculture classes for young and adult Negro farmers in South Carolina.* Pennsylvania State University, 1958. Status of out-of-school instruction in vocational agriculture in 1956.   **58-2268**

Cram, Leo L. *The cooperative extension service and the lower socioeconomic citizenry.* University of Wisconsin, 1965. Identifies problems confronting extension service as it seeks to deal with the needs of lower socio-economic population.   **65-6199**

Dellefield, Calvin J. *Aspirations of low socio-economic status adults and implications for adult education.* University of California at Los Angeles, 1965. Aspirations related mainly to obtaining jobs and producing adequate income, and to education for their children rather than for themselves. **66-216**

Floyd, Raymond B. *A plan to broaden guidance facilities for Negro adults through the establishment of church-affiliated centers in the city of New Orleans.* Columbia University, Teachers College, 1960.

Freeman, James N. *A program of education in agriculture for Negroes of Missouri based on an analysis of economic factors and of social activities of Negroes in selected communities in southeast Missouri.* Cornell University, 1946.

Hamilton, David A. *In-service teacher education programs for instruction in farm and home planning with low-income Negro farmers in Tennessee.* Pennsylvania State University, 1959. Relative effectiveness of three types of teacher education programs for vocational agriculture teachers who work with low-income Negro families. **59-6780**

Harris, Albert T. *An analysis of selected socio-economic status data for the purpose of determining the content of and the conditions under which a program of education may be carried on by and for the Negro adults of Chesterfield County, Virginia.* University of Michigan, 1948. Survey of heads of Negro families as basis for recommendations for content of a program of adult education. **1054**

Hill, William B. *A status study of program development in the Negro divisions of the Cooperative Extension Services of ten southern states.* University of Wisconsin, 1959. Status of extension work among Negroes in relation to accepted theories of program planning and needs of agents. **59-3196**

Perry, Benjamin L., Jr. *Alternative economic opportunities on the land for Negro veteran institutional on-the-farm trainees in the general farming area of northwest Florida.* Cornell University, 1954. An appraisal of a farm training program on the basis of economic progress of trainees. **10601**

Pinnock, Theodore J. *A comparison of the effectiveness of film and bulletin in transmitting knowledge to Negro 4-H Club local leaders in Alabama and Caucasian 4-H Club local leaders in Wisconsin.* University of Wisconsin, 1965. The amount of change in knowledge was attributable to the educational level completed by the subjects. **65-9257**

Roberts, Tommy L. *A comparative analysis of the achievement and training success of high school dropouts.* University of Oklahoma, 1965. Factors related to completion of a Manpower Development Training Program by Negroes and whites. **65-9137**

Stanbury, Harry D. *A study of adult education opportunities for an underprivileged community.* Michigan State University, 1965. Description of forced attachment of two suburban school districts and the extension of adult education opportunity to the disadvantaged community. **66-8492**

Webster, Sherman N. *A study of the patterns of adult education in selected Negro churches.* Indiana University, 1960. Patterns of adult education in 10 leading Negro Baptist churches in South Carolina. **60-3017**

Williams, Cornelius A. *An analysis of extension program projection procedures used by Negro county agents in Alabama.* Cornell University, 1962. Organizational and operational phases of county extension programs, with emphasis on long-term planning as practiced by 35 Negro county agents. **62-5838**

4. Higher Education

Abraham, Ansley A. *An investigation of the interaction of freshmen with their curriculum in the School of Education at Florida A & M University.* Indiana University, 1956. Relationship of freshman needs and abilities to the curriculum in a predominantly Negro college. **17755**

Anderson, Thelma H. *Dimensions of the characteristics related to the high- and low-achievement of a selected group of Negro college students.* University of Oklahoma, 1961. Significant differences found in personality needs and adjustment, interests, study habits and attitudes.   **61-4498**

Anderson, Tommie M. *The achievement in mathematics and science of students in the Negro schools and colleges in Mississippi.* Determination of the incidence of talent in science and mathematics among Mississippi Negroes in grades 9, 12 and 13.   **58-7902**

Armstrong, Byron K. *Factors in the formulation of collegiate programs for Negroes.* University of Michigan, 1938.

Bailey, Rubelia J. *The relationship of educational background, socio-economic status, level of aspiration, and intelligence to success in business education.* Temple University, 1965. Students at Virginia State College (Norfolk Division) were subjects of this study.   **65-9471**

Beck, James D. *Functions and responsibilities of deans of students in selected Negro institutions of higher learning.* Indiana University, 1959. Findings based on interviews in 16 Negro colleges. **59-4267**

Bell, James. *An appraisal of undergraduate teacher education in physical education in selected land-grant colleges and universities for Negroes: with special reference to Southern University.* Columbia University, Teachers College, 1959-60.

Berry, Charles A., Jr. *Student part-time employment policies and practices in Negro land-grant colleges.* Indiana University, 1954. Found colleges employed 21% of students enrolled 1951-52; non-college employment opportunities were limited.   **7904**

Bindman, Aaron M. *Participation of Negro students in an integrated university.* University of Illinois, 1965. Reported Negro students were isolated within the university social system and showed an increasingly poor academic performance relative to other students.   **65-7076**

Boger, Dellie L. *The problems of Morehouse College students.* Columbia University, Teachers College, 1956.

Bolton, Ina A. *The problems of Negro college women.* University of Southern California, 1949.

Bonner, Leon W. *Factors associated with the academic achievement of freshman students at a southern agricultural college.* Pennsylvania State University, 1956. Population drawn from predominantly Negro Alabama Agricultural and Mechanical College, 1955-56.   **19963**

Bowen, Hilliard A. *Student personnel services in the Negro land grant colleges.* Ohio State University, 1947.

Bradley, Nolen E., Jr. *The Negro undergraduate student: factors relative to performance in predominantly white state colleges and universities in Tennessee.* University of Tennessee, 1966. Selected characteristics, academic performance, personal problems and successes of Negro undergraduates in 7 predominantly white institutions in Tennessee, 1963-65.   **66-12606**

Brice, Edward W. *A study of the status of junior colleges for Negroes in the United States.* University of Pennsylvania, 1950.

Brooks, Thomas E. *The inception and development of student personnel services at Tuskegee Institute.* Indiana University, 1955. Surveyed development of the program from 1881 to 1953.   **13213**

Brown, Jessie L. *Writing opportunities at Hampton Institute in the student activities program.* Columbia University, Teachers College, 1954.

Brown, Jonel L. *A critical appraisal of the philosophy, organization and educational program of a landgrant college for Negroes.* University of Wisconsin, 1946.

Brown, Theresa K. *A study of home economics graduates at Morgan State College, Baltimore, Maryland from 1944 to 1953: an investigation for curriculum development.* New York University, 1958. Follow-up study of home economics graduates of a predominantly Negro college.   **59-1044**

Brown, William Crawford. *An evaluation of the course offerings and requirements in the secretarial science curriculum at Hampton Institute.* New York University, 1960. Curriculum revisions proposed as a result of evaluation by secretarial science graduates of a predominantly Negro college from 1948 to 1958.   **61-357**

Brown, William Crews. *An evaluation of the present status of health services in Negro land-grant colleges.* New York University, 1960. Criteria developed from the literature used to assess strengths and weaknesses.   **61-358**

Buck, James R., Jr. *Some identifiable characteristics of students entering Negro senior colleges in Mississippi.* George Peabody College for Teachers, 1964. The average Negro freshman was 19 years old, had an I.Q. of 90, and read at the eighth-grade level.   **65-344**

Caldwell, Marion M. *An evaluation of the undergraduate curriculum in agricultural education at South Carolina State College.* Ohio State University, 1959. Suggestions for curriculum improvement in a predominantly Negro college.   **60-1171**

Carpenter, Henry D., Jr. *A proposal for developing procedures for the community program of Grambling College of Louisiana.* Columbia University, Teachers College, 1961.

Chapman, Oscar J. *A historical study of Negro land-grant colleges in relationship with their social, economic, political, and educational background and a program for their improvement.* Ohio State University, 1940.   **325**

Christophe, LeRoy M., Sr. *A study of the provisions for the pre-service and in-service education of secondary-school principals in Arkansas Negro colleges with recommendations for improvement.* New York University, 1954. Reported vast differences between educational opportunity for Negro and white students in Arkansas.   **8016**

Clark, Geraldine L. *A comparative study of the fictional reading of Negro college freshmen and seniors.* University of Chicago, 1957.

Clary, George E. *The founding of Paine College – a unique venture in inter-racial cooperation in the New South, 1882-1903.* University of Georgia, 1965. Origin and development of Paine College, one of the earliest indigenous southern experiments in interracial higher education.   **65-10286**

Clem, William W. *Administrative practices in laboratory schools connected with land-grant and state teachers colleges for Negroes.* University of Wisconsin, 1950.

Clift, Virgil A. *An appraisal of curricular offerings in four Negro teacher education institutions in North Carolina.* Ohio State University, 1944.

Cohen, Arthur M. *Miami-Dade Junior College: a study in racial integration.* Florida State University, 1964. Emphasizes methods of policy formulation during the opening and first two years of operation.
64-10584

Cole, Earl L. *A study of the follow-up program of Grambling College with specific recommendations for further development and improvement.* Columbia University, Teachers College, 1958.

Collins, William M. *A study to determine practices in secondary student teaching programs in nine Negro colleges and universities in Texas and the improvements that are needed.* Cornell University, 1957. Analysis and evaluation of secondary student teaching programs in terms of national practices.
23127

Colson, Cortlandt M. *Appraisal of cadet teaching at Virginia State College.* Ohio State University, 1951. Program analysis at a predominantly Negro college, 1948-50.
24096

Colson, Elsie C. *A co-ordinated plan of organization and administration of certain phases of teacher education for all departments of Virginia State College concerned with the preparation of teachers.* Pennsylvania State University, 1960. Proposed plan for teacher education in a predominantly Negro college, following NCATE principles.
60-5423

Colston, James A. *Higher education in Georgia from 1932 to 1949 with specific reference to higher education for the Negro.* New York University, 1950.
2177

Connor, Miles W. *A study of the facilities and practices of laboratory-school departments of tax-supported normal schools and colleges for the preparation of Negro teachers of elementary schools.* New York University, 1936.

Conyers, Charline F. *A history of the Cheyney State Teachers College, 1837-1951.* New York University, 1960. Historical study of a predominantly Negro college.
60-3767

Conyers, James E. *Selected aspects of the phenomenon of Negro passing.* Washington State University, 1962. Includes attitudes of Negro and white college students toward passing.
63-3027

Cooper, Matthew N. *To determine the nature and significance, if any, of certain differences in the social and personal adjustment of fifty-one successful and fifty-one non-successful college students at Texas Southern University.* New York University, 1955. Population taken from students at a predominantly Negro college.
13600

Cooper, Theodore B. *Adjustment problems of undergraduate Negroes enrolled at Indiana University.* Indiana University, 1952.

Cope, William, Jr. *A study of selected characteristics of the drop-outs at Dillard University.* Indiana University, 1958. Population drawn from a predominantly Negro college, 1946-56.
59-71

Cordery, Sara B. *The training of business teachers in degree-granting institutions attended predominantly by Negroes.* Columbia University, Teachers College, 1957.

Cotton, George R. *Collegiate technical education for Negroes in Missouri with proposed plans for development.* Ohio State University, 1944.

Crawford, Harold W. *Organizational patterns for industrial education programs in selected land-grant colleges.* Wayne State University, 1960. Based on the 17 Negro land-grant colleges.
60-2318

Cuthbert, Marion V. *Education and marginality; a study of the Negro woman college graduate.* Columbia University, 1943.

Daniel, Walter G. *The reading interests and needs of Negro college freshmen regarding social science materials.* Columbia University, 1943.

Davis, Lawrence A. *A comparison of the philosophies, purposes and functions of the Negro land-grant colleges and universities with emphasis upon the program of the agricultural, mechanical, and normal college, Pine Bluff, Arkansas.* University of Arkansas, 1960. Concluded that the Negro colleges embrace 75% of the philosophy statements, 95% of the purposes and 52% of the functions of land-grant institutions. **60-2763**

Davis, Malcolm A. *A study of the personalities and social interests of a group of Negro college freshmen as revealed in their college compositions.* New York University, 1952. A comparison of results of standardized personality tests with analysis of a series of freshman compositions based on personal experience. **7129**

Derbyshire, Robert L. *Personal identity: an attitude study of American Negro college students.* University of Maryland, 1964. The most common characteristic was one of identity conflict and confusion; the primary group to which the students were willing to relate closely was socio-cultural and national rather than racial. **64-11098**

Diamonstein, Barbara L. D. *A study of some factors in relation to the potential acceptance of Negroes in the traditionally white institutions of higher learning in the commonwealth of Virginia, with specific reference to the years 1947, 1950, and 1957.* New York University, 1963. Emphasis placed on the changing economic and political position and the emerging positive self-concept of Negroes. **64-6528**

Dove, Pearlie C. *A study of the relationship of certain selected criteria and success in the student teaching program at Clark College, Atlanta, Georgia.* University of Colorado, 1959. Developed criteria for a selective admission plan in a predominantly Negro college. **60-1064**

Dowdy, Lewis C. *A critical analysis of the purpose, philosophy and objectives of the Agricultural and Technical College of North Carolina with implications for change.* Indiana University, 1965. Recommendations varied from restatement of purposes to certain reorganizations of the college. **66-3112**

Drake, Joseph F. *Occupational interests and opportunities as determinants in the construction of curricula for a Negro land-grant college in Alabama.* Cornell University, 1938.

Drew, Jesse M. *A study of the student personnel services of the Negro land-grant colleges of the United States.* Harvard University, 1950.

Duncan, Catherine W. *Pre-service teacher education for Negroes in Georgia.* Ohio State University, 1949.

DuValle, Sylvester H. *An evaluation of the standards of chemistry teaching in the universities and colleges for Negroes in the United States.* New York University, 1943.

Echols, Jack W. *Criteria for evaluating teacher education in the Negro colleges of Texas.* University of Denver, 1955.

Eddy, Edward D. Jr. *The development of the land-grant colleges: their program and philosophy.* Cornell University, 1956. Contains separate chapter on the 17 Negro land-grant colleges. **18272**

Espy, James A. *Factors influencing choice of college teaching as a career: a study of faculties in predominantly Negro institutions.* University of Minnesota, 1963. Chief factors in the decision were intellectual challenge, opportunity to contribute to society, interest in further study, desire to work with college-age students and unsolicited job offers.   **64-4061**

Fischer, Stephen J. *The development and implementation of a training program for teaching in urban disadvantaged schools.* Harvard University, 1966.

Forbes, Frank L. *A four-year undergraduate professional physical education curriculum for men at the Atlanta University Center.* New York University, 1953. Local, regional and national influences considered as basis for proposed curriculum in a predominantly Negro university center.   **6293**

Gallagher, Buell G. *American caste and the Negro college.* Columbia University, 1939.

Gayles, Anne R. *Proposed program for the improvement of college instruction at Florida Agricultural and Mechanical University.* Indiana University, 1961. An evaluation of teaching effectiveness at a predominantly Negro university, with a plan for the improvement of instruction.   **61-3207**

George, Arthur A. *The history of Johnson C. Smith University, 1867 to the present: to present and analyze the growth and development of the administrative and the curricular aims and practices of Johnson C. Smith University 1867 to the present.* New York University, 1954. History of a predominantly Negro college and theological seminary supported by the Presbyterian church.   **10661**

Goins, William F. *An evaluation of science courses offered for general education in selected Negro colleges.* Ohio State University, 1951.

Goodwin, Louis C. *A historical study of accreditation in Negro public and private colleges, 1927-1952 – with special reference to colleges in the Southern Association.* New York University, 1956. Primarily an analysis of strengths and weaknesses in the accrediting of Negro colleges.   **19989**

Graham, William L. *Patterns of intergroup relations in the cooperative establishment, control, and administration of Paine College (Georgia) by Southern Negro and white people: a study of intergroup process.* New York University, 1955. Historical account of a pioneer demonstration of mutual involvement of indigenous ethnic groups in a hostile environment.   **12215**

Graves, Linwood D. *Proposals for improving teacher education at Morris Brown College.* Columbia University, Teachers College, 1954.

Gray, William H., Jr. *A study of the needs of Negro high school graduates in Louisiana and the recognition accorded them in college.* University of Pennsylvania, 1942.

Grossley, Richard S. *The public-relations program of the Negro land-grant college. Determination of factors and trends in the recent development of the public relations program of the Negro land-grant colleges.* New York University, 1944.

Guines, James T. *Professional laboratory experience provided elementary majors in Negro teacher education programs.* University of Tennessee, 1961. Evaluation against professional criteria of lab experiences in 36 Negro institutions in 16 states for the year 1960-61.   **61-6727**

Hardy, Blanch B. *A follow-up study of Stillman College graduates.* Michigan State University, 1960. Reports results of questionnaire administered to the 1951-57 graduates of a predominantly Negro college.
                                                                                            60-3413

Harrison, General L. *A program of teacher training by Prairie View State College for the improvement of the rural Negro schools of Texas.* Ohio State University, 1937.

Haynes, Roland E. *The place of religiosity in the self-reports of Negro students in a church-related college.* Boston University Graduate School, 1961. Examined relationships between religiosity and various personality factors.   **61-3403**

Headd, Pearl W. *An evaluation of the effectiveness of Tuskegee Institute's basic course in audio-visual education with recommendations for improvement.* Indiana University, 1960. Developed recommendations for improvement in an introductory course in audio-visual education.   **60-6056**

Hedrick, James A. *The Negro in southern graduate education.* North Texas State College, 1954. An evaluation of interracial policies in nonsegregated graduate programs in the South.   **10816**

Henderson, Romeo C. *The academic adaptability of Negro junior college graduates to senior college.* Pennsylvania State University, 1951.

Hinton, William H. *A history of Howard Payne College with emphasis on the life and administration of Thomas H. Taylor.* University of Texas, 1957.

Holley, James M. *An evaluation of the pre-service teacher education curriculum in agricultural education at the Virginia State College.* Ohio State University, 1958. Evaluation of curriculum and competencies of 1944-54 graduates of a predominantly Negro school.   **58-2630**

Holmes, Dwight O. W. *The evolution of the Negro college.* Columbia University, Teachers College, 1935.

Hopson, Raymond W. *An evaluation of the general service programs of physical education of several Negro institutions of higher education as determined by criteria evolved from an examination of the purposes of higher education and of physical education.* Ohio State University, 1952.

Humiston, Thomas F. *Participation of ethnic groups in student activities at a junior college.* Stanford University, 1959. Minority-group students showed differences from dominant group in nature and extent of extracurricular participation.   **59-3665**

Hunter, Robert W. *An analysis and critique of the administrative organization and faculty personnel policies and practices at Alcorn A & M College.* Columbia University, Teachers College, 1954.

Jackson, Julia. *A plan for improving the beginning course in French at Morris Brown College, Atlanta, Georgia.* Columbia University, Teachers College, 1955.

Jackson, Reid E. *A critical analysis of curricula for educating secondary school teachers in Negro colleges of Alabama.* Ohio State University, 1938.

Jacobs, Mary G. *An evaluation of the physical education service program for women in certain selected colleges.* New York University, 1957. Colleges studied were public, four-year Negro colleges.   **25494**

Jenkins, Clara B. *An historical study of Shaw University, 1865-1963.* University of Pittsburgh, 1965.   **65-12946**

Johnson, Harry A. *A proposed plan for a communication materials center at Virginia State College, Petersburg, Virginia.* Columbia University, Teachers College, 1953.

Johnson, Norman J. *A comparative study of the interest patterns of students enrolled in selected curricula at Prairie View Agricultural and Mechanical College, Texas, 1956-1958.* University of Michigan, 1961. Mitchell-Rober Check List used to determine patterns of interest among students at a predominantly Negro college.   **61-1753**

Johnson, Ruth B. *Factors affecting the financing of private Negro colleges and universities in the U.S.* Fordham University, 1961.

Johnston, William E., Jr. *A study of the registrar in state-supported colleges for Negroes.* University of Oregon, 1952.

Kafka, Francis J. *A study and evaluation of the industrial arts teaching methodology at Millersville State College, Millersville, Pennsylvania, as reflected by the teaching methodology of recent graduates.* Columbia University, 1966.   **66-10298**

Kennedy, Joseph C. *A study of ethnic stereotypes of Negro college students.* Columbia University, 1958. Investigated stereotypes held by Negro students toward 5 ethnic groups, in relation to regional background and years in college.   **58-2690**

Kidd, Richard D. *Problems encountered by the faculty of Central State College, Wilberforce, Ohio.* Indiana University, 1959. Analysis of faculty problems in a predominantly Negro college.   **59-4278**

Knight, Charles L. *A study of student personnel programs in Negro colleges accredited by the Southern Association.* University of Denver, 1951.

Lanier, Raphael O. *The history of higher education for Negroes in Texas, 1930-1955, with particular reference to Texas Southern University.* New York University, 1957. Effect of social, political and legal forces; special emphasis on Prairie View College and Texas Southern University.   **58-634**

Le Beau, Oscar R. *Factors affecting the need among Negroes for graduate courses in agriculture.* Cornell University, 1937.

Lee, Lurline M. *The origin, development, and present status of Arkansas' program of higher education for Negroes.* Michigan State University, 1955. Includes analysis of economic and educational backgrounds of Negro college students, as well as quality and extent of educational offerings of Negro colleges.   **12151**

Lightfoote, William E. *The development of a plan for vocational training at the Alabama industrial school for Negro boys and girls.* Indiana University, 1961. Analysis of educational program with recommendations for improved vocational training.   **61-3214**

Lowry, Carmen E. *The prediction of academic success in a private liberal arts college for Negroes.* University of Texas, 1957. Developed a regression equation using scores from standardized tests for predicting academic success in a church-related liberal arts college for Negroes.   **23016**

Madden, Samuel A. *A plan for a conference service bureau at Virginia State College, Petersburg, Virginia.* Columbia University, Teachers College, 1953.

Marion, Claud C. *A qualitative and quantitative study of the effectiveness of instructional programs in technical agriculture in Negro land-grant colleges.* Cornell University, 1948.

Marshall, David C. *A history of the higher education of Negroes in the state of Louisiana.* Louisiana State University, 1956.   **17447**

Martin, Walter T., Jr. *Fundamentals learning laboratories in industrial education centers, technical institutes and community colleges in North Carolina.* Duke University, 1966. Includes racial data on users of the laboratories.   **66-12743**

McClellan, James F. *Seminary training in pastoral counseling at Howard University.* Columbia University, Teachers College, 1956.

McCuistion, Fred. *Graduate instruction for Negroes in the United States.* George Peabody College for Teachers, 1939.

McDaniel, Vernon. *Administering and supervising a program for preparing secondary teachers at Tuskegee Institute.* New York University, 1962. Application of existing knowledge to improvement of secondary education program at a predominantly Negro college.   **62-3301**

McGinnis, Frederick A. *A history of Wilberforce University.* University of Cincinnati, 1940.

McKinney, Richard I. *Religion in higher education among Negroes.* Yale University, 1942.

McMillan, Naman M. *Selected factors related to increased attendance at graduate schools of Negro secondary-school principals in the state of North Carolina between 1956-57 and 1960-61.* New York University, 1964. The factors of promotion, salary increase, and certification requirements were responsible for increased graduate school attendance by North Carolina Negro secondary school principals.   **65-6605**

McMillan, William A. *The evolution of curriculum patterns in six senior Negro colleges of the Methodist church from 1900 to 1950.* University of Michigan, 1957. Reported shift from liberal arts curriculum to more vocational orientation, especially teacher education.   **58-956**

McPheeters, Alphonso A. *The origin and development of Clark University and Gammon Theological Seminary, 1869-1944.* University of Cincinnati, 1944.

McQueen, Finley T. *An evaluation of the pre-service professional curriculum in agricultural education at Tuskegee Institute.* Ohio State University, 1957. Program evaluation in terms of desired competencies at a predominantly Negro college.   **58-2086**

Menchan, William M. *An evaluation of the Cheyney Training School for Teachers.* University of Pennsylvania, 1950.

Miller, Kenneth C. *The teaching and learning of modern foreign languages in colleges and universities for Negroes.* Ohio State University, 1953. Development, present status and evaluation of foreign language programs in Negro colleges.   **58-7188**

Minor, Edward O. *An analytical study of audio-visual programs in four-year accredited Negro colleges and universities.* Survey of extent and organizational structure of audio-visual programs in 49 Negro colleges and universities.   **8934**

Morgan, John W. *The origin and distribution of the graduates of the Negro colleges of Georgia.* Columbia University, 1941.

Murphy, Ella L. *Origin and development of Fayetteville State Teachers College, 1867-1959 — a chapter in the history of the education of Negroes in North Carolina.* New York University, 1960.   **61-341**

Murray, Thelma T. *An appraisal of reading programs in Negro colleges.* Northwestern University, 1951.

Neilson, Herman N. *The development of a professional curriculum in physical education for Hampton Institute in its reorganized program of teacher preparation.* New York University, 1956. Development of a 4-year undergraduate professional curriculum in physical education at a predominantly Negro college.   **16618**

Nicholas, James F. *Professional laboratory experiences provided in teacher education programs by Negro colleges in Virginia and nearby areas.* Pennsylvania State University, 1951.

Noble, Jeanne L. *The Negro woman looks at her college education.* Columbia University, 1955.

Nyabongo, Virginia S. *Achievement in modern foreign languages in Negro colleges of America.* University of Wisconsin, 1944.

Oak, Vishnu V. *Commercial education in Negro colleges.* Clark University, 1937.

Orr, Charles W. *Admissions policies and practices in Negro land-grant colleges.* Columbia University, Teachers College, 1954.

Orr, Clyde L. *An analytical study of the conference of presidents of Negro land-grant colleges.* University of Kentucky, 1959. The work and contributions to education of the conference. **65-15160**

Owens, Robert L., III. *Financial assistance for Negro college students in America: a social historical interpretation of the philosophy of Negro higher education.* State University of Iowa, 1953. A study of the influence of financial assistance on the general philosophy of Negro higher education.   **6548**

Paige, Joseph C. *Administrator faculty and student evaluations of science programs in the nine colleges associated with the African Methodist Episcopal Church.* American University, 1965. Analysis of judgments by administration, faculty and students regarding the improvement of science instruction; Southern Association standards applied to science programs.   **65-9937**

Patterson, Joseph N. *A study of the history of the contribution of the American Missionary Association to the higher education of the Negro — with special reference to five selected colleges founded by the Association, 1865-1900.* Cornell University, 1956. Schools studied are Fisk, Talladega, Atlanta, Hampton, and Straight.   **20423**

Payne, Joseph A. *An analysis of the role of the Association of Colleges and Secondary Schools for Negroes from 1934 to 1954.* Indiana University, 1957. Evaluation of the role of the Association, with emphasis on colleges and the 1954 desegregation ruling.   **24836**

Payne, William V. *A proposed program for the development and use of instructional media in industrial teacher education at Tuskegee Institute.* Ohio State University, 1965.   **66-1814**

Perry, James O. *A study of a selective set of criteria for determining success in secondary student teaching at Texas Southern University.* University of Texas, 1962. Study was designed to discover predictors of success in a teacher education program at a predominantly Negro college.   **62-4807**

Phelps, Ralph A., Jr. *The struggle for public higher education for Negroes in Texas.* Southwestern Baptist Theological Seminary, 1949.

Phillips, Augustus C. *Industrial education for Negroes in the South Atlantic Region — development of a program based on population and occupational changes.* Ohio State University, 1942.

Pierce, Juanita G. *The organization and administration of health, physical education, and recreation in the Atlanta University Center.* New York University, 1945. Analysis of curricula of institutions concerned with higher education of Negroes, with proposals for a coordinated plan of organization and administration. **803**

Pierro, Armstead A. *A history of professional preparation for physical education in some selected Negro colleges and universities.* University of Michigan, 1962. Traces the history of professional preparation for physical education from 1924 to 1958; organization is by problem areas. **63-429**

Pirkle, William B. *A study of the state scholarship aid program for Negroes in Georgia, 1944-1955.* Alabama Polytechnic Institute, 1956. Description and evaluation of a program to provide scholarship aid to Negroes for graduate and professional education. **19394**

Puckett, John R. *An evaluation of certain areas of physical education service programs of selected white and Negro colleges in Tennessee.* University of Tennessee, 1959. Little difference found between 5 white and 5 Negro colleges. **59-6287**

Rackley, Larney G. *The influence of the National Defense Education Act of 1958 on the seventeen original Negro land-grant colleges, with emphasis on audio-visual education.* University of Oklahoma, 1963. NDEA had little influence, except in the area of student loans. **63-3795**

Rand, Earl W. *An analysis of the boards of control of a group of selected Negro Protestant church-related colleges.* Indiana University, 1952.

Rea, Katharine. *A follow-up study of women graduates from the state colleges of Mississippi, class of 1956.* Ohio State University, 1958. Negro women comprised 26 percent of the sample. **59-418**

Reed, William T. *A partial selection of curriculum content for the improvement of industrial teacher education in colleges for Negroes.* University of Pittsburgh, 1947.

Richards, Violet K. *A study of teacher education programs in selected liberal arts colleges for Negroes.* Northwestern University, 1952.

Richardson, John F., III. *A comparison of certain characteristics of a group of Negro and non-education college students: an investigation to determine the nature and significance of the differences in various characteristics between Negro college students who select teaching and those who choose other vocational goals.* New York University, 1963. Found some differences in interests, but few personality differences between education and non-education students. **64-265**

Ridley, Walter N. *Prognostic values of freshman tests used at Virginia State College.* University of Virginia, 1953. Analysis of prognostic value of 6 tests used in freshman guidance at a predominantly Negro college. **7984**

Robinson, William H. *The history of Hampton Institute, 1868-1949.* New York University, 1954. An account of how one college sought to meet the needs of Negroes in the South. **10646**

Roche, Richard J. *Catholic colleges and the Negro students.* Catholic University of America, 1948.

Rochelle, Charles E. *Graduate and professional education for Negroes.* University of California, Berkeley, 1943.

Sanders, Charles D. *Student personnel service in Negro colleges of the South Atlantic States.* Oregon State University, 1963. Adequate provisions found in areas of religious life, functional student governing bodies and part-time jobs; weaknesses existed in areas relating to the personality of the student. **64-2380**

Sandford, Paul L. *The origins and development of higher education for Negroes in South Carolina to 1920.* University of New Mexico, 1965. Includes discussion of the SPG, the Port Royal experiment, constitutional convention of 1868, and the founding of colleges such as Claflin, Allen and Morris.
66-4451

Satneck, Walter J. *The history of the origins and development of the Delaware State College and its role in higher education for Negroes in Delaware.* New York University, 1962. Covers period from 1891 to 1960.
63-5380

Sawyer, Robert M. *The Gaines case: its background and influence on the University of Missouri and Lincoln University, 1936-1950.* University of Missouri, 1966. Historical study of the effect of the Gaines case upon Negro higher education in Missouri.
66-9000

Scott, Will B. *Race consciousness and the Negro student at Indiana University.* Indiana University, 1965. Negro students at Indiana University saw themselves as isolated, believed that University policies were not enforced and were unenforceable and tended to avoid interracial involvement.
65-14068

Shipman, F. George. *An evaluative study of the Southern Education Foundation's Regional Research and Leadership Development Program.* George Peabody College for Teachers, 1961. Evaluation of a program to prepare personnel above the M.A. degree level for southern Negro schools.
61-5828

Shoots, Queen Esther. *Gainful employment of Negro home economics graduates with implications for educational programs.* University of Wisconsin, 1965. Study of the employment situation of home economics graduates from 5 predominantly Negro southern colleges against English graduates as a control group.
65-6242

Silverman, Pincus. *Characteristics of a Negro college environment and its relationship to student value systems.* North Texas State University, 1964. Reports significant differences in college environment and student values between Negro and non-Negro colleges.
65-1151

Smith, William P., Jr. *A follow-up of selected graduates of Alabama State College.* Rutgers— The State University, 1959. Descriptive survey of graduates from an institution which trains nearly all Negroes employed in education in Alabama.
59-5329

Spann, Annabelle E. *A follow-up study of Alabama Agricultural Mechanical College home economics graduates with implications for curriculum improvement.* University of Wisconsin, 1958. Reports graduates' jobs, opinions as to adequacy of their education, strengths and weaknesses of home economics curriculum and recommendations for improvement.
58-1931

Speigner, Theodore R. *An analysis of the resource-use education program of North Carolina College at Durham.* University of Michigan, 1961. Evaluation of workshop at a predominantly Negro college.
61-1793

Strider, Rutherford H. *Music in the general college program: a plan for Morgan State College.* New York University, 1955. Proposes a music program for a predominantly Negro institution based on student needs and interests.
12241

Taylor, Cyrus B. *Mechanic arts programs in land-grant colleges, established for Negroes: a study of the types and status of the programs operating and an analysis of selected factors that influenced the development of these programs.* University of Minnesota, 1955. Curricula found to be different from other land-grant colleges because of employment practices under the caste-system.
15964

Taylor, Joseph T. *An analysis of some factors involved in the changing function and objectives of the Negro college.* Indiana University, 1952. Analysis of aims and objectives of the Negro college in selected historical periods. **7427**

Taylor, Paul L. *An analysis of religious counseling practices of nine selected Negro colleges.* Indiana University, 1958. Interviews and observation in public, private and church-related colleges. **58-5219**

Taylor, Prince A., Jr. *A history of Gammon Theological Seminary.* New York University, 1948. Development of a predominantly Negro theological seminary. **1155**

Thompson, Cleopatra D. *The Jackson State College graduate in American society: a follow-up study of 306 graduates, 1944-1953.* Cornell University, 1960. Appraisal of college experience by graduates of a predominantly Negro college. **61-1111**

Thompson, Ray. *Counselor training in state supported Negro colleges and universities in states with dual educational systems.* Michigan State College, 1953. Evaluation of training offered in terms of expert opinion. **5937**

Thornton, Peter B. *Analysis of the counselor-training program at Texas Southern University.* Colorado State College, 1963. Data collected from 1951 to 1960 graduates of a predominantly Negro university. **63-5901**

Toles, Caesar F. *Regionalism in southern higher education.* University of Michigan, 1953. Evaluation of interstate compacts leading to the Southern Regional Education Board according to concepts of regionalism and sectionalism. **5749**

Townes, Ross E. *A study of professional education in physical education in selected Negro colleges.* Indiana University, 1951.

Troup, Cornelius V. *A study of the student personnel services offered by the Negro colleges of Georgia.* Ohio State University, 1948.

Turner, Bridges A. *Objectives and problems of industrial education in Negro colleges.* Pennsylvania State University, 1941.

Van Wright, Aaron, Jr. *Factors relative to job selections in music faculties of the original Negro land-grant colleges since the 1954 Supreme Court decision.* University of Oklahoma, 1965. Job activities, rewards and satisfactions of music teachers in the Negro land-grant colleges. **65-9758**

Walker, George H. *A co-ordinated plan for a communication center at the Norfolk Division of Virginia State College.* New York University, 1949. A plan for teaching communications skills in a predominantly Negro college. **1569**

Walls, Jean H. *A study of the Negro graduates of the University of Pittsburgh for the decade 1926-36.* University of Pittsburgh, 1938.

Ward, John H. *The status of psychology in the seven Negro colleges of Alabama.* New York University, 1955. Analysis of course offerings, content, personal data and learning theories in the teaching of psychology. **12246**

Weatherford, Allen E., II. *Professional health education, physical education and recreation in Negro colleges and universities in the United States.* Pennsylvania State University, 1949.

Welch, Lucille S. *A critical analysis of Negro college catalogs to determine the course offerings in elementary education, particularly in the field of teacher training.* Indiana University, 1950.

West, Gordon L. *An appraisal of selected aspects of a teacher education program at Saint Augustine's College based upon a follow-up of beginning secondary school teachers.* Indiana University, 1959. Survey of graduates of a predominantly Negro college with no more than 4 years teaching experience.
59-6590

Whitehead, Matthew J. *Negro liberal arts college deans.* New York University, 1944. Status and duties of deans, as well as origin and development of the office.
677

Wilkinson, Rachel E. D. *A determination of goals for alumni relations in the colleges for Negroes in North Carolina.* New York University, 1952. Includes historical survey of alumni relations; proposes 5 major goals.
4539

William, Joshua L. *A plan for making more meaningful the course in freshman college algebra at State Agricultural and Mechanical College, Orangeburg, South Carolina.* Columbia University, Teachers College, 1955.

Wilson, Herbert A. *An analysis of the views of Alcorn A & M College held by its students, faculty and non-academic staff.* Columbia University, Teachers College, 1958.

Winder, Thelma V. *Financial experiences of families: family financial experiences of selected graduates of Morgan State College and the implications of these experiences for teaching family finance.* New York University, 1957. Family financial experiences of graduates one year after graduation from a predominantly Negro college.
58-501

Woodson, Grace I. *The implications of purpose for the definition of a college program, with special reference to the separate Negro college.* Ohio State University, 1940.

Young, Kenneth E. *Who can and should go to what kind of college.* Stanford University, 1953. Race was one of 8 variables in this temporal study of college admission requirements; notes effect of Depression and war.
5822

Young, Percy. *Guidance in Negro land-grant colleges.* Harvard University, 1946.

5. Secondary Education

Austin, Lettie J. *Programs of English in representative Negro high schools of Texas.* Stanford University, 1952.

Bell, William M. *A critical study of the physical education curricula in ten Negro high schools with respect to the relationship of principles to practice.* Ohio State University, 1960. Developed instrument to assess degree to which P.E. programs achieve goals of a democratic education.   **61-897**

Berry, Charles N. *Program improvement in Tennessee Negro secondary schools resulting from evaluations sponsored by the Southern Association of Colleges and Schools.* University of Tennessee, 1964. Greatest improvement occurred in instructional materials and in subject areas of mathematics, foreign language and music; least improvement was in methods of evaluating student progress. **65-1420**

Boney, Jew D. *A study of the use of intelligence, aptitude and mental ability measures in predicting the academic achievement of Negro students in secondary school.* University of Texas, 1964. Reported consistency of predictability for high school grade point average (GPA) with the STEP verbal tests and a positive relationship between SCAT total scores and high school GPA.
65-4283

Boose, Sidney S. *A study of the programs of vocational agricultural education in the secondary schools of Mississippi.* Indiana University, 1954. Data on all local programs of agricultural education in Mississippi; includes non-white programs.   **8925**

Boyd, Laurence E. *A study of the personnel in the Negro secondary schools in North Carolina for the school year 1937-1938.* University of Iowa, 1939.

Brodhead, John H. *The status of the Negro in the Philadelphia senior high schools with particular reference to his social and economic conditions.* Temple University, 1937.

Brooks, John W. *Attitudes and opinions of Negro parents and students concerning Shortridge High School.* Indiana University, 1960. Major dissatisfaction with this integrated high school was lack of Negro participation in extracurricular activities.   **60-2995**

Brown, Aaron. *An evaluation of the accredited secondary schools for Negroes in the South.* University of Chicago, 1944.

Brown, William H. *A critical study of secondary education for Negroes in Georgia.* Ohio State University, 1949.

Bryant, Ira B. *Administration of vocational education in Negro high schools in Texas.* University of Southern California, 1948.

Dean, Elmer J. *Social studies in the Negro high schools of Georgia, 1952.* Columbia University, Teachers College, 1955.

Dungee, Grant A. *A comparison of the health knowledge level of students in selected secondary Negro schools with the ratings of their schools' health service and health instruction programs.* Indiana University, 1964. Health knowledge of students in Mississippi related to quality of health service programs, size and location of schools and regional accreditation.   **65-420**

Fensch, Edwin A. *A critical study of Negro students in the John Simpson Junior High School, Mansfield, Ohio.* Ohio State University, 1944.

Fields, Marvin A. *Evaluation of selected departments of vocational agriculture in the Negro high schools of Virginia with implications for teacher-education and supervision.* Ohio State University, 1954. Revised Ohio criteria applied to the vocational agriculture programs in Negro high schools in Virginia.   **12023**

Gregg, Howard D. *The background study of Negro high school students in Ohio.* University of Pennsylvania, 1936.

Gunthorpe, Muriel B. *A comparison of Negro and white student participation in selected classes of the junior high school program.* New York University, 1964. Found integration most readily achieved in those activities which are voluntary and least readily accomplished in areas which depend upon teacher or administrative decision to include the student.   **64-8477**

Hall, John E. *A design for organizing and administering reading programs in consolidated high schools for Negroes in Mississippi.* New York University, 1961. Data for a handbook to guide principals in administering reading programs, considering the needs of principals of Negro schools.   **62-3310**

Harris, Nelson H. *An analysis and appraisal of North Carolina's provisions for furnishing teachers for her Negro secondary schools.* University of Michigan, 1938.

Harrison, Elton C. *An evaluation of industrial education programs in secondary schools for Negroes in Louisiana.* Ohio State University, 1949.

Hickerson, Nathaniel. *Comparisons between Negro and non-Negro students in participation in the formal and informal activities of a California high school.* University of California, Berkeley, 1963. Differences in participation found to exist between Negro, Filipino and Caucasian students were explained as a reflection within the high school of the role assigned in the total community. **63-6179**

Hindman, Baker M. *The emotional problems of Negro high school youth which are related to segregation and discrimination in a southern urban community.* New York University, 1953. Examines the relation between experience in interracial contacts and the attitudes of a group of Negro youth. **7101**

Hobson, Abigail K. *A study of values of rural and urban Negro families in Alabama with implications for homemaking education.* Michigan State University, 1962. Values explored in areas of food, relationships and management in home responsibilities, and compared with those taught in secondary school curricula. **63-3719**

Hutson, Darlene L. *The Jeanes Supervisory Program in Tennessee.* University of Tennessee, 1964. Development and present status of a program that provided the first administrative unit for Negro schools on a general basis in the southern states. **65-1437**

Kaiser, Louis H. *Factors related to the educational aspiration level of selected Negro and white secondary students and their parents.* University of Arkansas, 1961. Aspiration levels were significantly related to all factors for white students but only to education of fathers and aspirations of parents for Negro students. **61-1343**

Keeler, Kathleen F. R. *Post-school adjustment of educable mentally retarded youth educated in San Francisco.* Colorado State College, 1963. Recommends training in homemaking skills as being of special importance for the Negro and the Mexican-American group. **64-4194**

Kiah, Calvin L. *A study to determine the degree to which the Maryland County colored high school program is functional, based upon an inquiry into the occupational status of graduates from selected high schools.* Columbia University, Teachers College, 1951.

Kupferer, Harriet J. *An evaluation of selected physical education activities to determine their worth in bettering intergroup relations: a sociometric analysis of Negro-white relationships in physical education classes in a Connecticut high school.* New York University, 1954. The four activities studied did not substantially alter social structure in terms of increased racial acceptance. **10672**

Mahaffey, Theodore. *A critical study of business education in the West Virginia secondary schools for Negroes with implications for business teacher education.* Ohio State University, 1950.

McCown, George W. *A critical evaluation of the four track curriculum program of the District of Columbia senior high schools with recommendations for improvement.* University of Maryland, 1960. Concluded that the 4-track curriculum was meeting needs of students in D.C. with different backgrounds and abilities. **60-4928**

Miller, George R., Jr. *Adolescent Negro education in Delaware. A study of the Negro secondary school and community (exclusive of Wilmington).* New York University, 1944.

Moore, Parlett L. *Analysis of the factors determining elimination in the Negro secondary schools in Maryland.* Temple University, 1952.

Pender, William M. *Curriculum and instructional problems of the smaller secondary schools for Negroes in East Texas.* University of Texas, 1960. Survey of problems in secondary schools with less than 300 pupils during 1957-58 school year. **60-4574**

Poulos, Nicholis. *Negro attitudes toward pictures for junior high school social studies textbooks.* University of Michigan, 1965. Attitudes of Negro P.T.A. members toward hypothetical pictures of Negro personalities for junior high social studies texts. **66-6680**

Redcay, Edward E. *County training schools and public secondary education for Negroes in the South.* Columbia University, Teachers College, 1935.

Reuben, Anna M. *The American Negro and American nationality: a book of readings.* Columbia University, 1965. Meaning, nature and problems of American nationality as illustrated by the Negro; general essay plus readings on the senior high or college levels. **66-2664**

Roberts, John L. *A study of business education in the Negro public secondary schools of Tennessee.* State University of Iowa, 1962. Analysis of status of business education in accredited Negro public high schools in terms of philosophy, purposes, courses, enrollment and equipment. **62-2409**

Rogers, Oscar A., Jr. *Factors related to the educational aspiration level of selected Negro and white secondary students and their parents.* University of Arkansas, 1960. No racial differences found in educational aspiration levels. **60-2772**

Rowland, Monroe K. *Opinions of goals of secondary education held by parents and educators.* University of Michigan, 1960. Variables, including race, related to parental disagreement with educators regarding goals of secondary education. **60-6924**

Sills, Joe F. *Alcohol education: assessment of selected characteristics of Negro secondary school students as a basis for development of an alcohol education program.* University of North Carolina, 1964. Knowledge and behavior of Negro students in North Carolina with reference to alcohol. **64-12530**

Smith, Bettie M. *An evaluation of the health education program in the accredited Negro high schools of Georgia. An appraisal of health education programs based on validated principles and their relationship to local factors and current practices.* New York University, 1962. Comparison of present practices with established principles; recommendations for improving practices. **62-5352**

Spellman, Cecil L. *The basis for a program of rural secondary education for Negroes in Wilson County, North Carolina, with implications for curriculum content.* Cornell University, 1943.

Stegall, Alma L. *A critical analysis of the pre- and in-service education of the Jeanes supervisors in Georgia.* Indiana University, 1950.

Sullivan, Floyd W. *A study of the holding power of two selected Negro high schools of Atlanta, Georgia.* New York University, 1963. Students in the 9th and 10th grades found to be most vulnerable for leaving school; overall holding power of the two schools was 30 percent. **64-6543**

Svoboda, William S. *Negro-white problems in the United States: implications for secondary schools.* University of Kansas, 1964. Includes a complete hypothetical problem-solving unit as an example of how social studies classes might deal with racial problems. **65-7673**

Taylor, Henry L. *A study of the supervised farming programs of Negro pupils studying vocational agriculture in high schools in Tennessee.* Cornell University, 1951.

Ten Houten, Warren D. *Socialization, race, and the American high school.* Michigan State University, 1965. The effect on socialization of the racial composition of high schools.

66-444

Vardeman, Martha H. *A study of the relation between size and accreditation of school and certain aspects of the instructional program in public Negro high schools, Alabama, 1958.* University of Alabama, 1959. Significant relationships found between accreditation, size of senior class and aspects of instructional program.

60-1729

Wooden, Ralph L. *Industrial arts in the public secondary school programs for Negroes in North Carolina.* Ohio State University, 1956. Identification of needs, analysis of program and projections for improvement.

20735

6. Preschool and Elementary Education

Ametjian, Armistre. *The effects of a pre-school program upon the intellectual development and social competency of lower class children.* Stanford University, 1966. Reported that early intervention can produce significant differences in mental age, social competence and language development. **66-6316**

Benjamin, William F. *The attitudes of elementary school children toward the granting of privileges.* George Peabody College for Teachers, 1961. Influence of race, grade level, sex and socioeconomic and scholastic achievement status on children's attitudes toward privilege. **61-5797**

Bergin, Sister Marie L. *The effects of the summer vacation on the reading ability of children who had just completed first grade.* Fordham University, 1963. Urban whites tested lower, Negro children showed no significant difference and white suburban children tested higher after the summer vacation.

63-5583

Byrd, Laurie L. *The development of supervision of instruction in North Carolina with emphasis on state efforts to provide local supervision to rural elementary schools, 1900-1937.* Duke University, 1966. Includes supervision of Negro schools under Peabody Fund, General Education Board and Jeanes Fund, as well as state supervision.

66-12723

Chappat, Janine S. A. *"Race" prejudice and preschool education.* Radcliffe College, 1945.

Coker, Donald R. *The relationship of readiness test scores to selected socio-economic factors of lower class families.* University of Arkansas, 1966. A study of families and children who participated in Head Start and those not in program in Fayetteville, Arkansas, summer, 1965. **66-11605**

Dawson, Carrie B. *Art education at the elementary level and the improvement of Negro-white relations.* University of Illinois, 1957. Projection of an elementary art program aimed at improving Negro-white relations.

20857

Fodor, Eugene M. *The effect of systematic reading of stories on the language development of culturally deprived children.* Cornell University, 1966. Experimental group (mainly Negro) showed significantly greater gains than control group. **66-10261**

Hall, Mary A. *The development and evaluation of a language experience approach to reading with first grade culturally disadvantaged children.* University of Maryland, 1965. Greater gains in reading readiness, word recognition and sentence reading found with language experience approach than with visual approach.

66-3080

Hast, Eugene E. *Administering an experimental program at the primary level designed to meet the needs of disadvantaged children.* Harvard University, 1965.

Johnson, Mayme E. L. *The educational needs of Negro youth.* Stanford University, 1951.

Jones, Katherine L. S. *The language development of Head Start children.* University of Arkansas, 1966. A comparison of Head Start and non-Head Start children on language development in Little Rock, Arkansas, summer, 1965. **66-11609**

Kleiman, Bert M. *Planning and implementing a modified Higher Horizons Program in the Dade County, Florida, public schools.* Harvard University, 1964.

Kostiuk, Nick. *Attitude changes of culturally deprived school children in a large metropolitan gray areas project.* Pennsylvania State University, 1963. The attitudes of all groups underwent significant changes on such items as attitudes toward school, home and people. **64-5373**

Lepper, Robert E. *A cross cultural investigation of the relationship between the development of selected science-related concepts and social status and reading readiness of Negro and white first graders.* Florida State University, 1965. No racial differences found in the non-experience based tasks. **65-15475**

Loper, Doris J. *Auditory discrimination, intelligence, achievement, and background of experience and information in a culturally disadvantaged first-grade population.* Temple University, 1965. Concluded that culturally disadvantaged children have the experiences and concepts necessary to handle early reading materials but lack the oral language tools to describe and organize these experiences. **66-659**

Mermelstein, Egon. *The effect of lack of formal schooling on number development.* Michigan State University, 1965. Study of a group of Prince Edward County, Virginia, children showed that lack of schooling does not affect the stages of number development on either verbal or non-verbal tasks. **65-8396**

Moore, William, Jr. *A portrait: the culturally disadvantaged pre-school Negro child.* St. Louis University, 1964. Detailed description of the disadvantaged child based on a group of Negro children in St. Louis, Missouri. **64-13475**

Nicholson, Elsie M. *An investigation of the oral vocabulary of kindergarten children from three cultural groups with implications for readiness and beginning reading programs.* Western Reserve University, 1965. A study of oral vocabulary of children as related to social class, race and sex. **66-8020**

Robinson, Andrew A., Jr. *Retention in grade in predominantly Negro schools of Duval County, Florida.* Columbia University, 1963. For the 27 percent of Negro ninth-graders who had been retained in grade, the greatest incidence was in the first and ninth grades. Retention itself, not test scores, seemed the strongest concomitant of retention. **64-1499**

Sandmeier, Thelma L. *A study of the differences in aims for public elementary education as related to selected sociological factors.* Rutgers— The State University, 1964. Divergence in aims for public elementary education were reported to be related to sociological factors of sex, age, religion, level of education and occupation, but not to race. **65-6566**

Tyrrell, Frank E. *Administrative policies and practices of programs for the culturally disadvantaged in elementary schools of the U.S.* University of Southern California, 1965. Reports on 136 elementary school districts with programs for culturally disadvantaged children. **65-8925**

Wallace, Elsie H. *Negro elementary education in Northern Alabama.* Northwestern University, 1948.

Williams, Johnetta K. *The development of the processes of curriculum improvement in the Negro schools of Chattanooga, Tennessee: a critical analysis and appraisal of the processes of curriculum improvement and their development in the Negro schools of Chattanooga, Tennessee.* New York University, 1952. Processes used included classroom research, staff research, system-wide study and cooperative study.   4553

Williams, Percy V. *School designed programs and projects on selected socio-economic problems of Negroes in Maryland.* New York University, 1955. Study of extent to which schools for Negroes designed programs and projects on problems of the Negro community.   15555

Wishart, Claire K. *A comparison of the problems of boys and girls in four elementary schools in the city of New York, Higher Horizons and non-Higher Horizons programs, grades 5 and 6.* Fordham University, 1964. Compared problem areas and frequency of problems.   65-2008

7. Guidance and Occupational Choice

Blee, Myron R. *Factors associated with the college attendance plans of Florida high school seniors.* University of Illinois, 1958. Includes race as a variable.   59-476

Blossom, Herbert H. *Some factors influencing high school graduates' attendance at different types of colleges.* University of California, Berkeley, 1966. Factors considered included race, academic ability, socio-economic level, sex and motivation.   66-8240

Brown, Louis P. *The status of guidance services in twenty-two accredited secondary schools for Negroes in Virginia.* University of Michigan, 1954. General inadequacies found using USOE criteria.   7615

Cobb, Willie L. *Vocational interests of white and Negro pupils at the secondary level.* University of California, Berkeley, 1949.

Connors, Maureen. *A comparative study of the occupational interests of Negro and white adolescent boys.* Catholic University of America, 1965. Reported no significant differences in the occupational interests of Negro and white adolescent boys when matched for age, IQ and socio-economic level.
65-10366

Cooper, Charles L. *Major factors involved in the vocational choices of Negro college students.* Cornell University, 1936.

Craine, James F. *A comparison of the occupational aspirations of Negroes and whites.* University of Southern California, 1953.

English, Walter H. *A study of minority group attitudes of Negroes in Springfield, Massachusetts, and the implications for guidance services in the public schools.* Columbia University, Teachers College, 1954.

Fisher, John. *The effects of counseling on levels of aspiration and school performance of underachieving lower class Negro children.* University of Michigan, 1962. Reported counseling did not produce more realistic aspirations or reduce underachievement.   62-3238

Franklin, George W. *An evaluation of counseling and employment activities of disabled Negro veterans.* Purdue University, 1955. Evaluation of counseling at Tuskegee Institute, 1944 to 1949.   13922

Gilbert, Jean P. *Psychocultural implications of vocational behavior of Negro college students.* University of Buffalo, 1962. Significance of the educational status of the like-sexed parent for persistence, interests, academic potential and success of Negro students.

62-5219

Holtzclaw, Thelbert E. *An analysis of the vocational preferences of seniors in the Negro secondary schools of Arkansas with implications for possible curriculum modification.* University of Arkansas, 1955. Reports findings of questionnaire and vocational interest inventory administered to a stratified sample of students. **8151**

Jackson, Ervin, Jr. *Students' expressed opinions relative to the use and adequacy of certain guidance practices in selected Negro high schools.* University of Oklahoma, 1963. Varying degrees of correlation were found between school achievement, type of counseling program available and the use of the counseling services. **63-6705**

Johnson, Autrey B. *A comparative study of white and Negro guidance programs and the administrators' attitudes toward these programs in selected school districts of Arkansas.* University of Arkansas, 1962. Found differences mainly in the professional preparation of guidance staffs. **62-6564**

Jones, Samuel O. *An analysis of guidance services and practices in the Negro secondary schools resulting from evaluations sponsored by the Southern Association of Colleges and Schools.* University of Oklahoma, 1964. Reasonably well trained counselors and programs organized on the basis of established practice. **64-5965**

Macklin, Arnett G. *A critical study of the Virginia revised program for improving secondary education of Negroes: based upon the high school counseling program.* Ohio State University, 1945.

McKinney, Frederick J. D. *The guidance program in selected Negro institutions for higher education.* Indiana University, 1953. Survey and evaluation of guidance programs of 37 Negro colleges. **7011**

Morrow, Robert O. *A study of evaluation of the guidance services in the Virginia public secondary schools.* University of Virginia, 1961. Evaluation of guidance services; data presented for urban and rural, white and Negro schools. **61-4556**

Morse, Carlton H. *Guidance services and practices in the Negro secondary schools of Georgia.* University of Oklahoma, 1959. Normative survey with recommendations for improvement. **59-5497**

Muse, Charles S. *A comparison of factors influencing the decision of academically able high school Negro and white seniors to attend or not to attend college.* University of Oklahoma, 1964. More Negroes than whites stated plans to attend college; white students' plans were more diversified and definite. **64-13353**

Nicholson, Lawrence E. *The Urban League and the vocational guidance and adjustment of Negro youth.* Columbia University, 1950.

Pemberton, Zelda C. *Social guidance needs in the secondary Negro schools, Cleveland County, North Carolina.* New York University, 1946. Survey of health, recreation and social welfare needs and provisions to meet those needs. **821**

Pierro, Earl H. *A comparative analysis of the occupational aspirations of rural and urban Negro adolescents.* State University of Iowa, 1955. A study of the effect of social systems on occupational aspirations. **12119**

Powell, Christus N. *Factors affecting the educational and vocational plans of high ability Negro students in the high schools of Alabama.* Pennsylvania State University, 1963. Many factors significant in the college plans of other youth were not found significant for Negro youth.   **64-5382**

Sain, Leonard F. *Occupational preferences and expectations of Negro students attending a high school located in a lower socio-economic area.* Wayne State University, 1965. Students found to be vocationally immature, had little exploration of vocations; school was a minor source of information and parents and relatives were the major influence.   **66-10119**

Satterwhite, Mildred M. *The vocational interests of Negro teachers college students.* University of California, Berkeley, 1949.

Smith, Benjamin F. *A critical analysis of the relationship between occupational goals, social adjustment and social status of high school seniors in urban Negro high schools in two states.* New York University, 1951. Each social class tends to aspire to occupations which the regional culture has established as Negro jobs.   **3452**

Stout, Charles O. *A comparison between vocational offerings and job placement in five vocational schools for Negroes and five vocational schools for whites in Oklahoma.* Indiana University, 1950.

Uzzell, Odell. *Occupational aspirations of Negro male high school students in North Carolina.* Ohio State University, 1958. Occupational aspirations of urban youth as related to social background characteristics.   **59-432**

Waters, E. Worthington. *Vocational aspirations, intelligence, problems and socio-economic status of rural Negro high school seniors on the eastern shore of Maryland – their implications for vocational guidance.* Temple University, 1952.

Watson, William H. *The establishment of a functional guidance program in the rural Negro high schools of eastern North Carolina.* New York University, 1949. Survey of existing programs, criteria for and steps necessary to inaugurate program.   **1498**

Yancey, Sadie M. *A study of racial and sectional differences in the ranking of occupations by high school boys.* Cornell University, 1951.

8. School Personnel

Allman, Reva W. *A study of selected competencies of prospective teachers in Alabama.* University of Michigan, 1952. Data on measures of teacher competencies for prospective teachers in Alabama Negro colleges.   **3461**

Barnett, William J. *A study of teacher perception of selected community attitudes concerning the personal life, civil rights, and academic freedom of teachers in one central western New York community.* University of Buffalo, 1958. Reports significant difference between teacher perceptions and actual community attitudes in direction of teacher pessimism.   **58-2335**

Blanton, Harry S. *The relationship of behavioral patterns of selected superintendents to the process of public school desegregation.* University of Tennessee, 1959. Showed importance of careful planning, involving citizens in cooperative planning, and making formal plans in the desegregation process.   **59-4253**

Bracey, Isaac C. *The high school principalship in South Carolina.* University of Oklahoma, 1961. Characteristics and problems of Negro secondary school principals in South Carolina.   **61-2862**

Cappelluzzo, Emma M. *Ethnic distance as it appears in teachers from three elementary schools of differing ethnic composition.* University of Arizona, 1965. No discriminating data were obtained from scales of social distance and dogmatism, but distinct patterns emerged from open-ended interviews. **65-9844**

Claiborne, Montraville I. *Classroom mental hygiene practices of teachers in Negro public schools and the relation between these practices and certain factors which influence the quality of teaching.* New York University, 1949. Survey of classroom mental hygiene practices of teachers in Negro public schools. **1814**

Collins, Gladys B. *Community activities of rural elementary teachers: a study of the community participation of Negro rural elementary teachers in Louisiana.* New York University, 1953. No differences found in community activities of teachers prepared with different institutional emphases. **7128**

Combs, Willie E. *The principalship of the Negro secondary schools of Florida.* Indiana University, 1964. Tasks performed and judgments as to their importance by Negro principals compared with criteria applied in other studies. **65-387**

Dohlstrom, Arthur H. *A study to determine how the emotional attitudes of Dade County, (Miami) Florida teachers may aid or hinder desegregation in public school classes.* New York University, 1955. Majority ready to accept their role in desegregation. **13602**

Drake, E. Maylon. *Employment of Negro teachers.* University of Southern California, 1963. Analyzed changes in the employment of Negro teachers by Los Angeles County school districts following enactment in 1959 of FEPA legislation. **64-2572**

Draper, Dorothy W. *The status of the elementary school principalship in Negro schools of Alabama.* University of Pittsburgh, 1958. Findings based on questionnaires and interviews with 320 principals and 113 superintendents of schools. **58-5608**

Elliott, Theodore B. *A comparative study of the attitudes of Negro teachers towards two articles on social equality.* University of Arkansas, 1964. Attitudes were affected by amount of education, but not by age, by whether one taught in an integrated or segregated school or the level of teaching experience. **65-1522**

Farrell, James E. *The self-perceived role of the Negro principal in improving instructional supervision in Tennessee.* University of Oklahoma, 1963. Significant differences found between what principals should be doing and were doing. **64-231**

Franklin, Laline O. *A study of problems relative to desegregation encountered by selected teachers during the first year of desegregation in the Washington, D.C. public schools.* New York University, 1956. Questionnaire used to determine problems and interview used to learn methods of solutions. **20281**

Funches, DeLars. *The superintendent's expectations of the Negro high school principal in Mississippi.* University of Oklahoma, 1961. Comparison of principal's self-reported role and role expected by superintendent. **61-5019**

Gamblin, Hance. *The relative importance of selected factors indicative of teacher effectiveness among graduates in elementary education at Jackson State College.* University of Oklahoma, 1962. Based on graduates of a predominantly Negro college from 1954 to 1958. **62-1752**

Gilmore, Henry F. *A study of attitudes of Negro teachers toward the Supreme Court decision and other issues of desegregation in education.* Columbia University, Teachers College, 1958.

Gore, George W., Jr. *In-service professional improvement of Negro public school teachers in Tennessee.* Columbia University, 1940.

Grant, Ernest A. *A proposed program for the improvement of pre-employment teacher training in agriculture for Negroes in Alabama based upon an analysis and evaluation of what teachers of agriculture do.* Cornell University, 1941.

Grantham, James W. *A study of the problems of beginning teachers in selected secondary schools of Mississippi.* Indiana University, 1961. Subjects were graduates of two predominantly Negro colleges in Mississippi from 1957 to 1959.   **61-4437**

Graves, Lawrence E. *First-year teachers' development in community relations: a study of the activities affecting teachers' development in good community relations with specific reference to first-year teachers in the Negro junior high schools of Washington, D.C.* New York University, 1956. A study of first-year teachers' community relationships with a view to making recommendations for preparing teachers of urban schools.   **20283**

Gunter, Pearl K. *Problems and patterns of staff desegregation with implications for Tennessee.* University of Tennessee, 1963. Survey of southern schools which had initiated plans for staff desegregation.   **64-4878**

Harris, Ruth M. *Teachers' social knowledge and its relation to pupils' responses; a study of four St. Louis Negro elementary schools.* Columbia University, 1941.

Hatch, Robert H. *A study of the leadership ability of Negro high school principals.* Colorado State College, 1964. Behavioral characteristics that distinguish effective from less effective leaders in a group of Negro principals.   **65-4772**

Hendricks, Harry G. *The full-time Negro principalship in Texas.* University of Colorado, 1960. Evaluation of the status of the Negro principal.   **61-830**

Johnston, Andrew V. *An investigation of elementary school teachers information concepts and generalizations about races, cultures and nations.* University of Oregon, 1963. A study of factors influencing the extent of knowledge possessed by elementary school teachers about races and their international understanding.   **64-7971**

Kaufman, Mae E. *Some problems of Negro teachers related to integration of pupils in public schools.* Indiana University, 1960. Problems of Negro teachers in Louisville, Kentucky, and Jeffersonville and New Albany, Indiana, resulting from pupil integration.   **60-6059**

Kelley, Glen E. *An analysis of white and Negro teachers' knowledge of good teaching practices.* University of Arkansas, 1962. Differences in "How I Teach" inventory favoring white teachers led to conclusion that there are differences in quality of instruction offered Negro and white students.   **62-2278**

Kettig, Thomas H. *Attitudes of Ohio public school teachers toward racial integration.* Ohio State University, 1957. Examination of interrelationships between factual knowledge of Negroes, authoritarianism, race and attitude toward racial integration.   **21481**

Koepper, Robert C. *Psychological correlates of teacher attitudes toward school desegregation.* George Peabody College for Teachers, 1966. Investigation of relationship between expressed attitudes of teachers toward school desegregation and selected personality traits; population selected from a southern and a border state. **66-11231**

Lamanna, Richard A. *The Negro public school teacher and school desegregation: a survey of Negro teachers in North Carolina.* University of North Carolina, 1966.

Lopez, Juan F. *Problems of Negro teachers of the Orange Belt counties of Central Florida in selected areas of supervision.* Fordham University, 1966. Identified problems and concluded that they affect the quality of education in schools for Negroes. **66-7106**

Major, Anthony J. *An investigation of supervisory practices for the improvement of instruction in Negro public schools.* University of Pittsburgh, 1941.

Martin, William H. *The development and appraisal of a program for promoting the in-service professional improvement of Negro teachers.* Ohio State University, 1945.

Matthew, Eunice S. *An evaluative study of the attitudes of Negro elementary school teachers in one-teacher schools of Tennessee toward certain educational principles.* Cornell University, 1948.

McPhail, James H. *Classroom teachers' amenability toward additional factors upon which to base teachers' salaries in Mississippi.* Boston University School of Education, 1963. Experience and degrees are currently the criteria for determining teacher salaries in Mississippi; non-Caucasians were more agreeable than Caucasians to the various alternatives presented. **64-4046**

Moore, Bradley G., Jr. *Implications for the teacher education programs of two Florida Negro colleges found in problems of recent graduates who taught and of senior students.* Ohio State University, 1959. Study based on Bethune-Cookman College and Florida A & M. **60-1203**

Moss, James A. *Utilization of Negro teachers in the colleges of New York State.* Columbia University, 1957. Supply lagged behind absorption into the colleges from 1945 to 1955. **25148**

Nelum, Junior N. *A study of the first seventy years of the colored teachers state association of Texas.* University of Texas, 1955.

Phillips, Ernest C., Jr. *A comparative study of the performance of white and Negro teachers on the individual items of a standardized test of teaching competence.* University of Georgia, 1956. An analysis of racial differences in scores on a test of teaching competence. **20011**

Pitkin, Victor E. *A resource unit for the training of secondary teachers in problems and issues involving minority groups, with special reference to Negro-white relationships.* New York University, 1950. Readings in ten concept areas of the race problem designed to help secondary teachers understand problems of intergroup relationships. **2195**

Rall, Clifford L. *A study of public school administration practices relating to Negroes and Negro groups in selected cities of the New York metropolitan area.* Columbia University, Teachers College, 1953.

Rivers, Marie D. *Peer acceptance and rejection of Negro teachers who were first or among the first to be employed in white or predominantly white schools north of the Mason-Dixon Line.* University of Michigan, 1959. Study of factors determining acceptance or rejection. **59-3954**

Ryder, Jack M. *A study of personnel practices and policies with relation to utilization of teachers from the Negro minority group in certain Michigan public school districts.* Michigan State University, 1962. Factors involved in employment and integration of Negro teachers.   **63-3740**

Scott, John I. E. *Professional functions of Negro principals in the public schools of Florida in relation to status.* University of Pittsburgh, 1942.

Shaw, William H. *A study of the behavior and beliefs of public school principals in the Muscogee County School District, Georgia.* Auburn University, 1963. The behavior and beliefs of 58 principals were studied and related to race, sex, level and size of school.   **64-1540**

Simpson, Hazel D. *An analysis of the relationship between scores attained on the national teacher examinations and certain other factors.* University of Georgia, 1963. Data offered to support generalizations as to the greater competence of white school personnel over Negro, high school personnel over elementary, males over females, non-teaching personnel over teachers and University of Georgia graduates over those from other institutions.   **63-7465**

Stephenson, Chester M. *A study of the attitudes toward Negroes of white prospective school teachers.* Ohio State University, 1950.

Stewart, William W. *Activities and training of Louisiana Negro high school teachers.* University of Nebraska, 1946.

Stoker, Winfred M. *A comparison of white and Negro elementary school teachers in Galveston County.* University of Houston, 1958. Based on a 30-minute visit to class and questionnaire.   **58-2654**

Stosberg, William K. *A study of the relation between quality of education and the morale status of the faculty.* New York University, 1957. Part of the problem was to determine whether morale factors appear in different relationship patterns between white and Negro schools.   **58-668**

Thompson, Daniel C. *Teachers in Negro colleges (a sociological analysis).* Columbia University, 1956. Comparative analysis of career patterns of teachers in Negro colleges with emphasis on differences from colleagues in white colleges.   **17084**

Wayson, William W. *Expressed motives of teachers in slum schools.* University of Chicago, 1966.

Wirth, Janina W. *Relationships between teacher opinions of disadvantaged children and measures of selected characteristics of these children.* University of Florida, 1966. The mutuality or discrepancy between teacher opinions and children's potential regarding personality, creative thinking and social acceptance; study of grades 5 and 6 in New York City.   **66-11144**

Yancey, Maude J. *A study of some health misconceptions of prospective teachers in Negro colleges of North Carolina.* University of Michigan, 1952. Found health misconceptions prevalent in all groups with little difference by college, sex, field of study and classification.   **3680**

9. Curriculum Materials

Bryson, Ralph J. *The promotion of interracial understanding through the study of American literature.* Ohio State University, 1953. Proposes materials, methods and techniques of instruction in the study of American literature which will help foster understanding and remove prejudices.   **58-676**

Carlsen, George R. *A study of the effect of reading books about the Negro on the racial attitudes of a group of eleventh grade students in northern schools.* University of Minnesota, 1949.

Carpenter, Marie E. *The treatment of the Negro in American history school textbooks; a comparison of changing textbook content, 1826 to 1939, with developing scholarship in the history of the Negro in the United States.* Columbia Universtiy, 1941.

Colson, Edna M. *An analysis of the specific references to Negroes in selected curricula for the education of teachers.* Columbia University, 1941.

Golden, Loretta. *The treatment of minority groups in primary social studies textbooks.* Syracuse University, 1964. Content analysis showed that the less frequently used textbooks may have more meaningful presentations of minorities. **64-13549**

Gustafson, Lucile. *Relationship between ethnic group membership and the retention of selected facts pertaining to American history and culture.* New York University, 1957. Ethnic groups (Caucasian, Jewish, Negro) tended to remember better facts associated with the contributions of their group. **21703**

Jackson, Earl C. *What is being taught about Negroes at the secondary level in American schools?* Harvard University, 1951.

Lash, John S. *The academic status of the literature of the American Negro: a description and analysis of curriculum inclusions and teaching practices.* University of Michigan, 1946.

Miller, Ruth V. *Nationalism in elementary schoolbooks in the United States from 1776 to 1865.* Columbia University, 1952. Patterns of social concepts presented in schoolbooks as typically American; includes reference to attitudes toward Negroes. **3906**

Mudd, Sister Rita. *A content analysis: the treatment of intergroup relations in social studies curriculum materials used in Catholic schools.* St. Louis University, 1961. Nine group categories (included Negro); five analytical categories. **61-6480**

Sawyers, Emanuel C. G. *An analysis of the content of later elementary basic readers in relation to their treatment of selected minority groups.* Wayne State University, 1962. An analysis of 20 readers used in Detroit Public Schools to ascertain differential treatment of majority and minority groups regarding behavior and consequent rewards and punishments; found similarity of treatment. **63-8086**

Thomas, Ruth M. *Selected readings by Negro authors for the young adolescent.* New York University, 1946. Selections in fiction, poetry and biography published since 1915. **820**

Wargny, Frank O. *The good life in modern readers.* University of Maryland, 1963. An analysis of the characters and way of life portrayed in seven series of widely used readers (grades 2 through 6). **63-5656**

10. Achievement

Anderson, Louis V. *The effects of desegregation on the achievement and personality patterns of Negro children.* George Peabody College for Teachers, 1966. Reported no personality or social adjustment differences, but gains in achievement depended on early entry into desegregated schools. **66-11237**

Brown, Donald V. *An investigation of the influence of prejudice, race, and sex factors in a testing situation.* Purdue University, 1956. Effect of examiner's race on test performance of high and low prejudiced groups. **19399**

Downing, Gertrude L. *The effects of systematic phonics instruction on the reading achievement of adolescent retarded readers with problems of dialect speech: a study of the relative effectiveness of systematic phonics instruction and incidental phonics instruction on the improvement in phonic knowledge, word knowledge and silent reading achievement of seventh and eighth grade retarded readers in a community characterized by American Negro dialects.* New York University, 1965. Concluded that daily directed reading instruction with high interest, low difficulty materials is the most practical approach.   **66-9495**

Einstein, Florence. *A comparative study of reading achievement of seventh-grade junior high school boys in a low socio-economic area of New York City 1945 and 1957.* New York University, 1960. Comparison of Negro boys entering 7th grade in 1945 and 1957 as to age, I.Q. and reading achievement.   **60-3741**

Fortenberry, James H. *The achievement of Negro pupils in mixed and non-mixed schools.* University of Oklahoma, 1959. Mixing seemed to benefit 8th- and 9th-grade Negro students in all areas, but more in arithmetic and language than in reading.   **59-5492**

Geisel, Paul N. *I Q performance, educational and occupational aspirations of youth in a southern city: a racial comparison.* Vanderbilt University, 1962. A study of Negro and white differences in performances and aspirations related to underlying social factors.   **63-1838**

Geller, Max. *Some social factors related to the educational achievement of 100 Negro secondary school students residing in the Bedford-Stuyvesant area of Brooklyn, City of New York.* New York University, 1943.

Jackson, William S. *Housing as a factor in pupil growth and development: a comparison of select factors of growth and development of pupils living in a low rent public housing project with those from slum housing through three and one-half years of elementary school experience.* New York University, 1954. Subjects were 5th- and 6th-grade Negro pupils in Harlem: public housing pupils showed greater mental, social and emotional growth; slum pupils showed greater physical growth.
                                                     10623

Jaffe, Bernard. *The relationship between two aspects of socio-economic disadvantage and the school success of 8th grade Negro students in a Detroit junior high school.* Wayne State University, 1965. Effect of absence of gainfully employed father in the home and dependence upon public agency assistance on number of grade failures, intelligence test scores and achievement scores.   **66-10112**

Jones, Arlynne L. *An investigation of the response patterns which differentiate the performance of selected Negro and white freshmen on SCAT.* University of Colorado, 1960. Strength of positive relationship between sentence understandings and word meaning differentiated Negro and white performance at both upper and lower levels.   **61-800**

Jones, Tom M. *Comparisons of test scores of high school graduates of 1954 who go to college with those who do not go, and a study of certain factors associated with going to college.* University of Arkansas, 1956. Data reported by race.   **16959**

Matzen, Stanley P. *The relationship between racial composition and scholastic achievement in elementary school classrooms.* Stanford University, 1965. Studied the relation between the percentage of Negroes in a classroom and mean scholastic achievement of 5th- and 7th-grade classes; concluded that the relationship is largely a function of school grouping practices.   **66-2518**

McGurk, Frank C. *Comparison of the performance of Negro and white high school seniors on cultural and non-cultural questions.* Catholic University of America, 1952.

Merrill, Pierce K. *Race as a factor in achievement in plantation areas of Arkansas.* Vanderbilt University, 1951. Various objective manifestations of discrimination directed against Negro sharecroppers in delta areas of Arkansas. **4505**

Miller, James O. *Rule perception and reinforcement conditions in discrimination learning among culturally deprived and non-deprived children.* George Peabody College for Teachers, 1963. Learning efficiency found to be equal among the groups tested, which the researcher interpreted to mean that the culturally deprived can compete effectively on learning tasks with similar stimuli. **64-5086**

Miner, John B. *Verbal ability in the U.S.* Princeton University, 1955. Scores on a vocabulary test of a representative sample of U.S. population related to occupation, education, race, social class, sex, religion and other factors. **13713**

Mose, Ashriel I. *To what extent do certain factors influence the academic success of freshman students in social science courses at South Carolina State College.* New York University, 1957. Based on a predominantly Negro college. **25498**

Rodgers, E. George. *The relationship of certain measurable factors in the personal and educational backgrounds of two groups of Baltimore Negroes, identified as superior and average in intelligence as fourth grade children, to their educational, social and economic achievement in adulthood.* New York University, 1956. A study of childhood factors which correlate with adult success. **21716**

Samuels, Ivan G. *Desegregated education and differences in academic achievement.* Indiana University, 1958. A study of achievement differences between white and Negro students and among Negro students in integrated and mixed schools with intelligence, readiness, health and socio-economic factors held constant. **58-2934**

Savoca, Anthony F. *The effects of reward, race, I.Q., and socio-economic status of creative production of preschool children.* Louisiana State University, 1965. Reported reward and socio-economic index to be important factors and the race-IQ interaction as significant. **65-11405**

Shrader, Donald R. *A study of the relations among sex, social position, ethnic groups, manifest needs, and academic achievement in high school.* Purdue University, 1964. Ethnic differences affected academic achievement more significantly for males than females; ethnic differences in manifest needs were not predictive of achievement. **64-8710**

Smith, William N. *An investigation of certain factors in tests of mental ability and achievement to determine their influence on scores obtained by southern Negro students.* Indiana University, 1952.

Stewart, Richard H. *A study of selected factors in the instructional program of the public schools of Alabama.* Auburn University, 1964. Reports extensive data on racial differences in achievement and other factors. **64-7602**

St. John, Nancy H. *The relation of racial segregation in early schooling to the level of aspiration and academic achievement of Negro students in a Northern high school.* Harvard University, 1962.

Sullivan, Troy G. *Predicting readiness and achievement in reading by use of socio-economic and Howe reading material availability scales.* North Texas State University, 1965. Compared the relative effectiveness of certain reading readiness predictors for Negro and white subjects. **65-10074**

Swinton, Sylvia P. *Pupil progress: a problem of elementary school principals in South Carolina.* Indiana University, 1956. Age-grade status study of pupils; includes racial comparisons. **17781**

Theman, Viola. *A follow-up study of superior Negro youth.* Northwestern University, 1943.

Threatt, Robert. *A study of selected characteristics and college success of high and low-achieving Negro students on the CEEB Scholastic Aptitude Test in Georgia.* University of Oklahoma, 1963. High achievers were relatively younger, select humanities and natural science majors and have the highest grade point average.   **63-5785**

Tullis, David S. *A comparative study of Negro, Latin, and Anglo children in a West Texas community.* Texas Technological College, 1964.   **65-1464**

Willis, Larry J. *A comparative study of the reading achievement of white and Negro children.* George Peabody College for Teachers, 1940.

Wilson, Alan B. *The effect of residential segregation upon educational achievement and aspirations.* University of California, Berkeley, 1961.

11. Desegregation

Blanton, Milburn W. *The effect on resistance to desegregation in selected communities of a tendency toward a cultural status quo as identified by given characteristics.* University of Arkansas, 1960. Communities which did and did not experience resistance to desegregation were compared on a wide range of factors thought to indicate a tendency toward status quo.   **60-1319**

Brittain, David J. *A case study of the problems of racial integration in the Clinton, Tennessee, high school: a study concerned with the problems faced by school officials in the racial integration of a public secondary school in compliance with a Federal court order.* New York University, 1959. Planning for integration, nature of opposing or supporting forces, role of students and methods used by school personnel.   **59-6215**

Campbell, Ernest Q. *The attitude effects of educational desegregation in a southern community: a methodological study in scale analysis.* Vanderbilt University, 1956. Exploration of the utility of the Guttman scale analysis as a technique, using junior and senior high school students before and after desegregation in 1955.   **20489**

Cramer, Miles R. *School desegregation and new industry: the southern community leader's viewpoint.* Harvard University, 1962.

Dalomba, Roland F. *The racial integration movement in the state universities of the South, 1933-1954: a study of the recent movement in education which has seen the partial breaking down of Negro segregation in the southern state universities.* New York University, 1956. Important factors identified in the movement to get Negroes into southern state universities.   **20279**

Daniels, Roland H. *A case study of desegregation in the public schools of Trenton, New Jersey.* Rutgers— The State University, 1959. Traces the desegregation of Trenton schools in terms of factors leading to the decision, reactions of the community and methods of making policy decisions. **59-5321**

Dunn, Frederick L. *Programs and procedures of desegregation developed by the Board of Education, Montgomery County, Maryland.* University of Maryland, 1959. Analysis of procedures used, problems met in a successful desegregation program.   **59-6845**

Dwyer, Robert J. *A study of desegregation and integration in selected school districts of central Missouri.* University of Missouri, 1957. Administrative policies, evaluation of the situation by administrators, teachers and pupils, and patterns of interaction in seven school districts.   **22767**

Eddy, Elizabeth M. *Attitudes towards desegregation among southern students on a northern campus.* Columbia University, 1961. Attitudes toward integration related to length of time in the North of southern freshmen and seniors against northern undergraduates as control. **61-2210**

Ervin, John B. *Improving the educational experiences of the Negro child in a non-segregated school environment at Akron, Ohio.* Columbia University, 1950.

Fort, Edward B. *A case study of the struggle to secure an administrative plan for eliminating de facto segregation in the junior high schools of Sacramento, California.* University of California, Berkeley, 1964. Emphasis placed on the decision-making process as it pertained to superintendent-board-community interaction. **65-2985**

Gates, Robbins L. *The making of massive resistance: Virginia's politics of public school desegregation, 1954-1956.* Columbia University, 1962. Chronological, historical study of Virginia's response to school desegregation decision in 1954. **62-4230**

Greenfield, Robert W. *Factors associated with white parents' attitudes toward school desegregation in a central Florida community.* Ohio State University, 1959. Reports social background characteristics associated with various attitudes toward school desegregation; findings were at variance with the literature in this field. **60-745**

Haigwood, Thomas J. *A study of desegregation problems that may affect the instructional program of junior high school industrial arts in North Carolina.* Pennsylvania State University, 1959. Comparison of incidence of instructional problems in segregated and desegregated schools. **59-2886**

Ingram, Sam H. *Behavioral patterns of selected superintendents during the process of public school desegregation.* University of Tennessee, 1959. Survey of factors influencing behavior of school superintendents in Kentucky. **59-4257**

Johnson, Howard M. *The coordination of a study of racial imbalance in the Englewood Public Schools, Englewood, New Jersey.* Harvard University, 1965.

Johnson, Norman C. *An analysis of certain problems related to integration of Negro students into interracial schools.* Indiana University, 1954. Attitudes of Negro students and parents to integration; action taken to prepare Negro students for integration. **7906**

Jones, Douglas R. *An opinion poll on attitudes of white adults about desegregation in the public schools of Knoxville, Tennessee.* George Peabody College for Teachers, 1958. Personal interviews indicated 77% of adults favored segregation but 44% indicated acceptance of any plan the Board might draw up; 6% would use violence. **59-1106**

Koponen, Niilo E. *Observational follow-up and the dissemination of proposals for school integration.* Harvard University, 1966.

May, Clifford B. *The forced attachment of two culturally differing school districts: a problematic analysis.* Wayne State University, 1963. Historical treatment of the forcible (by state and county) annexation of a predominantly Negro school district to the adjoining (white) Oak Park district on the edge of Detroit. **64-5105**

McCarrick, Earlean M. *Louisiana's official resistance to desegregation.* Vanderbilt University, 1964. The reaction of Louisiana state officials to the 1954 Supreme Court decision and its impact on Louisiana's internal political processes. **65-4551**

McPherson, Philip E. *Coordination of efforts for the improvement of race relations in the Pittsburgh public schools.* Harvard University, 1966.

Meyer, Alan S. *The not-so-solid South: a study of variability in southern sentiment on school desegregation.* Columbia University, 1962. The relationship between variability in county voting on school desegregation referenda and the course of social and cultural change in the South.   **63-1504**

Quinn, Alfred T. *Persistent patterns and problems peculiar to selected schools and communities in racial transition.* University of California at Los Angeles, 1964. Identified and codified 53 persistent patterns and problems faced by schools, based on examination of 7 cities in various stages of racial transition.   **64-7312**

Reuter, Frederick W. *An administrator's guide to successful desegregation of the public schools: a study of thirty techniques used and thirty-two conditions under which they were used to desegregate successfully one-hundred-forty-six schools or school systems in eleven southern and border states.* New York University, 1961. Assesses frequency of use and superintendents' rating of helpfulness of 30 techniques used in school desegregation.   **62-1448**

Sartain, James A. *Attitudes of parents and children toward desegregation.* Vanderbilt University, 1966. Data gathered at Oak Ridge, Tennessee, summer, 1955.   **66-10999**

Scharf, Richard K. *Pupil placement and public school desegregation.* University of Chicago, 1963.

Smith, Wilfred R. *A normative study of desegregation in public education – a crisis of meanings in culture.* Wayne State University, 1959. Scientific defense of desegregation as consistent with main themes of our culture.   **59-4706**

Spruill, Albert W. *Consequences encountered by Negro teachers in the process of desegregation of schools in four southern states.* Cornell University, 1958. Employment and other consequences experienced in Delaware, Kentucky, Maryland and West Virginia.   **59-1518**

Stoff, Sheldon. *Factors related to the non-violent desegregation of public elementary and secondary schools in the South and border states.* Cornell University, 1965. Statistical analysis of 189 communities desegregated between September, 1960 and October, 1963; 17 variables identified as related to nonviolence.   **65-6975**

Turner, Harold E. *A study of public school integration in two Illinois communities.* George Peabody College for Teachers, 1956. Analysis of desegregation experiences of East St. Louis and Alton, Illinois from 1949 to 1952.   **19765**

Whitmore, Paul G. *A study of school desegregation: attitude change and scale validation.* University of Tennessee, 1956. Results of test of attitude toward the Negro, administered to junior and senior high school students before and after desegregation.   **20501**

Wiley, Alfred D. *A study of desegregation in the Evansville School Corporation, Evansville, Indiana.* Indiana University, 1961. Focuses on desegregation as a social process and the role of various community factors.   **62-203**

Williams, Wyman L. *A study of school desegregation: self-prediction of behavior and correlates of self-prediction.* University of Tennessee, 1955. Data designed to aid in anticipation of problems arising in desegregation of Oak Ridge, Tennessee, school system.   **15802**

Zion, Carol L. *The desegregation of a public junior college: a case study of its Negro faculty.* Florida State University, 1965. The Negro faculty at Miami-Dade Junior College before and after desegregation. **66-5462**

12. History of Education

Alexander, Frederick M. *Education for the needs of the Negro in Virginia.* Columbia University, 1944.

Beasley, Leon O. *A history of education in Louisiana during the Reconstruction period, 1862-1877.* Louisiana State University, 1957. Includes discussion of schools for Negroes, and the administration of William G. Brown as State Superintendent. **21981**

Bond, Horace M. *Social and economic influences on the public education of Negroes in Alabama, 1865-1930.* University of Chicago, 1937.

Boom, Kathleen W. *The Julius Rosenwald's Aid to Education in the South.* University of Chicago, 1950.

Brigham, Robert I. *The education of the Negro in Missouri.* University of Missouri, 1946. Historical analysis of the development of schools for Negroes in Missouri. **1274**

Butler, Loretta M. *A history of Catholic elementary education for Negroes in the diocese of Lafayette, Louisiana.* Catholic University of America, 1963. Concluded that the educational program in this enclave of colored Catholics had failed to cope with the preparation needed to earn a living. **63-7975**

Capps, Marian P. *The Virginia Out-of-State Graduate Aid Program, 1936-1950.* Columbia University, Teachers College, 1954.

Christopher, Nehemiah M. *The history of Negro public education in Texas, 1865-1900.* University of Pittsburgh, 1949.

Dabney, Lillian G. *The history of schools for Negroes in the District of Columbia, 1807-1947.* Catholic University of America, 1949.

Davis, William R. *The development and present status of Negro education in East Texas.* Columbia University, Teachers College, 1935.

Ellis, Frankie N. *The Southern Education Foundation and its role in the improvement of Negro elementary school personnel in the South.* University of Texas, 1965. Showed that the Foundation shifted from support to the use of funds to stimulate change. **65-10698**

Erickson, Leonard E. *The color line in Ohio public schools, 1829-1890.* Ohio State University, 1959. Traces efforts to achieve equality of educational opportunity for Negroes in 19th-century Ohio.
60-735

Goldaber, Irving. *The treatment by the New York City Board of Education of problems affecting the Negro, 1954-1963.* New York University, 1965. Analyzed 35 cases of protest in the New York City schools as a means of understanding the manner in which the Board of Education handled educational problems affecting Negroes. **65-7293**

Hall, Clyde W. *A survey of industrial education for Negroes in the U.S. up to 1917.* Bradley University, 1953. Apprenticeship programs of slavery; type, scope, philosophy, leaders and foundation support of industrial education. **6494**

Handorf, William G. *An historical study of the superintendency of Dr. Frank W. Ballou in the public school system of the District of Columbia.* American University, 1962. The development of public education in Washington, D.C., from 1920 to 1943.   **62-4187**

Harlan, Louis R. *Separate and unequal: public school campaigns and the race issue in the southern seaboard states, 1901-1915.* Johns Hopkins University, 1956.

Heller, Herbert L. *Negro education in Indiana from 1816 to 1869.* University of Indiana, 1952.

Johnson, Henry M. *The Methodist Episcopal church and the education of Southern Negroes (1862-1900).* Yale University, 1939.

Kegley, Tracy M. *The Peabody Scholarships, 1877-1899.* George Peabody College for Teachers, 1949.

Lewis, Elmer C. *A history of secondary and higher education in Negro schools related to the Disciples of Christ.* University of Pittsburgh, 1957.   **22853**

Lewis, William J. *The educational speaking of Jabez L. M. Curry.* University of Florida, 1955. Addresses to white and Negro audiences from 1861 to 1903; ideas paralleled B. T. Washington; influenced the establishment of Southern Education Board.   **14319**

Lofton, Williston H. *The development of public education for Negroes in Washington, D.C. (a study of "separate but equal accommodations").* American University, 1945.

Long, John C. *The Disciples of Christ and Negro education.* University of Southern California, 1960. By 1955, 10 schools had been established but only 2 remained in operation.   **60-2779**

Mann, George L. *The historical development of public education in St. Louis, Missouri, for Negroes.* Indiana University, 1949.

Parker, Marjorie H. *The educational activities of the Freedman's Bureau.* University of Chicago, 1952.

Peck, Richard C. *Jabez Lamar Monroe Curry: educational crusader.* George Peabody College for Teachers, 1943.

Pfanner, Daniel J. *The thought of Negro educators in Negro higher education, 1900-1950.* Columbia University, Teachers College, 1958.

Reynolds, Jack Q. *Historical and current issues in racial integration in the public schools of Arkansas.* University of Arkansas, 1957. Chronological account of significant events in the development of race relations in Arkansas and a description of the views of Arkansas educators on current issues.   **21955**

Rice, Jessie P. *J.L.M. Curry, Southerner, statesman and educator.* Columbia University, 1950.

Robert, Edward B. *The administration of the Peabody Education Fund from 1880 to 1905.* George Peabody College for Teachers, 1936.

Samples, Ralph E. *The development of public education in Tennessee during the Bourbon Era, 1870-1900.* University of Tennessee, 1965. Includes attitudes toward and provisions for the education of Negroes.   **66-8205**

Shannon, Irwin V. *Negro education and the development of a group tradition.* Vanderbilt University, 1934.

Strong, Evelyn R. *Historical development of the Oklahoma Association of Negro Teachers: a study in social change.* University of Oklahoma, 1961. Origin, development and deactivation of a Negro teachers organization. **61-5206**

Swint, Henry L. *The Northern teacher in the South, 1862-1870.* Vanderbilt University, 1939.

Thomas, Leland C. *Some aspects of biracial public education in Georgia, 1900-1954.* George Peabody College for Teachers, 1960. Comparative development of Negro and white public elementary and secondary schools. **60-5867**

Thompkins, Robert E. *A history of religious education among Negroes in the Presbyterian Church in the United States of America.* University of Pittsburgh, 1951.

Thompson, Herbert W. *A history of Negro education in the Catawba County school system from 1865-1960.* Pennsylvania State University, 1964. Study based in North Carolina. **65-6769**

Turner, Howard. *Robert Mills Lusher, Louisiana educator.* Louisiana State University, 1945. Biography of superintendent of public instruction; includes material on Negro education in Louisiana during Reconstruction.

Vaughan, William P. *The sectional conflict in southern public education: 1865-1876.* Ohio State University, 1961. Impact of sectionalism on education in the South, 1865 to 1876. **61-5130**

Venable, Tom C. *A history of Negro education in Kentucky.* George Peabody College for Teachers, 1953.

West, Earle H. *The life and educational contributions of Barnas Sears.* George Peabody College for Teachers, 1961. Includes account of activities of Peabody Education Fund in behalf of Negro education in the South, 1867 to 1882. **61-5832**

Wright, Marion T. *The education of Negroes in New Jersey.* Columbia University, 1942.

Wright, Stephen J. *A study of certain attitudes toward the education of Negroes since 1865.* New York University, 1943.

HISTORY

1. Biography

Abbott, Richard H. *Cobbler in Congress: life of Henry Wilson, 1812-1875.* University of Wisconsin, 1965. Includes Wilson's work as abolitionist and his efforts in Congress to aid the Negro during Reconstruction. **65-13709**

Bates, Jack W. *John Quincy Adams and the antislavery movement.* University of Southern California, 1953.

Broderick, Francis L. *W. E. B. Du Bois: the trail of his ideas.* Harvard University, 1955.

Cheek, William F., III. *Forgotten prophet: the life of John Mercer Langston.* University of Virginia, 1961. Traces work of Langston as educational director of BRFAL, dean of Howard Law School and congressman. **61-4534**

Cooke, Jacob E. *The life of Frederick Bancroft and the colonization of American Negroes by Frederick Bancroft.* Columbia University, 1955.

Cooper, Alice A. *Harriet Beecher Stowe: a critical study.* Harvard University, 1964.

Coyner, Martin B., Jr. *John Hartwell Cocke of Bremo. Agriculture and slavery in the ante-bellum South.* University of Virginia, 1961. Cocke (1780-1866) held antislavery views and pioneered in the education of slaves, but later accepted Confederate rationale for slavery.   **61-4536**

Durham, Francis M. *Dubose Heyward: the Southerner as artist, a critical and biographical study.* Columbia University, 1953. Detailed consideration of Heyward, author of *Porgy and Bess.*   **6608**

Eby, Cecil D., Jr. *A critical biography of David Hunter Strother. ("Porte Crayon").* University of Pennsylvania, 1958. Biography of a 19th-century Southern writer and illustrator important for his realistic portrayal of southern Negroes.   **58-3320**

Fladeland, Betty L. *James Gillespie Birney: exponent of political action against slavery.* University of Michigan, 1952. Biography of Southerner and slaveholder who became an outstanding figure in the antislavery movement in the U.S.   **3746**

Gottfried, Alex. *A. J. Cermak, Chicago politician: a study in political leadership.* University of Chicago, 1953.

Holmes, William F., III. *The white chief: James K. Vardaman in Mississippi politics, 1890-1908.* Rice University, 1964. The career of a racist governor.   **64-10174**

Hooper, Robert E. *The political and educational ideas of David Lipscomb.* George Peabody College for Teachers, 1965. Includes discussion of his thought relative to the Negro question.   **66-10702**

Horowitz, Murray M. *Ben Butler: the making of a radical.* Columbia University, 1955. Includes Butler's treatment of the Negro as a Union general and during his administration of Louisiana.   **15631**

Humes, Dollena J. *Oswald Garrison Villard: a study in American liberalism, 1918-1932.* Syracuse University, 1956. Includes Villard's efforts in behalf of minority groups, including the Negro.   **18019**

Johnson, Everett O. *Oliver P. Morton: a study of his career as a public speaker and of his speaking on slavery, Civil War, and Reconstruction issues.* University of Michigan, 1957. Study of a leading spokesman for the Republican Party in Indiana, 1860 to 1876.   **58-1420**

Lashley, Leonard C. *Anthony Benezet and his anti-slavery activities.* Fordham University, 1939.

Lewis, Ruth B. *Angelina Grimke Weld, reformer.* Ohio State University, 1962. Miss Grimke's contributions to the abolition and women's rights movements (1835-1870).   **63-65**

Ludlum, Robert P. *Joshua R. Giddings, antislavery radical.* Cornell University, 1936.

Maddocks, Lewis I. *Justice John Marshall Harlan: defender of individual rights.* Ohio State University, 1959. Includes Harlan's views on rights of Negroes; early dissenter to separate-but-equal doctrine.   **59-5918**

Mann, Harold W. *The life and times of Atticus Greene Haygood.* Duke University, 1962. Includes Haygood's work as agent of the Slater Fund.   **63-3600**

McCulloch, Samuel C. *The life and times of Dr. Thomas Bray (1656-1730): a study in humanitarianism.* University of California at Los Angeles, 1945.

McKee, James W., Jr. *William Barksdale: the intrepid Mississippian.* Mississippi State University, 1966. Includes Barksdale's (1821-1863) views on the extension of slavery, southern rights and institutions.
66-12773

Orr, Oliver H., Jr. *Charles Brantley Aycock: a biography.* University of North Carolina, 1958. Evaluation of life of North Carolina governor (1901-05), who directed state normal school for Negroes and defended the right of the Negro to adequate schools.
59-55

Powers, Thomas J. *Benjamin Franklin and his views and opinions on education.* Michigan State University, 1965. Includes Franklin's thinking on Negro slavery.
66-6161

Quarles, Benjamin A. *The public life of Frederick Douglass.* University of Wisconsin, 1941.

Rudwick, Elliott M. *W. E. B. DuBois: A study in minority group leadership.* University of Pennsylvania, 1956. Appraisal of type of minority-group leadership represented by Du Bois.
17269

Simon, Walter A. *Henry O. Tanner – a study of the development of an American Negro artist: 1859-1937.* New York University, 1961. Evolution of an American Negro painter.
61-2570

Smith, Richard W. *The career of Martin Van Buren in connection with the slavery controversy through the election of 1840.* Ohio State University, 1959. Describes Van Buren as a "Northern man with Southern policies."
59-5870

St. Clair, Saide D. *The national career of Blanche Kelso Bruce.* New York University, 1947. An interpretation of the career of Bruce, emphasizing years 1875 to 1898.
938

Tate, Ernest C. *The social implications of the writings and the career of James Weldon Johnson.* New York University, 1959. An evaluation of the influence of Johnson on race relations in America.
59-2092

Taylor, Lloyd C. *To make men free: an interpretative study of Lydia Maria Child* Lehigh University, 1956. Examines role of Child (1802-1880) in humanitarian movement, especially her plea for racial equality.
19367

Tillman, Nathaniel P. *Walter Francis White: a study in interest group leadership.* University of Wisconsin, 1961. Career of the executive secretary of the NAACP.
61-6003

2. Before Emancipation

Anderson, Godfrey T. *The slavery issue as a factor in Massachusetts politics from the Compromise of 1850 to the outbreak of the Civil War.* University of Chicago, 1944.

Aptheker, Herbert. *American Negro slave revolts.* Columbia University, 1944.

Bahney, Robert S. *Generals and Negroes: education of Negroes by the Union Army, 1861-65.* University of Michigan, 1965. Need for centralized authority led to BRFAL, which used procedures and leadership similar to those of the army.
66-5035

Bannan, Phyllis M. *Arthur and Lewis Tappan: a study of religious and reform movements in New York City.* Columbia University, 1950. Includes the Tappans' interest in aid to free Negroes (Phoenix Society), Negro schools and the American Colonization Society. **1829**

Berwanger, Eugene H. *Western anti-Negro sentiment and laws, 1846-60: a factor in the slavery extension controversy.* University of Illinois, 1964. The role of anti-Negro sentiment in the controversy over the western extension of slavery between 1846 and 1860. **65-3179**

Boucher, Morris R. *The free Negro in Alabama prior to 1860.* University of Iowa, 1950.

Brewer, James H. *An apocalypse on slavery: the story of the Negro slave in the Lower Cape Fear region of North Carolina.* University of Pittsburgh, 1949.

Brown, Letitia W. *Free Negroes in the original District of Columbia.* Harvard University, 1966.

Carnathan, Wiley J. *American Negro slavery during the Revolutionary era.* University of Texas, 1949.

Carroll, Joseph C. *Slave insurrections in the United States, 1800-1865.* Ohio State University, 1937.

Cavanagh, Helen M. *Anti-slavery sentiment and politics in the Northwest, 1844-1860.* University of Chicago, 1938.

Cole, Charles C., Jr. *The secular ideas of the northern evangelists, 1826-1860.* Columbia University, 1951. Includes views on slavery of Nathaniel Emmons, Asahel Nettleton, Lyman Beecher, Peter Cartwright, Francis Wayland, Albert Barnes, Horace Bushnell and Charles G. Finney. **3329**

Constantine, James R. *The African slave trade: a study of eighteenth century propaganda and public controversy.* Indiana University, 1953. Analysis of propaganda responsible for public interest in abolition in England following Peace of Paris, 1783. **6436**

Cook, Lester H. *Anti-slavery sentiment in the culture of Chicago, 1844-1858.* University of Chicago, 1953.

Cope, Robert S. *Slavery and servitude in the Colony of Virginia in the seventeenth century.* Ohio State University, 1951.

Cornish, Dudley T. *Negro troops in the Union Army, 1861-1865.* University of Colorado, 1950.

Davis, Charles S. *The plantation system in Alabama before 1860.* Duke University, 1938.

Del Porto, Joseph A. *A study of American anti-slavery journals.* Michigan State College, 1953. Traces the rise of abolitionist papers, their editorial objectives and practices, editors and their relationship to the total antislavery movement. **6850**

DesChamps, Margaret B. *The Presbyterian church in the South Atlantic states, 1801-1861.* Emory University, 1952. Social history of attitudes toward morals, education, westward migration, slavery and secession. **58-5132**

Dillon, Merton L. *The anti-slavery movement in Illinois: 1809-1844.* University of Michigan, 1951. Before 1824 Illinois was friendly to slavery; people moved in to escape southern slavery and provided leadership for antislavery cause. **2582**

Dusinberre, William W. *Civil War issues in Philadelphia, 1856-1865.* Columbia University, 1960. Includes discussion of abolitionist attitudes and status of Negroes. **61-2209**

Ellsworth, Clayton S. *Oberlin and the anti-slavery movement up to the Civil War.* New York University, 1930. A description of the antislavery character of the town and the college from 1833 to 1866. **618**

Engelder, Conrad J. *The churches and slavery. A study of the attitudes toward slavery of the major Protestant denominations.* University of Michigan, 1964. Described the vacillatory policies of Baptist, Congregational, Methodist, Presbyterian and Episcopal churches before the Civil War. **64-12589**

England, James M. *The free Negro in ante-bellum Tennessee.* Vanderbilt University, 1941.

Everett, Donald E. *Free persons of color in New Orleans, 1803-1865.* Tulane University, 1941.

Fichett, Elijah H. *The free Negro in Charleston, South Carolina.* University of Chicago, 1950.

Fife, Robert O. *Alexander Campbell and the Christian church in the slavery controversy.* Indiana University, 1960. Attitudes toward slavery instrumental in preventing a church split over the issue. **60-6289**

Finnie, Gordon E. *The antislavery movement in the South, 1787-1836: its rise and decline and its contribution to abolitionism in the West.* Duke University, 1962. A study of the nature and extent of antislavery sentiment in the South, 1787-1836, and its relationship to emigration and the rise of abolitionism in the West. **63-3585**

Floan, Howard R. *The South in northern eyes, 1831-1861: a study of ante-bellum attitudes toward the South among the major northern men of letters who were actively writing on the eve of the Civil War.* Columbia University, 1954. Includes discussion of attitudes toward slavery. **8657**

Foner, Philip S. *Business and slavery: the New York merchants and the irrepressible conflict.* Columbia University, 1941.

Franklin, John H. *The free Negro in North Carolina, 1790-1860.* Harvard University, 1941.

Genovese, Eugene D. *The limits of agrarian reform in the slave South.* Columbia University, 1959. Concludes that a general reformation of agriculture was impossible so long as slavery was retained. **60-1139**

Greene, Lorenzo J. *The Negro in colonial New England, 1620-1776.* Columbia University, 1943.

Harkness, Donald R. *Crosscurrents: American anti-democracy from Jackson to the Civil War (1829-1860).* University of Minnesota, 1955. Anti-Negro sentiment treated as one of several types of anti-democracy. **15928**

Harrell, David E., Jr. *A social history of the Disciples of Christ to 1866.* Vanderbilt University, 1962. Includes discussion of attitudes toward slavery and an assessment of influence on such movements as the slavery controversy. **62-4508**

Harris, Alfred G. *Slavery and emancipation in the District of Columbia, 1801-1862.* Ohio State University, 1947

Hart, Charles R. D. *Congressmen and the expansion of slavery into the territories: a study in attitudes, 1846-61.* University of Washington. A study of public opinion in the 1850's with reference to expansion of slavery, as inferred from expressions in Congress. **65-15384**

Harwood, Thomas F. *Great Britain and American antislavery.* University of Texas, 1959. Effect of British antislavery movement upon the parallel movement in U.S., 1776-1860. **59-4720**

Hazel, Joseph A. *The geography of Negro agricultural slavery in Alabama, Florida, and Mississippi, circa 1860.* Columbia University, 1963. Study of relations between slavery and the physical environment, agricultural products and transportation.   **64-2755**

Hendricks, George L. *Union army occupation of the southern seaboard, 1861-1865.* Columbia University, 1954. Discusses superintendence of labor, homesteading, education and relief for freedmen during Union occupation of Port Royal, Fernandina, and St. Augustine.   **10265**

Hirsch, Charles B. *The experiences of the S.P.G. in eighteenth century North Carolina.* Indiana University, 1954. Includes discussion of efforts to reach Indians and Negroes.   **7532**

Holland, Timothy J. *The Catholic church and the Negro in the United States prior to the Civil War.* Fordham University, 1950.

Howard, Victor B. *The anti-slavery movement in the Presbyterian church, 1835-1861.* Ohio State University, 1961. Traces development of two independent but interwoven controversies (slavery and orthodoxy) leading to divisions within the church.   **62-778**

Howard, Warren S. *The United States Government and the African slave trade, 1837-1862.* University of California at Los Angeles, 1960.

Jackson, Luther P. *Free Negro labor and property holding in Virginia, 1830-1860.* University of Chicago, 1938.

Jackson, Margaret Y. *An investigation of biographies and autobiographies of American slaves published between 1840 and 1860: based upon the Cornell Special Slavery Collection.* Cornell University, 1954.

Johnson, Clifton H. *The American Missionary Association, 1846-1861: a study of Christian abolitionism.* University of North Carolina, 1959. Formation of the AMA and its missions and antislavery activities before the Civil War.   **59-5561**

Johnson, Lulu M. *The problem of slavery in the old Northwest, 1787-1858.* University of Iowa, 1942.

Johnston, James H. *Race relations in Virginia amd miscegenation in the South, 1776-1860.* University of Chicago, 1937.

Jones, Bobby F. *A cultural middle passage: slave marriage and family in the ante-bellum South.* University of North Carolina, 1965. Found matricism not as extreme as previously presumed and that family strength depended upon individual commitment and support from the master.   **65-14357**

Jordan, Winthrop D. *White over black: the attitudes of the American colonists toward the Negro, to 1784.* Brown University, 1960. Description of attitudes toward the Negro both before and after firm establishment of slavery.   **62-5752**

Kooker, Arthur R. *The anti-slavery movement in Michigan, 1796-1840: a study in humanitarianism on an American frontier.* University of Michigan, 1941.

Leslie, William R. *The fugitive slave clause, 1787-1842: a study in American constitutional history and in the history of the conflict of laws.* University of Michigan, 1945.

Lindsay, Crawford B. *The Cornell University special collection on slavery: American publications through 1840.* Cornell University, 1950.

Lines, Stiles B. *Slaves and churchmen: the work of the Episcopal church among southern Negroes, 1830-1860.* Columbia University, 1960. Discusses work and motivation of clergy and laity of Episcopal church in relation to slavery. **60-3107**

Lipscomb, Patrick L., III. *William Pitt and the abolition of the slave trade.* University of Texas, 1960. Detailed history of British Abolition Movement from 1783 to 1807. **60-1984**

Litwack, Leon F. *North of slavery: the Negro in the free states, 1790-1860.* University of California, Berkeley, 1959.

Lloyd, Arthur V. *The slavery controversy, 1831-1860.* Vanderbilt University, 1934.

Lord, Francis A. *The federal volunteer soldier in the American Civil War, 1861-1865.* University of Michigan, 1949. Chronological treatment of the federal soldier's military life in its main phases; includes contributions of foreigners and Negroes in considerable detail. **1162**

Lumpkins, Josephine. *Antislavery opposition to the annexation of Texas, with special reference to John Quincy Adams.* Cornell University, 1941.

Mandel, Bernard. *The northern working class and the abolition of slavery.* Western Reserve University, 1952.

McManus, Edgar J. *Negro slavery in New York.* Columbia University, 1959. History of slavery in New York from 1626 to abolition in 1817. **59-4077**

Meldrum, George W. *The history of the treatment of foreign and minority groups in California, 1830-1860.* Stanford University, 1949.

Merkel, Benjamin. *The anti-slavery movement in Missouri, 1819-1865.* Washington University, 1939.

Mooney, Chase C. *Slavery in Tennessee.* Vanderbilt University, 1939.

Moore, Wilbert E. *Slavery, abolition and the ethical valuation of the individual.* Harvard University, 1940.

Moseley, Thomas R. *A history of the New York Manumission Society, 1785-1849.* New York University, 1963. **65-1691**

Myers, John L. *The agency system of the anti-slavery movement, 1832-1837, and its antecedents in other benevolent and reform societies.* University of Michigan, 1961. Efforts of 100 agents in producing a change in northern sentiment toward slavery. **61-1895**

Murray, Alexander L. *Canada and the Anglo-American anti-slavery movement: a study in international philanthropy.* University of Pennsylvania, 1960. Efforts of Canadian, British and American philanthropists to aid fugitive slaves who escaped to Canada prior to the Civil War. **60-3674**

Murray, Constance C. *Portland, Maine, and the growth of urban responsibility for human welfare, 1830-1860.* Boston University Graduate School, 1960. Traces growth of governmental concern for human welfare in Portland, Maine, 1830-1860, including care of poor, antislavery movements and education of Negroes. **60-3472**

Newbold, Catharine. *The anti-slavery background of the principal State Department appointees in the Lincoln Administration.* University of Michigan, 1962. Backgrounds of territorial governors, ministers and consuls appointed by the Lincoln Administration with regard to views on slavery and motives for appointment. **63-1920**

O'Dell, Richard F. *The early antislavery movement in Ohio.* University of Michigan, 1948. Discusses antislavery movement and status of the Negro in Ohio from 1802 to the Civil War. **1069**

Olson, Edwin. *Negro slavery in New York, 1628-1827.* New York University, 1938.

Pendleton, Lawson A. *James Buchanan's attitude toward slavery.* University of North Carolina, 1964. Describes Buchanan as occupying middle ground between extreme pro- and antislavery groups. **65-9047**

Pendleton, Othniel A. *The Influence of the Evangelical Churches Upon Humanitarian Reform: A Case Study Giving Particular Attention to Philadelphia, 1790-1840.* University of Pennsylvania, 1945.

Powell, Milton B. *The abolitionist controversy in the Methodist Episcopal church, 1840-1864.* State University of Iowa, 1963. Traces the conflict within northern Methodism respecting the role of the church in society and the attitude of the church toward existing institutions, with particular reference to abolitionism. **64-3415**

Purifoy, Lewis M., Jr. *The Methodist Episcopal church, South, and slavery, 1844-1865.* University of North Carolina, 1965. Traces the church's relation to slavery from its founding as an antislavery institution through gradual acceptance of slavery as issue for the state to decide. **66-4728**

Qualls, Youra T. *Friend and freedman: the work of the Association of Friends of Philadelphia and its vicinity for the relief and education of freedmen during the Civil War and Reconstruction, 1862-1872.* Radcliffe College, 1956.

Ratner, Lorman A. *Northern opposition to the anti-slavery movement, 1831-1840.* Cornell University, 1961. Abolitionists were viewed as threats to the social order who were being used by aliens to destroy American institutions. **61-4888**

Refsell, Oliver M. *The Massies of Virginia: a documentary history of a planter family.* University of Texas, 1959. Includes description of methods of handling slaves, slave rosters with details on births, deaths, morals, health and family relations of slaves. **59-4735**

Reid, Robert D. *Slavery in Alabama.* University of Minnesota, 1946.

Reilley, Edward C. *The early slavery controversy in the Western Reserve.* Western Reserve University, 1940.

Reinders, Robert C. *A social history of New Orleans, 1850-1860.* University of Texas, 1957. Study of class structure, schools, press, opera and recreations of ante-bellum New Orleans; includes treatment and status of Negroes. **25174**

Robinson, Donald L. *Slavery and sectionalism in the founding of the United States, 1787-1808.* Cornell University, 1966. A study of slavery as an obstacle to "more perfect union" among the American states during the constitutional and early national periods. **66-11043**

Roethler, Michael D. *Negro slavery among the Cherokee Indians, 1540-1866.* Fordham University, 1964. Treats slaves as an important element in civilizing the Cherokee Nation. **64-13299**

Savage, William S. *The controversy over the distribution of abolition literature, 1830-1860.* Ohio State University, 1935.

Scarborough, William K. *Plantation management in the ante-bellum South: the overseer.* University of North Carolina, 1962. Examines the general performance of the overseer class. **63-3516**

Schnell, Kempes Y. *Court cases involving slavery: a study of the application of anti-slavery thought to judicial argument.* University of Michigan, 1955. Evolving trend of constitutional argument to 1860.
12643

Seifman, Eli. *A history of the New York State Colonization Society.* New York University, 1965. Traces policy from one of removal of free Negroes to concern for improving population of Liberia.
66-9519

Schoen, Harold. *The free Negro in the Republic of Texas.* University of Texas, 1938.

Senior, Robert C. *New England Congregationalism and the anti-slavery movement, 1830-1860.* Yale University, 1954.

Shaw, Warren C. *The fugitive slave issue in Massachusetts politics, 1780-1837.* University of Illinois, 1938.

Simpson, Albert F. *The political significance of slave representation, 1787-1821.* Vanderbilt University, 1941.

Sio, Arnold A. *The legal and social structure of slavery in the U.S.* University of Illinois, 1958. Restructuring of interpretations of slavery in the ante-bellum South.
59-577

Smith, Robert Gordon. *The arguments over abolition petitions in the House of Representatives in December, 1835: a Toulmin analysis.* University of Minnesota, 1962. Characteristics of arguments in the House of Representatives relating to abolition of slavery and slave trade in the District of Columbia.
63-5043

Spraggins, Tinsley L. *Economic aspects of Negro colonization during the Civil War.* American University, 1957. Analysis of the economic phases of the Negro colonization movement.
21968

Stanton, William R. *The leopard's spots: science and the American idea of equality: 1815-1860.* Brown University, 1956. Evolving scientific views on the equality of men from Jefferson to Darwin.
19545

Staudenraus, Philip J. *The history of the American Colonization Society.* University of Wisconsin, 1958. Organized in 1817: group viewed Negro as alien; established Liberia as its colony.
60-6792

Stavisky, Leonard P. *The Negro artisan in the South Atlantic States, 1800-1860: a study of status and economic opportunity with special reference to Charleston.* Columbia University, 1958. Traces development of Negro labor in America; emphasis on the South.
58-2246

Steely, Will F. *Antislavery in Kentucky, 1850-1860.* University of Rochester, 1956.

Stirton, Thomas. *Party disruptions and the rise of the slavery extension controversy, 1840-1846.* University of Chicago, 1957.

Stowe, William M. *The influence of Thomas Jefferson's democratic principles upon Abraham Lincoln's thinking on the question of slavery.* Boston University, 1938.

Stump, William D. *The English view Negro slavery, 1660-1780.* University of Missouri, 1962. Traces rise of antislavery feeling in England from the introduction of Negro slavery.
62-3345

Sweat, Edward F. *The free Negro in ante-bellum Georgia.* Indiana University, 1957. Historical treatment of origin, status and laws affecting free Negroes.   **22709**

Taylor, Hubert V. *Slavery and the deliberations of the Presbyterian General Assembly, 1833-1838.* Northwestern University, 1964. Traced the influence of the slavery controversy upon events which resulted in a Presbyterian split in 1838.   **65-3316**

Taylor, Joe G. *Negro slavery in Louisiana.* Louisiana State University, 1952.

Taylor, Orville W. *Negro slavery in Arkansas.* Duke University, 1956.

Thornbrough, Emma L. *Negro slavery in the North, its legal and constitutional aspects.* University of Michigan, 1947.

Todd, Willie G. *The slavery issue and the organization of a Southern Baptist Convention.* University of North Carolina, 1964.   **65-9067**

Towner, Lawrence W. *A good master well served: a social history of servitude in Massachusetts, 1620-1750.* Northwestern University, 1955. Factors shaping the servant class, various servant types and their common characteristics.   **13145**

Twersky, Atarah S. *The attitude of the ante-bellum North toward the Negro.* Radcliffe College, 1959.

Voegeli, Victor J., III. *The Northwest and the Negro during the Civil War.* Tulane University, 1965. The Civil War intensified racism in a region which was a stronghold of white supremacy.   **66-1586**

Wax, Darold D. *The Negro slave trade in colonial Pennsylvania.* University of Washington, 1962. Historical account from 1681 to 1788.   **63-3147**

Wight, Willard E. *Churches in the Confederacy.* Emory University, 1958. Work of churches during secession, in support of Confederacy, on home front, in army, among Negroes and in education.
                    58-5190

Yanuck, Julius. *The fugitive slave law and the Constitution.* Columbia University, 1953. Constitutional and statutory remedies for the fugitive slave problem.   **5218**

Zilversmit, Arthur. *Slavery and its abolition in the northern states.* University of California, Berkeley, 1962. Traced legal and other efforts to free the slave from colonial period to 1804.   **63-5469**

3. After Emancipation

Abbott, Martin L. *The Freedmen's Bureau in South Carolina, 1865-1872.* Emory University, 1954. Describes and evaluates the work of BRFAL in relief, labor, education, and inter-racial relations.
                    58-5108

Alderson, William T. *The influence of military rule and the Freedmen's Bureau on Reconstruction in Virginia, 1865-1870.* Vanderbilt University, 1952. Includes BRFAL efforts in education, labor contracts and physical aid.   **3968**

Alexander, Thomas B. *Reconstruction in Tennessee.* Vanderbilt University, 1947.

Bacote, Clarence A. *The Negro in Georgia politics, 1880-1908.* University of Chicago, 1956.

Baker, Robert A. *The American Baptist Home Mission Society and the South, 1832-1894.* Yale University, 1947.

Banks, Melvin J. *The pursuit of equality: the movement for first class citizenship among Negroes in Texas, 1920-1950.* Syracuse University, 1962. Historical account of the struggle for political and educational equality. **63-3620**

Bentley, George R. *A history of the Freedmen's Bureau.* University of Wisconsin, 1949.

Boyd, Willis. *Negro colonization in the national crisis, 1860-1870.* University of California at Los Angeles, 1954.

Brown, Donald N. *Southern attitudes toward Negro voting during the Bourbon period, 1877-1890.* University of Oklahoma, 1960. Bourbon attitudes moved from moderate in 1877 toward a more radical position; defeat of Bourbons brought an end to the Negro as a force in southern elections. **60-5185**

Buckland, Roscoe L. *Anglo-Saxonism in America, 1880-1898.* State University of Iowa, 1955. Belief in Anglo-Saxon superiority examined in writings, speeches of public figures, works of scholars and literature of the period. **12883**

Buni, Andrew. *The Negro in Virginia politics, 1902-1950.* University of Virginia, 1965. Traced the participation of Negroes in Virginia politics from exclusion by the 1902 constitution to the election of 1950. **66-3147**

Caldwell, Martha B. *The attitude of Kansas toward Reconstruction of the South.* University of Kansas, 1933. Includes discussion of attitudes toward Negro immigrants after the Civil War. **1543**

Carper, Noel G. *The convict-lease system in Florida, 1866-1923.* Florida State University, 1964. Detailed history of the system, a majority of whose victims were Negro. **65-5569**

Cheaney, Henry E. *Attitudes of the Indiana pulpit and the press toward the Negro, 1860-1880.* University of Chicago, 1961.

Cobb, Henry E. *Negroes in Alabama during the Reconstruction period, 1865-1875.* Temple University, 1953.

Cochrane, William G. *Freedom without equality: a study of northern opinion and the Negro issue, 1861-1870.* University of Minnesota, 1957. Detailed study of a decade of debate over Negro suffrage, education and employment. **23928**

Corlew, Robert E. *The Negro in Tennessee, 1870-1900.* University of Alabama, 1954.

Cox, LaWanda F. *Agricultural labor in the United States, 1865-1900, with special reference to the South.* University of California, 1942.

Drake, Richard B. *The American Missionary Association and the Southern Negro, 1861-1888.* Emory University, 1957. Historical survey of the changing role of the AMA, 1846-1888, with emphasis on work in the South. **58-5136**

Edmonds, Helen G. *The Negro and fusion politics in North Carolina, 1895-1901.* Ohio State University, 1946.

EssienUdom, Essien. *Black nationalism: the search for an identity.* University of Chicago, 1962.

Fishel, Leslie H., Jr. *The North and the Negro, 1865-1900: a study in race discrimination.* Harvard University, 1954.

Fuller, Luther M. *The Negro in Boston, 1864-1954.* Columbia University, 1956.

Going, Allen J. *Bourbon democracy in Alabama, 1874-1890.* University of North Carolina, 1948.

Gossett, Thomas F. *The idea of Anglo-Saxon superiority in American thought, 1865-1915.* University of Minnesota, 1953. Traces influence of this idea in ethnology, social theory, history writing, religious thought, language and literature, and politics; treats novels of Frank Norris, Jack London and Owen Wister.   **6381**

Hair, William I. *The agrarian protest in Louisiana, 1877-1900.* Louisiana State University, 1962. Treats dissatisfaction of agrarian elements with conservative regimes and the attempted alliance with Negroes.   **62-3648**

Harrell, Kenneth E. *The Ku Klux Klan in Louisiana, 1920-1930.* Louisiana State University, 1966.
                                                                    66-10903

Hirshson, Stanley P. *Farewell to the bloody shirt: northern Republicans and the southern Negro, 1877-1893.* Columbia University, 1959. A study of the shift in Republican policy toward the Negro.
                                                                    62-1919

Jackson, Kenneth T. *The decline of the Ku Klux Klan, 1924-1932.* University of Chicago, 1963.

Kearney, Kevin E. *Speaking in Florida on the issues of presidential Reconstruction, 1865-1867: a rhetoric of reunion.* University of Florida, 1960. One chapter discusses speaking of William Marvin to Negroes on the responsibilities of freedom.   **60-1904**

Kelsey, George D. *The social thought of contemporary southern Baptists.* Yale University, 1946. Southern Baptist views on major social topics from 1917 to 1944.   **65-2492**

Kifer, Allen F. *The Negro under the New Deal, 1933-1941.* University of Wisconsin, 1961. Policies of New Deal organizations (CCC, NYA, WPA, Farm Security Administration) toward Negroes.   **61-3124**

Knuth, Helen E. *The climax of American Anglo-Saxonism, 1898-1905.* Northwestern University, 1958. Explores roots and effects of Anglo-Saxonism.   **58-5763**

Krueger, Thomas A. *The Southern Conference for Human Welfare.* University of Minnesota, 1965. The work of the first integrated southern organization to demand complete abolition of segregation.
                                                                    65-15202

Lawrence, Charles R. *Negro organizations in crisis: Depression, New Deal, World War II.* Columbia University, 1952. Goals and programs of NAACP; National Negro Congress, National Urban League, March-On-Washington Movement in relation to national crises.   **4577**

Lindsay, Inabel B. *The participation of Negroes in the establishment of welfare services, 1865-1900, with special reference to the District of Columbia, Maryland, and Virginia.* University of Pittsburgh, 1952.

Logan, Frenise A. *The Negro in North Carolina, 1876-1894.* Western Reserve University, 1954.

Lowe, Robert A. *Racial segregation in Indiana, 1920-1950.* Ball State University, 1965. Traces rise of segregation after World War I, increased segregation in the Depression, the end of segregation in 1949.
66-1988

Mabry, William A. *The disfranchisement of the Negro in the South.* Duke University, 1933.

McConnell, Roland C. *The Negro in North Carolina since Reconstruction.* New York University, 1945.

Meier, August. *Negro racial thought in the age of Booker T. Washington, circa 1880-1915.* Columbia University, 1957. Analysis of ideas of self help, racial solidarity, economic development and industrial education as exemplified by Booker T. Washington.
22058

Mellette, Peter. *Reconstruction, expansion, and change: America as reported by British travelers during the period 1865-1890 with a focus upon intergroup relations.* Columbia University, Teachers College, 1951.

Miller, Robert M. *An inquiry into the social attitudes of American Protestantism, 1919-1939.* Northwestern University, 1955. Attitudes of 15 major denominations on civil liberties, race relations, labor, war and capitalism-socialism-communism.
13115

Mitchell, Frank J. *The Virginia Methodist conference and social issues in the twentieth century.* Duke University, 1962. Includes attitudes toward the race problem.
63-1407

Moore, Ross H. *Social and economic conditions in Mississippi during Reconstruction.* Duke University, 1938.

Neyland, Leedell W. *The Negro in Louisiana since 1900: an economic and social study.* New York University, 1959. Social and economic aspects of Negro life in Louisiana since 1900.
59-2450

Nolen, Claude H. *Aftermath of slavery: Southern attitude toward Negroes, 1865-1900.* University of Texas, 1963. The political, educational and economic steps are traced in detail by which Southerners reduced free Negroes to a lower caste in the social order.
64-101

Osofsky, Gilbert. *Harlem, the making of a ghetto: a history of Negro New York, 1900-1920.* Columbia University, 1963.
65-7467

Phillips, Paul D. *A history of the Freedmen's Bureau in Tennessee.* Vanderbilt University, 1964. **65-1813**

Rawick, George P. *The New Deal and youth: the Civilian Conservation Corps, the National Youth Administration and the American Youth Congress.* University of Wisconsin, 1957. Includes involvement of Negroes in these programs.
60-1883

Record, Cy W. *The role of the Negro intellectuals in contemporary racial movements.* University of California, Berkeley, 1954.

Reimers, David M. *Protestant churches and the Negro: a study of several major Protestant denominations and the Negro from World War One to 1954.* University of Wisconsin, 1961. Includes Congregational, Methodist Episcopal, Presbyterian and Protestant Episcopal churches.
61-2975

Richardson, Joe M. *The Negro in the Reconstruction of Florida.* Florida State University, 1963. Rejecting the Dunning view of Reconstruction, this study asserts that the abilities and acts of the legislators compared favorably with both previous and subsequent all-white governments.
64-3611

Robinson, James H. *A social history of the Negro in Memphis and in Shelby County.* Yale University, 1934.

Scheiner, Seth M. *The Negro in New York City, 1865-1910.* New York University, 1963. The move from Greenwich Village into Harlem, the increasing trend of Negroes going into business or trades, conflict with other nationality groups and the decline of the Negro clergy as a political and social force.   **63-7231**

Scroggs, Jack B. *Carpetbagger influence in the political Reconstruction of the South Atlantic States, 1865-1876.* University of North Carolina, 1953.

Seshachari, Candadai. *Gandhi and the American scene: an intellectual history and inquiry.* University of Utah, 1964. American interest in the ideas of Gandhi, with emphasis on the intellectual involvement of Reinhold Niebuhr and the practical involvement of Martin Luther King, Jr.   **64-8259**

Shaw, Van B. *Nicodemus, Kansas, a study in isolation.* University of Missouri, 1951. Study of an all-Negro community founded in 1877.   **2901**

Sheeler, John R. *The Negro in West Virginia before 1900.* University of West Virginia, 1954.

Silvestro, Clement M. *None but patriots: the Union leagues in Civil War and Reconstruction.* University of Wisconsin, 1959. Work of secret Union leagues in promoting patriotism; includes work in South during Reconstruction.   **60-4645**

Singletary, Otis A. *The Negro militia movement during Radical Reconstruction.* Louisiana State University, 1954.

Sisk, Glenn N. *Alabama Black Belt, a social history, 1875-1917.* Duke University, 1951.

Smith, James D. *Virginia during Reconstruction, 1865-1870 – a political, economic and social study.* University of Virginia, 1960. Account of the relatively tranquil and moderate course of Reconstruction in Virginia; includes status of freedmen.   **60-4621**

Spain, Rufus B. *Attitudes and reactions of southern Baptists to certain problems of society, 1865-1900.* Vanderbilt University, 1961. Includes discussion of race relations.   **61-3604**

Spangler, Earl. *A history of the Negro in Minnesota.* University of Oklahoma, 1961. Sees the Negro as a catalyst of American democracy.   **61-2722**

Spear, Allan H. *Black Chicago, 1900-1920: the making of a Negro ghetto.* Yale University, 1965. Account of the factors involved in transformation of a segregated community into a ghetto.   **65-9716**

Stocking, George W., Jr. *American social scientists and race theory: 1890-1915.* University of Pennsylvania, 1960. Traces development of the concept of race in the scholarly journals of anthropology and social science.   **60-3698**

Stone, Olive M. *Agrarian conflict in Alabama: sections, races, and classes in a rural state from 1800-1938.* University of North Carolina, 1940.

Strickland, Shirley W. *A functional analysis of the Garvey movement.* University of North Carolina, 1956.

Taylor, Alrutheus A. *The Negro in the Reconstruction of Virginia.* Harvard University, 1936.

Thorpe, Earlie E. *Negro historiography in the United States.* Ohio State University, 1954.

Tindall, George B. *The Negro in South Carolina after Reconstruction, 1877-1900.* University of North Carolina, 1951.

Tingley, Donald F. *The rise of racialistic thinking in the United States in the nineteenth century.* University of Illinois, 1953.

Tolson, Arthur L. *The Negro in Oklahoma Territory, 1889-1907: a study in racial discrimination.* University of Oklahoma, 1966. Role of Negroes in Oklahoma through *Brown* decision, 1954.

66-11792

Ulrich, William J. *The northern military mind in regard to Reconstruction, 1865-1872: the attitudes of ten leading Union generals.* Ohio State University, 1959. Attitudes toward the Negro problem, civil rights, labor relations and military governments. **60-802**

Valentine, Foy D. *A historical study of southern Baptists and race relations, 1918-1947.* Southwestern Baptist Theological Seminary, 1949.

Vander Zanden, James W. *The southern white resistance movement to integration.* University of North Carolina, 1958. Southern resistance analyzed by ideology, foundations, resistance organizations and resistance at state and national levels. **58-5972**

Walz, Robert B. *Migration into Arkansas, 1834-1880.* University of Texas, 1958. From where and at what rate families moved into Arkansas; racial data given. **58-1675**

Ward, Judson C. *Georgia under the Bourbon Democrats, 1872-1890.* University of North Carolina, 1948.

Warnock, Henry Y. *Moderate racial thought and attitudes of southern Baptists and Methodists, 1900-1921.* Northwestern University, 1963. From published denominational materials the author found predominantly conservative attitudes with respect to Negro education, voting rights, segregation and mob violence. **64-2539**

Webb, Allie B. W. *A history of Negro voting in Louisiana, 1877-1906.* Louisiana State University, 1962. Traces Negro voting from Reconstruction to disfranchisement in 1906. **62-3674**

Weston, M. Moran. *Social policy of the Episcopal church in the twentieth century.* Columbia University, 1954. Includes racial policies and problems. **8860**

Wharton, Vernon L. *The Negro in Mississippi, 1865-1890.* University of North Carolina, 1940.

White, Frank H. *The economic and social development of Negroes in North Carolina since 1900.* New York University, 1960. Population trends, economic activities, social aspects such as educational, religious, fraternal associations, recreational activities; begins 1865 but focuses on 1900-1957. **61-705**

White, Howard A. *The Freedmen's Bureau in Louisiana.* Tulane University, 1956. Evaluation of Bureau's work in Louisiana between 1865 and 1872.   **59-1082**

Wiley, Bell I. *The Negro in the Confederacy.* Yale University, 1938.

Williamson, Edward C. *The era of the Democratic county leader: Florida politics, 1877-1893.* University of Pennsylvania, 1954. Includes analysis of Negro political activity.   **8593**

Williamson, Joel R. *The Negro in South Carolina during Reconstruction, 1861-1877.* University of California, Berkeley, 1964. The role of the Negro in politics, labor and religion.   **64-9108**

Wilson, Raleigh A. *Negro and Indian relations in the five civilized tribes from 1865 to 1907.* University of Iowa, 1950.

Wood, Forrest G. *Race demagoguery during the Civil War and Reconstruction.* University of California, Berkeley, 1965. Not slavery or abolition, but race — the Negro himself and his place — was the central theme of political oratory from 1862 to 1872.   **65-8284**

Wynes, Charles E. *Race relations in Virginia, 1870-1902.* University of Virginia, 1960. Attitudes toward the role of Negroes during Reconstruction and the period of liberalism around 1880, to the legal definition of the Negro's place in 1900.   **60-4627**

POLITICAL AND CIVIL RIGHTS

1. Patterns and Conditions

Akiwowo, Akinsola A. *Status inconsistency in relation to social participation and political activity in a Boston Negro community: an application of the status inconsistency concept to the study of a local community.* Boston University Graduate School, 1961. A study of the relationship between status inconsistency of Negro men in Boston to their attitudes and social-political acitivites.   **61-714**

Berman, William C. *The politics of civil rights in the Truman Administration.* Ohio State University, 1963. The efforts of the Truman Administration concerning civil rights, traced from creation of the President's Commission in 1946 to the administrative brief to the Supreme Court in late 1952.
64-6875

Bond, J. Max. *The Negro in Los Angeles.* University of Southern California, 1936.

Bowman, Robert L. *Negro politics in four southern counties.* University of North Carolina, 1964. Factors related to the amount and effectiveness of Negro participation in politics in four southern counties.   **65-8994**

Brittain, Joseph M. *Negro suffrage and politics in Alabama since 1870.* Indiana University, 1958. Describes the Negro's role and influence in Alabama politics.   **58-2902**

Cohen, Leon S. *The southern Negro: a model of ethnic political assimilation.* University of North Carolina, 1965. Developed a model of ethnic political assimilation to which data concerning the Negro may be used to understand and predict political behavior of ethnic groups.   **65-14324**

Collins, Ernest M. *The political behavior of the Negroes in Cincinnati, Ohio, and Louisville, Kentucky.* University of Kentucky, 1950. Factors affecting voting behavior of Negroes, 1928-1948.   **60-643**

Cosman, Bernard. *Republicanism in the metropolitan South.* University of Alabama, 1960. One chapter analyzes "who-votes-how" for 12 southern cities and includes racial analysis.   **62-71**

Dreer, Herman. *Negro leadership in St. Louis: a study in race relations.* University of Chicago, 1956.

Farris, Charles D. *Effects of Negro voting upon the politics of a southern city: an intensive study, 1946-48.* University of Chicago, 1953.

Eichhorn, Robert L. *Patterns of segregation, discrimination and inter-racial conflict: analysis of a nationwide survey of intergroup practices.* Cornell University, 1954. Survey of extent of segregation in urban areas and types of action effective in eliminating discriminatory practices.   **10577**

Gooden, John E. *Negro participation in civil government with emphasis on public education in Texas.* University of Southern California, 1950.

Hoot, John W. *Lynch-law: the practice of illegal popular coercion.* University of Pennsylvania, 1935.

Kaplan, Harold. *The politics of slum clearance. A study of urban renewal in Newark, New Jersey.* Columbia University, 1961. The political preconditions of rapid social change, using Newark as a case study; includes role of Negro leaders, migration and other factors.   **61-3442**

Ladd, Everett C., Jr. *Negro political leadership in the urban South.* Cornell University, 1964. Pattern of Negro leadership since 1954 was found to be "issue leadership" with high fluidity potential. **64-13810**

Lindenfeld, Frank. *An analysis of political involvement.* Columbia University, 1961. Differences in levels of political involvement based on 1956 survey; race as a factor.   **62-1923**

Martin, Robert E. *Negro-white participation in the A.A.A. cotton and tobacco referendum in North and South Carolina: a study in differential voting and attitudes in selected areas.* University of Chicago, 1948.

Miller, James E. *The Negro in Pennsylvania politics with special reference to Philadelphia since 1932.* University of Pennsylvania, 1946.

Morsell, John A. *The political behavior of Negroes in New York City.* Columbia University, 1951. Analysis of political behavior of Negroes in Harlem since 1920; case study of the 1944 campaign.
                                                                                          2842

Seasholes, Bradbury. *Negro political participation in two North Carolina cities.* University of North Carolina, 1962. Variables associated with political participation in Winston-Salem and Durham, North Carolina.   **63-3518**

Smolka, Richard G. *The emergence of a party system in the District of Columbia.* American University, 1966. A study of factors involved in the emergence of a party system in D.C.   **66-12815**

Solomon, Thomas R. *Participation of Negroes in Detroit elections.* University of Michigan, 1939.

Starlard, Victor D. *Factors associated with Negro voting in a delta county of Arkansas.* University of Arkansas, 1961. Generally supported other findings that certain educational and economic factors are related to voting behavior.   **61-1350**

Turner, James D. *Dynamics of criminal law administration in a biracial community of the Deep South.* Indiana University, 1956. Study of modifications in the differential application of criminal law to white and Negro persons in a 5-year period following World War II as compared to period before the war.   **17983**

Whitaker, Hugh S. *A new day: the effects of Negro enfranchisement in selected Mississippi counties.* Florida State University, 1965. Benefits such as fairer law enforcement, rate of desegregation, equality of real estate assessment significantly correlated with the extent of Negro registration.   **66-2102**

Williams, Frank B., Jr. *The poll tax as a suffrage requirement in the South, 1870-1901.* Vanderbilt University, 1950. Rejects prevention of Negro voting as the main factor in poll tax requirement. **4411**

Wilhoit, Francis M. *The politics of desegregation in Georgia.* Harvard University, 1958.

2.   The Courts and the Law

Anderson, Robert L. *Negro suffrage in relation to American Federalism, 1957-63.* University of Florida, 1964. Found that the issue of Negro suffrage drastically altered the boundary of the division of powers.   **65-2411**

Andresen, Karl A. *The theory of state interposition to control federal action: a study of the Kentucky and Virginia resolutions of 1798, of Calhoun's doctrine of nullification, and the contemporary interposition resolutions of some southern states.* University of Minnesota, 1960. Examines interposition doctrine from 1798 to the 1954 desegregation decision.   **61-555**

Berger, Morroe. *Equality by statute: law and group discriminations in the U.S.* Columbia University, 1950. An assessment of law as a means of social control in intergroup relations.   **1740**

Borinski, Ernst. *Sociology of judge-made law in civil rights cases.* University of Pittsburgh, 1954. A study of the principles of judge-made law controlling Supreme Court decisions in civil rights cases.   **8880**

Caldwell, Wallace F. *Use of the administrative process by states to secure civil rights.* University of Washington, 1965. The extent to which states have used regulatory and nonregulatory activities to prohibit discrimination.   **65-8509**

Christensen, Janice E. *The constitutional problems of national control of the suffrage in the U.S.* University of Minnesota, 1952. Problems of Negro suffrage, poll tax and soldiers' voting.   **4849**

Dallmayr, Winfreid R. *Equal protection of the laws: a comparative study of its background and early development, 1750-1850.* Duke University, 1960. Background and meaning of the principle and reasons why equal protection emerged in modern society.   **60-6026**

Dew, Lee A. *The racial ideas of the authors of the Fourteenth Amendment.* Louisiana State University, 1960. Concludes that many who voted for the Amendment interpreted it narrowly and saw it as a political expedient.   **60-5906**

Hamilton, Charles V. *Southern federal courts and the right of Negroes to vote, 1957-1962.* University of Chicago, 1964.

Hamilton, Howard D. *The legislative and judicial history of the Thirteenth Amendment.* University of Illinois, 1950. The Congressional and state debates over the amendment and subsequent interpretations of its meanings.   **2070**

Hazel, David W. *The National Association for the Advancement of Colored People and the national legislative process, 1940-1954.* University of Michigan, 1957. Methods and effectiveness of the NAACP in influencing national legislation.   **58-1411**

Higbee, Jay A. *New York State law against discrimination*. Syracuse University, 1955. Analysis of the effects of the law. **15052**

Jans, Ralph T. *Negro civil rights and the Supreme Court, 1865-1949*. University of Chicago, 1951.

Mawhinney, Eugene A. *The development of the concept of liberty in the Fourteenth Amendment*. University of Illinois, 1955. Traces Supreme Court development of concept of liberty since 1868.
15239

Mayhew, Leon H. *Law and equal opportunity: anti-discrimination law in Massachusetts*. Harvard University, 1964.

McGuinn, Henry J. *The courts and the changing status of Negroes in Maryland*. Columbia University, 1940.

Mosby, Reba S. *The evolution of constitutional, legislative and judicial protection of civil and human rights in Missouri: a critical and interpretative analysis*. St. Louis University, 1960. Historical progression of the concept of civil and human rights in Missouri in relation to racial and religious restrictions. **61-761**

Nelson, Bernard H. *The Fourteenth Amendment and the Negro since 1920*. Catholic University of America, 1945.

Newsom, Lionel H. *Court treatment of intra- and inter-racial homicide in Saint Louis*. Washington University, 1956. Data from 1943 to 1947 supports hypothesis that the courts mete out differential treatment in intraracial and interracial homicides. **16629**

Stone, Raymond P. *'Separate But Equal': the evolution and demise of a constitutional doctrine*. Princeton University, 1964. Historical account developed with assumption that legal decisions are the product of interaction between social forces and personal values of the judges. **64-12140**

Sullivan, Donald F. *The civil rights programs of the Kennedy Administration: a political analysis*. University of Oklahoma, 1965. Kennedy administration civil rights programs summarized and analyzed, especially executive acts of Kennedy; evaluation of use of Presidential powers. **65-4953**

Ware, Gilbert. *The National Association for the Advancement of Colored People and the Civil Rights Act of 1957*. Princeton University, 1962. An empirical study of the legislative life of the NAACP.
63-572

3. Protest

Abramowitz, Jack. *Accommodation and militancy in Negro life, 1876-1916*. Columbia University, 1950. A study of the major economic, political and social activities of Negroes from 1876 to 1916, oriented around themes of accommodation and militancy. **1823**

Banks, Walter R. *A source of social protest: the predicament of the status inconsistent Negro*. Michigan State University, 1963. Reported that education, rather than occupation or income, was most predictive of desire to reduce discrimination. **64-4934**

Bell, Howard H. *A survey of the Negro convention movement, 1830-1861*. Northwestern University, 1953. Thought and action of various free Negro assemblies respecting slavery, communal settlements, suffrage, education and discrimination. **6179**

Bowen, Harry W. *The persuasive efficacy of Negro non-violent resistance.* University of Pittsburgh, 1962. Limitations of and results obtained by non-violent resistance.   **63-2419**

Bozeman, Herman H. *Attitudes of selected racial leadership organizations towards educational policies and practices for Negroes during the twentieth century.* University of Michigan, 1956. Comparison of educational concerns of the National Urban League and the NAACP.   **17417**

Brisbane, Robert H., Jr. *The rise of protest movements among Negroes since 1900.* Harvard University, 1949.

Caine, Augustus F. *Patterns of Negro protest: a structural-functional analysis.* Michigan State University, 1964. Patterns of response among Negroes in Lansing, Michigan, to racial discrimination, with emphasis on the structural features of the protest groups.   **65-6055**

Chasteen, Edgar R. *Public accommodations: social movements in conflict or the race is on.* University of Missouri, 1966. A study of the Public Accommodations Movement in Missouri, including the nature of its Negro leadership and Negro-white relations.   **66-8970**

Clarke, Jacquelyne M. J. *Goals and techniques in three Negro civil rights organizations in Alabama.* Ohio State University, 1960. Reports data on Alabama Christian Movement for Human Rights, Montgomery Improvement Association and Tuskegee Civic Association collected in 1959.   **60-6355**

Garfinkel, Herbert. *Black march on the White House: the Negro March on Washington Movement in the organization politics for FEPC.* University of Chicago, 1957.

Gerner, Henry L. *A study of the Freedom Riders with particular emphasis upon three dimensions: dogmatism, value-orientation, and religiosity.* Pacific School of Religion, 1963. Data from various value and religious concepts scales used with Mississippi "Freedom Riders."   **64-8258**

Gross, James A. *The NAACP, The AFL-CIO and the Negro worker.* University of Wisconsin, 1962. Impact on ALF-CIO by NAACP regarding the civil rights issue.   **62-2242**

McBee, Susanna B. *Sit-in demonstrations and the law.* University of Chicago, 1962.

Oppenheimer, Martin. *The genesis of the southern Negro student movement (sit-in movement): a study in contemporary Negro protest.* University of Pennsylvania, 1963. Origin, development, structure and results of some one hundred demonstrations during 1960.   **63-7075**

Orbell, John M. *Social protest and social structure: southern Negro college student participation in the protest movement.* University of North Carolina, 1965. The social and individual variables associated with college student participation in the protest movement; socio-economic status was the most powerful variable tested.   **66-4724**

Powe, Alphonso S. *The role of Negro pressure groups in interracial integration in Durham City, North Carolina.* New York University, 1954. Activities of six Negro pressure groups are described and analyzed.   **11948**

Powell, Ingeborg B. *Ideology and strategy of direct action: a study of the Congress of Racial Equality.* University of California, Berkeley, 1965. The ideology of the Congress of Racial Equality, contrasted with Gandhian, Quaker and other ideologies.   **65-13566**

White, Robert M. *The Tallahassee sit-ins and CORE: a non-violent revolutionary submovement.* Florida State University, 1964. A microcosmic analysis of the structure, framework, development of leadership and disciplinary processes of the Tallahassee Sit-Ins.   **65-339**

Zangrando, Robert L. *The efforts of the NAACP to secure passage of a federal anti-lynching law.* University of Pennsylvania, 1963. Concludes that NAACP lacked success with the immediate objective but did reorient the nation's conscience and stimulated united Negro action.   **64-3516**

HUMANITIES

1. Literature and Folklore

Abrahams, Roger D. *Negro folklore from South Philadelphia, a collection and analysis.* University of Pennsylvania, 1961. Presentation of folklore materials collected in a lower class neighborhood of South Philadelphia, with annotations.   **62-2817**

Bailey, Dale S. *Slavery in the novels of Brazil and the U.S.: a comparison.* Indiana University, 1961. Compares treatment of slavery in Brazilian and American novels.   **61-4420**

Blankenstein, Mark E. *The southern tradition in minor Mississippi writers since 1920.* University of Illinois, 1965. Described the treatment of the aristocrat, the poor white, and the Negro in works of minor Mississippi writers.   **66-4146**

Blue, Ila J. *A study of literary criticism by some Negro writers, 1900-1955.* University of Michigan, 1960. Concludes that Negro critics contributed especially to the understanding of irony in modern fiction.   **60-2508**

Briney, Martha M. *Ellen Glasgow: social critic.* Michigan State University, 1956. Analysis of attitudes toward poor whites, Negroes, formalized religion and the South in the novels of Ellen Glasgow.
        21049

Burrows, Robert N. *The image of urban life as it is reflected in the New York City novel, 1920-1930.* University of Pennsylvania, 1959. Novel treatment of major themes (migrant and immigrant; Negro and Jew) related to sociological data to determine extent of distortion.   **59-4601**

Butcher, Charles P. *George W. Cable as a social critic: 1887-1907.* Columbia University, 1956. Study of local-color writer who championed the cause of the freedman.   **16892**

Byrd, James W. *The portrayal of white character by Negro novelists, 1900-1950.* George Peabody College for Teachers, 1955. 110 novels examined, certain trends noted.   **13304**

Clark, Joseph E. *The American critique of the democratic idea, 1919-1929.* Stanford University, 1958. Treats the critical reflection on the democratic faith found in nonfiction books, periodicals and the *New York Times.*   **58-3598**

Clayton, Bruce L. *Southern critics of the New South, 1890-1914.* Duke University, 1966. The social criticism of John Spencer Bassett, William Garrott Brown, Edgar Gardner Murphy, Walter Hines Page and William P. Trent, in which race was a dominant theme.   **66-12726**

Cook, Raymond A. *Thomas Dixon: his books and his career.* Emory University, 1953. Emphasizes sociological significance of Dixon's novels, *The Leopard's Spots* and *The Clansmen.*   **58-5125**

Dickinson, Donald C. *A bio-bibliography of Langston Hughes, 1920-1960.* University of Michigan, 1964. Analysis of the writing of Langston Hughes from a biographic and bibliographic view.   **65-5891**

Doster, William C. *William Faulkner and the Negro.* University of Florida, 1955. Describes Faulkner's representation of the conduct of Negroes and traces development of his attitude toward the Negro.
        59-3557

Eckley, Wilton E. *The novels of T.S. Stribling: a socio-literary study*. Western Reserve University, 1965. Stribling's theory of life as a vast evolutionary process was the frame of reference for his idea of Negro progress.   **66-3028**

Emanuel, James A. *The short stories of Langston Hughes*. Columbia University, 1962. Sixty-five short stories of Langston Hughes analyzed with reference to themes, images and symbols, characterization and style.   **65-7484**

Erno, Richard B. *Dominant images of the Negro in the ante-bellum South*. University of Minnesota, 1961. Examines images of the Negro as Janus, Caliban, Satan, Sambo, Friday, Mammy and Uncle Tom.   **62-1776**

Farrell, Harold A. *Theme and variation: a critical evaluation of the Negro novel, 1919-1947*. Ohio State University, 1949.

Ford, Nick A. *The Negro author's use of propaganda in imaginative literature*. University of Iowa, 1946.

Galvin, Emma C. B. *The lore of the Negro in Central New York State*. Cornell University, 1943.

Gast, David K. *Characteristics and concepts of minority Americans in contemporary children's fictional literature*. Arizona State University, 1965. Complimentary, middle-class, Anglo-American virtues comprise a new stereotype of minority Americans.   **66-6902**

Gilbert, Robert B. *Attitudes toward the Negro in southern social studies and novels: 1932-1952*. Vanderbilt University, 1953. Rapid changes in southern society were reflected in treatment of the Negro in both novels and nonfiction.   **5508**

Gloster, Hugh M. *American Negro fiction from Charles W. Chesnutt to Richard B. Wright*. New York University, 1943.

Goldman, Hannah S. *American slavery and Russian serfdom; a study in fictional parallels*. Columbia University, 1955. Comparative literary analysis of novels concerned with human bondage; includes discussion of social forces in both countries giving rise to this fiction.   **11453**

Goldman, Morris M. *The sociology of Negro humor*. New School for Social Research, 1960.

Goldstone, Richard H. *The pariah in modern American and British literature: an illustration of a method for teachers of literature*. Columbia University, 1960. Treatment in literature of the fallen woman and the Negro is set against anthropological, social and psychological analysis of the pariah concept.   **60-3073**

Gross, Theodore L. *Albion W. Tourgee: reporter of the Reconstruction*. Columbia University, 1960. Analysis of Tourgee's fictional description of his Reconstruction experiences, contrasted with the southern interpretation of the same period.   **60-3075**

Hall, Wade H. *A study of southern humor: 1865-1913*. University of Illinois, 1961. Includes analysis of the Negro as the most popular subject for southern humor.   **62-616**

Hillger, Martin E. *Albion W. Tourgee: critic of society*. Indiana University, 1959. Analysis of Tourgee's novels reflecting the fundamental social differences of North and South.   **59-4011**

Hopson, James O. *Attitudes toward the Negro as an expression of English romanticism*. University of Pittsburgh, 1948.

Ives, Chauncey B. *Development in the fictional themes of Negro authors.* University of North Carolina, 1957.

Jackson, George B. *Of irony in Negro fiction: a critical study.* University of Michigan, 1953. Evaluation of irony in fiction of Walter White, Jessie R. Fauset, Ann Petry and William G. Smith. **5049**

James, Stuart B. *Race relations in literature and sociology.* University of Washington, 1960. Analysis of contemporary American literature in which Negro characters appear on the thesis that literary artists must be socially responsible beings. **60-4288**

Johnson, Beulah V. *The treatment of the Negro woman as a major character in American novels, 1900-1950.* New York University, 1955. Comparison between white and Negro authors in characteristics attributed to Negro women in novels. **15566**

Landa, Bjarne E. *The American scene in Friedrich Gerstacker's works of fiction.* University of Minnesota, 1952. Includes discussion of racial groups and Negro slavery. **3949**

Lash, John S. *The academic status of the literature of the American Negro: a description and analysis of curriculum inclusions and teaching practices.* University of Michigan, 1946.

Liedel, Donald E. *The antislavery novel, 1836-1861.* University of Michigan, 1961. Examined 60 antislavery novels; found emphasis on deleterious effects of slavery on white society but tended to lose sight of the Negro's cause. **61-6385**

Linneman, William R. *American life as reflected in illustrated humor magazines: 1877-1900.* University of Illinois, 1960. Includes treatment of Negroes, political issues, rural life and labor unions. **60-3947**

Lombard, Lee R. *Contemporary Negro writers of New York: an inquiry into their social attitudes.* New York University, 1949.

Margolies, Edward L. *A critical analysis of the works of Richard Wright.* New York University, 1964. Found Wright's principal achievement to have been his ability to illuminate the immense gulf between white and black. **66-9543**

Mason, Julian D., Jr. *The critical reception of American Negro authors in American magazines, 1800-1885.* University of North Carolina, 1962. Used 56 American magazines; found patterns of reviewing corresponded to the changing patterns of the Negro's place in American society. **63-3505**

Mays, Benjamin E. *The idea of God in contemporary Negro literature.* University of Chicago, 1936.

Montell, William L. *The folk history of the Coe Ridge Negro colony.* Indiana University, 1964. Used principally oral traditions for preparing history of a Negro colony in Cumberland County, Kentucky. **65-3502**

Moore, William L. *The literature of the American Negro prior to 1865: an anthology and a history.* New York University, 1942.

Moreland, Agnes L. *A study of Faulkner's presentation of some problems that relate to Negroes.* Columbia University, 1960. Problems discussed include slave origins of economic, social and moral problems, miscegenation and self-assertiveness in Negroes. **60-3118**

Nelson, John H. *The Negro character in American literature.* Cornell University, 1923. **OP 41753**

Nichols, Charles H., Jr. *A study of the slave narrative.* Brown University, 1949.

Nilon, Charles H. *Some aspects of the treatment of Negro characters in five representative American novelists: Cooper, Melville, Tourgee, Glasgow, Faulkner.* University of Wisconsin, 1952. **S-214**

Oliver, Clinton F., Jr. *The name and nature of American Negro literature: an interpretative study in genre and ideas.* Harvard University, 1965.

Pettit, Paul B. *The important American dramatic types to 1900: a study of the Yankee, Negro, Indian and frontiersman.* Cornell University, 1949.

Player, Raleigh P., Jr. *The Negro character in the fiction of William Faulkner.* University of Michigan, 1965. Found Negro characters in William Faulkner's fiction portrayed with integrity and compassion. **66-6678**

Rabassa, Gregory. *The Negro in Brazilian fiction since 1888.* Columbia University, 1954. No movement in Brazilian fiction devoted to the Negro, but Negroes have assumed importance at times in the Brazilian novel. **10182**

Reeves, Walter P., Jr. *Race and nationality in the works of Thomas Wolfe.* Duke University, 1963. An examination of Wolfe's published writings to determine the nature and extent of his social criticism in his treatment of racial types. **64-2838**

Smith, Helena M. *Negro characterization in the American novel: a historical survey of work by white authors.* Pennsylvania State University, 1959. Analysis of the Negro as a literary figure in historical perspective. **59-6799**

Starke, Catherine J. *Negro stock characters, archetypes, and individuals in American literature: a study for college teachers.* Columbia University, 1963. Suggests a technique for objectively handling literature which contains offensive stereotypes. **63-5730**

Steinberg, Aaron. *Faulkner and the Negro.* New York University, 1963. Examination of Faulkner's treatment of the Negro based on detailed examination of pertinent novels and stories. **66-9531**

Starling, Marion W. *The slave narrative; its place in American literary history.* New York University, 1946.

Taylor, Walter F., Jr. *The roles of the Negro in William Faulkner's fiction.* Emory University, 1964. Concludes that Faulkner's most important contribution has been his attempt to dramatize the meaning of the Negro for white society. **64-11221**

Timmons, F. Alan. *A content analysis of romance and biography story types in Negro magazine communication.* University of Southern California, 1958.

Wiley, Electa C. *A study of the noble savage myth in characterizations of the Negro in selected American literary works.* University of Arkansas, 1964. Literary works in which American writers have characterized the Negro as a thinking, feeling individual who contributes significantly to the themes of the works where he appears. **65-1521**

Woolridge, Nancy B. *The Negro preacher in American fiction before 1900.* University of Chicago, 1943.

Wormley, Margaret J. *The Negro in southern fiction, 1920-1940.* Boston University, 1948.

Wright, Howard E. *Racial humor: a value analysis.* Ohio State University, 1947.

2. Drama, Theater, Movies

Archer, Leonard C. *The National Association for the Advancement of Colored People and the American theatre: a study of relationships and influences (Vols. I & II).* Ohio State University, 1959. Evaluation of influence of NAACP in regard to stereotyping in literature, motion pictures, broadcasting and on the stage. **59-2728**

Bloom, Samuel W. *A social psychological study of motion picture audience behavior: a case study of the Negro image in mass communication.* University of Wisconsin, 1956. A case study of the film "Lost Boundaries," its content and its effects on the members of a small college community. **16145**

Bond, Frederick W. *The direct and indirect contribution which the American Negro has made to drama and the legitimate stage, with the underlying conditions responsible.* New York University, 1939.

Collins, John D. *American drama in anti-slavery agitation.* State University of Iowa, 1963. Found that abolition playwrights were generally successful in adapting drama to persuasive ends. **63-4727**

Davidson, Frank C. *The rise, development, decline and influence of the American minstrel show.* New York University, 1952. Concluded that the minstrel show is the only indigenous American contribution to drama and melodies the Negro minstrel inspired are America's only approach to national music. **4515**

Goldberg, Albert L. *The effects of two types of sound motion pictures on attitudes of adults toward minority groups.* Indiana University, 1956. Study of effects of film types, age, education, religion and sex on changes of attitude regarding race. **17769**

Hicklin, Fannie E. F. *The American Negro playwright, 1920-64.* University of Wisconsin, 1965. Trends in both dramatic and non-dramatic writing by Negroes were noted and compared with trends in general American drama. The appendix lists 237 plays with publication and production data. **65-6217**

Lawson, Hilda J. *The Negro in American drama.* University of Illinois, 1939.

Linnehan, Edward G. *We wear the mask: the use of Negro life and character in American drama.* University of Pennsylvania, 1948. Traces the development of the American Negro in drama from Ridgley Torrence's *Three Plays for a Negro Theatre* (1917) to Richard Wright's *Native Son* (1941). **3967**

Pembrook, Carrie D. *Negro drama through the ages – an anthology.* New York University, 1947.

Sandle, Floyd L. *A history of the development of the educational theatre in Negro colleges and universities from 1911 to 1959.* Louisiana State University, 1959. Influence of pioneer playwrights and actors; work of Southern Association of Dramatic and Speech Arts; growth of speech and drama. **59-5527**

Sherman, Alfonso. *The diversity of treatment of the Negro character in American drama prior to 1860.* Indiana University, 1964. Analysis of 40 plays with Negro characters written between 1770 and 1860; found a wide range of cultural and social ranks and attitudes portrayed. **65-3518**

Silver, Reuben. *A history of the Karamu Theatre of Karamu House, 1915-1960.* Ohio State University, 1961. History of an interracial community theater in Cleveland, Ohio. **62-811**

Troesch, Helen De R. *The Negro in English dramatic literature and on the stage and a bibliography of plays with Negro characters.* Western Reserve University, 1940.

3. The Press

Beatty-Brown, Florence R. *The Negro as portrayed by the St. Louis Post-Dispatch from 1920-1950.* University of Illinois, 1951. Content analysis showed *Post-Dispatch* relatively liberal and moving further in that direction. **3127**

Bohn, Dorothy A. *A sociological study of some newspaper reporting of the March on Washington.* Ohio State University, 1966. Study of differences in newspaper reporting of the 1963 march to clarify processes of social change and control. **66-10002**

Brooks, Maxwell R. *Content analysis of leading Negro newspapers.* Ohio State University, 1953.

Brown, Warren. *Social change and the Negro press, 1860-1880.* New School for Social Research, 1950.

Dixon, Frank J. *Anti-slavery sentiment in the New York City press: 1830-1850; a consideration of its origin, development, extent and quality.* Fordham University, 1939.

Ellen, John C., Jr. *Political newspapers of the Piedmont Carolinas in the 1850's.* University of South Carolina, 1958. Includes data on miscegenation, prices of slaves and slave conditions based on analysis of advertising as a reflector of culture. **59-668**

Fenderson, Lewis H. *Development of the Negro Press: 1827-1948.* University of Pittsburgh, 1949.

Graham, Hugh D. *Tennessee editorial response to changes in the bi-racial system, 1954-60.* Stanford University, 1965. Examination of editorial views (1954-60) as to whether and to what degree the bi-racial system of education should be modified. **65-6296**

Hogen, Mildred E. *The attitude of the New York press towards Lincoln and the slavery question.* Marquette University, 1944.

Jones, Wendell P. *The Negro press and the higher education of Negroes, 1933-1952; a study of news and opinion on higher education in the three leading Negro newspapers.* University of Chicago, 1954.

Kephart, John E. *A voice for freedom: the Signal of Liberty, 1841-1848.* University of Michigan, 1960. Analysis of *Signal of Liberty,* official newspaper of Michigan Anti-Slavery Society. **60-2543**

Norton, L. Wesley. *The religious press and the Compromise of 1850: a study of the relation of the Methodist, Baptist and Presbyterian press to the slavery controversy, 1846-1851.* University of Illinois, 1959. Analysis of weekly religious press regarding slavery; comparison of northern and southern editors. **60-222**

Oaks, Harold R. *An interpretative study of the effects of some upper Mid-West productions of Uncle Tom's Cabin as reflected in local newspapers, between 1852 and 1860.* University of Minnesota, 1964. Evidence found of subtle changes in audience attitudes but no direct influence on political action. **65-139**

Pride, Armistead S. *A register and history of Negro newspapers in the United States, 1827-1950.* Northwestern University, 1950. **62-6508**

Reddick, Lawrence D. *The Negro in the New Orleans press, 1850-60: a study in attitudes and propaganda.* University of Chicago, 1939.

Simpson, George E. *The Negro in the white newspapers of Philadelphia.* University of Pennsylvania, 1934.

Traber, Michael. *The treatment of the Little Rock, Arkansas, school integration incident in the daily press of the Union of South Africa, West Nigeria and Ghana from September 1 to October 31, 1957.* New York University, 1960. Frequency of reference and focus on attention given by 25 daily newspapers.   60-3762

4. Music

Adams, Rosemary F. *A study of community services as professional laboratory experiences in the preservice preparation of teachers in music at Knoxville College, Tennessee.* New York University, 1961. Proposed program for a predominantly Negro college combining laboratory experiences with community services.   61-2572

Anderson, Edison H., Sr. *The historical development of music in the Negro secondary schools of Oklahoma and at Langston University.* State University of Iowa, 1957. Covers the period from 1878 to 1954.   20916

Bluestein, Eugene. *The background and sources of an American folksong tradition.* University of Minnesota, 1960. Includes discussion of Negro folksong in terms of the Lomax thesis that folksongs illustrate the democratic traditions historically associated with American development.   60-5156

Boggs, Grace B. *Laboratory experiences in music education prior to student teaching at Morris Brown College, Atlanta, Georgia.* Columbia University, Teachers College, 1956.

Braithwaite, Coleridge. *A survey of the lives and creative activities of some Negro composers.* Columbia University, Teachers College, 1952.

Charles, Norman. *Social values in American popular songs.* University of Pennsylvania, 1958. A study of the national state of mind as revealed by content of popular songs; categories included minority groups, romantic love, war and patriotism.   58-3313

Christian, Edwin C. *A plan for improving the music curriculum for educating music teachers at Morris Brown College, Atlanta, Georgia.* Columbia University, Teachers College, 1960.

Davis, Henderson S. *The religious experience underlying the Negro spiritual.* Boston University, 1950.

Fisher, Miles M. *The evolution of slave songs in the United States.* University of Chicago, 1949.

Gatlin, F. Nathaniel. *A plan for housing the department of music at Virginia State College involving alterations to an existing structure and recommendations for equipment.* Columbia University, Teachers College, 1960.

George, Zelma W. *A guide to Negro music: an annotated bibliography of Negro folk music, and art music by Negro composers or based on Negro thematic material.* New York University, 1953. Bibliography based on the card catalogue of Howard University Library compiled by the author in 1944.   8021

Goines, Leonard. *Music and music education in predominantly Negro colleges and universities offering a four-year-program of music study terminating in a degree.* Columbia University, 1963. Concluded that the colleges studied are not producing the leaders of school and community music who are needed.
                                                                                                        64-1476

Hansen, Chadwick C. *The ages of jazz: a study of jazz in its cultural context.* University of Minnesota, 1956. Traces development of jazz as a modification of the African cultural heritage by the American experience.   **59-6054**

Hubert, Gadus J. *An examination of the music programs of four selected Negro colleges in the Atlanta University Center with recommendations for Morris Brown College.* Columbia University, Teachers College, 1961.

Leonard, Neil, Jr. *The acceptance of jazz by whites in the United States, 1918-1942.* Harvard University, 1960.

Myers, James G. *God's Trombones.* Columbia University, 1965. Used the text of James Weldon Johnson's *God's Trombones* as the basis for an original work for solo voices, mixed chorus and brass instruments.   **65-8825**

Patterson, Cecil L. *A different drum: the image of the Negro in the nineteenth century popular song book.* University of Pennsylvania, 1961. Content analysis of 260 song books and 96 other 19th-century writings yielded general image of the Negro as an exotic and inferior being.   **61-3577**

Ricks, George R. *Some aspects of the religious music of the United States Negro: an ethnomusicological study with special emphasis on the gospel tradition.* Northwestern University, 1960. Defines the variety of styles and relates these to their cultural background.   **60-4788**

5.   Rhetoric, Speech, Dialect

Denison, Ronald H. *A rhetorical analysis of speeches by segregationists in the Deep South.* Purdue University, 1961. Study of kind and quality of speeches on the integration issue by segregationists from the Deep South.   **61-6528**

Dexter, Erwin B. *A study of the speech development of primary grade children in relation to certain perceptual, intellectual, and sociological factors.* Boston University School of Education, 1961. Racial comparisons included in a study of the predictive value of factors in the speech development of children.   **61-3324**

Dorne, William P. *The comprehensibility of the speech of representative sixth-grade Negro children in Lee County Schools, Alabama.* University of Florida, 1959. Panels of white southern judges rated Negro children's speech more comprehensible than panels of northern or Negro judges.   **59-6094**

Everhart, Rodney W. *The growth and development of Negro and white elementary children with articulatory defects.* University of Michigan, 1953. Comparison of articulatory handicapped Negro and white children related to growth and developmental factors.   **5033**

Farrison, William E. *The phonology of the illiterate Negro dialect of Guilford County, North Carolina.* Ohio State University, 1937.

Hibler, Madge B. *A contemporary study of speech patterns of selected Negro and white kindergarten children.* University of Southern California, 1960. Racial differences in speech patterns found significant at the 1% level.   **60-5479**

Kennedy, James S. *A study of the teacher-education aspects of speech in Negro colleges of America: including the relationship between training received and the teaching activities of teachers of speech to speech programs in Negro colleges.* New York University, 1961. Primary concern was whether speech training in Negro colleges was equal to that in other colleges.   **62-1470**

McDaniel-Teabeau, Hazel. *Wilberforce's speeches on the abolition of the slave trade.* University of Missouri, 1959. Investigated historical-social-political forces that produced Wilberforce and his means of persuasion.   **59-6387**

Murray, Thomas J. *A language analysis of the treatment of the civil rights issue by the Presidential candidates in their 1956 campaign speeches.* University of Michigan, 1961. Treatment of civil rights issue by Eisenhower and Stevenson in 1956 campaign speeches.   **61-1770**

Pardoe, T. Earl. *A historical and phonetic study of Negro dialect.* Louisiana State University, 1937.

Pitts, Willis N., Jr. *A critical study of Booker T. Washington as a speech-maker with an analysis of seven selected speeches.* University of Michigan, 1952. Traces political, social and economic philosophy of Washington in his speeches; rhetorical judgment applied to 7 speeches.   **3790**

Reeves, Elizabeth W. *A program in speech for the College of Liberal Arts at Howard University.* Columbia University, Teachers College, 1956.

Schnitzer, Maxine M. *A rhetorical analysis of the anti-slavery speaking of Cassius M. Clay of Kentucky.* Michigan State University, 1962.   **62-4460**

Sherman, Sam. *A history of speech education in New Orleans public elementary and secondary schools.* Louisiana State University, 1955. Includes speech education for Negroes.   **14081**

Smith, Donald H. *Martin Luther King, Jr.: rhetorician of revolt.* University of Wisconsin, 1964. Analysis of King's rhetoric in connection with the Montgomery bus boycott, the Birmingham movement of 1963 and the Washington March in 1963.   **64-12753**

Thomas, Dominic R. *Oral language sentence structure and vocabulary of kindergarten children living in low socio-economic urban areas.* Wayne State University, 1962. Comparison of white and Negro children on sentence length, sentence structure, grammatical errors, parts of speech and vocabulary.   **62-3918**

Todd, Hollis B. *An analysis of the literary dialect of Irwin Russell and a comparison with the spoken dialect of certain native informants of west central Mississippi.* Louisiana State University, 1965. Concluded that the dialect in Russell's poetry was a reasonably accurate representation of what he had heard.   **66-753**

Williams, Hazel B. *A semantic study of some current, pejoratively regarded language symbols involving Negroes in the United States.* New York University, 1953. The functioning of language in relation to social groupings using language symbols involving Negroes.   **5429**

Williams, Jamye C. *A rhetorical analysis of Thurgood Marshall's arguments before the Supreme Court in the public school segregation controversy.* Ohio State University, 1959. Analysis of the brief and oral argument of *Brown* v. *Board of Education* to determine Marshall's persuasive techniques. **59-5949**

Williamson, Juanita V. *A phonological and morphological study of the speech of the Negro of Memphis, Tennessee.* University of Michigan, 1961. Systematic analysis of speech patterns of Negro subjects with differences noted by age and amount of education.   **61-1811**

AUTHOR INDEX

DISSERTATION ABSTRACTS

For many years the great wealth of useful knowledge recorded in doctoral dissertations was almost inaccessible to academic and commercial researchers. Thousands of dissertations were carefully prepared, submitted, published and then lost in the wide scattering of libraries and repositories around the world.

Since 1938, this storehouse of valuable, useful thought has been indexed and published by University Microfilms as abstracts in *Dissertation Abstracts*.

Abstracts of many of the dissertations listed in this bibliography have been published in *Dissertation Abstracts*. These are noted in the Author Index. Reference to their location (volume/issue) in *Dissertation Abstracts* is provided in the column headed DA.

HOW TO ORDER DISSERTATIONS

Dissertations in this bibliography can be ordered on 35mm positive roll microfilm or as xerographic copies. Prices are quoted in the Author Index.

Block orders can be made with the help of a special *order guide* which is available on request. A block order consists of dissertations listed in any of the forty subject groups. Reference to block order numbers in the *order guide* obviates the need to itemize individual dissertations on a purchase order.

Bound copies of dissertations produced by xerography, a type of electrostatic printing are approximately 2/3 the size of the original typescript pages, or about 5 1/2 x 8 1/2 inches. Xerographic prices quoted in the Author Index include perfect (glued) binding with a 65-lb. paper cover. Cloth covers can be ordered for an additional $2.25 per dissertation. Modest handling and shipping prices are additional.

When ordering individual dissertations, please specify:

- quantity
- microfilm copy *or* xerographic copy
- order number
- author's name

Mail orders to:

University Microfilms
300 N. Zeeb Road
Ann Arbor, Michigan 48106

All prices quoted are subject to change without notice.

	Page	DA	Order No.	Xerographic Copy	Microfilm Copy
Abbott, Martin L.	82	19/11	58-5108	$11.95	$3.40
Abbott, Richard H.	73	27/6	65-13709	21.15	6.00
Abraham, Ansley A.	39	16/12	17755	10.15	3.00
Abrahams, Roger D.	93	23/3	62-2817	19.35	5.50
Abrahamson, Mark J.	33				
Abramowitz, Jack	91	5/3	1823	12.40	3.55
Adams, Rosemary F.	99	22/2	61-2572	14.85	4.20
Adams, Samuel C. Jr.	10				
Adler, Manfred	21	27/1	66-4366	9.00	3.00
Akiwowo, Akinsola A.	88	22/3	61-714	11.25	3.20
Alderson, William T.	82	12/5	3968	15.30	4.35
Alexander, Frederick M.	71				
Alexander, Thomas B.	82				
Alexis, Marcus	31	20/10	60-906	19.35	5.50
Allman, Reva W.	60	12/2	3461	7.60	3.00
Almond, John F.	35	24/7	64-1219	7.80	3.00
Amerman, Helen E.	11				
Ametjian, Armistre	56	27/1	66-6316	6.60	3.00
Amir, Menachem	18	27/4	66-4597	36.85	10.35
Amos, Robert T.	23	11/2	2373	7.20	3.00
Amos, William E.	18	21/10	61-876	6.40	3.00
Anderson, Edison H., Sr.	99	17/5	20916	15.75	4.45
Anderson, Floydelh	7	16/2	13643	8.40	3.00
Anderson, Godfrey T.	75				
Anderson, Louis V.	65	27/5	66-11237	7.40	3.00
Anderson, Mable B.	5	26/8	65-14731	10.15	3.00
Anderson, Robert L.	90	25/10	65-2411	9.00	3.00
Anderson, Thelma H.	40	22/4	61-4498	5.40	3.00
Anderson, Tommie M.	40	19/9	58-7902	7.60	3.00
Andresen, Karl A.	90	21/10	61-555	16.20	4.60
Aptheker, Herbert	75				
Archer, Leonard C.	97	20/2	59-2728	25.65	7.20
Armstrong, Byron K.	40				
Austin, Lettie J.	52				
Bacote, Clarence A.	82				
Badger, William V.	37	13/4	5391	28.60	8.05
Baehr, Rufus F.	23				
Bahney, Robert S.	75	26/11	66-5035	13.75	3.95
Bahr, Howard M.	9	26/12	66-1888	4.20	3.00
Bailer, Lloyd H.	33				
Bailey, Dale S.	93	22/5	61-4420	10.60	3.05
Bailey, Rubelia J.	40	26/3	65-9471	8.20	3.00
Baker, Paul E.	11				
Baker, Robert A.	83				
Banks, Melvin J.	83	24/1	63-3620	23.85	6.75
Banks, Walter R.	91	25/2	64-4934	11.05	3.15
Bannan, Phyllis M.	76	10/3	1829	10.35	3.00
Barban, Arnold M.	23	25/1	64-7162	11.50	3.25
Barnett, Suzanne E.	11	23/6	62-5007	10.35	3.00

	Page	DA	Order No.	Xerographic Copy	Microfilm Copy
Barnett, William J. 60		19/12	58-2335	7.20	3.00
Bates, Jack W. 73					
Beall, John W. 1		14/2	9035	8.80	3.00
Beasley, Leon O. 71		17/11	21,981	14.85	4.20
Beatty-Brown, Florence R. . . .98		12/1	3127	19.80	5.60
Bechtol, Paul T., Jr. 33		23/4	62-4505	11.95	3.40
Beck, Elizabeth J. 21		25/2	64-8571	6.80	3.00
Beck, James D. 40		20/4	59-4267	9.00	3.00
Bell, Howard H. 91		13/6	6179	13.95	3.95
Bell, James 40					
Bell, John A. 11		27/3	66-9247	9.90	3.00
Bell, William M. 52		21/10	61-897	12.15	3.45
Benjamin, Lawrence H. 23		25/10	65-1606	5.00	3.00
Benjamin, William F. 56		22/8	61-5797	5.60	3.00
Bentley, George R. 83					
Berg, Kenneth R. 11		23/1	62-2820	4.00	3.00
Berger, Morroe 90		10/3	1740	9.90	3.00
Bergin, Sister Marie L. 56		24/2	63-5583	15.30	4.35
Berman, William C. 88		24/11	64-6875	9.25	3.00
Berry, Charles A., Jr. 40		14/4	7904	7.60	3.00
Berry, Charles N. 52		25/9	65-1420	7.80	3.00
Berwanger, Eugene H. 76		26/1	65-3179	14.40	4.10
Better, Norman M. 33		26/10	66-4944	8.80	3.00
Bieber, Toby B. 5		24/9	64-3254	6.60	3.00
Biggers, John T. 36					
Bindman, Aaron M. 40		26/1	65-7076	13.30	3.80
Blake, Dudley A. 23		26/4	65-9967	6.20	3.00
Blake, Elias Jr. 23		20/12	60-1616	5.40	3.00
Blanding, James D. 36		17/1	24461	14.65	4.15
Blankenstein, Mark E. 93		26/12	66-4146	11.95	3.40
Blanks, Augustus C. 21		15/7	12199	9.25	3.00
Blanton, Harry S. 60		20/4	59-4253	6.60	3.00
Blanton, Milburn W. 68		20/11	60-1319	9.25	3.00
Blee, Myron R. 58		19/11	59-476	8.20	3.00
Bloch, Herman D. 33					
Bloom, Samuel W. 97		16/6	16145	19.80	5.60
Bloom, Wallace 23		25/9	65-4294	8.20	3.00
Blossom, Herbert H. 58		27/3	66-8240	7.80	3.00
Blue, Ila J. 93		21/2	60-2508	11.50	3.25
Blue, John T., Jr. 5		19/8	58-3028	19.35	5.50
Bluestein, Eugene 99		21/7	60-5156	9.45	3.00
Blumenfeld, Ruth 20		26/9	66-251	11.05	3.15
Boger, Dellie L. 40					
Boggs, Grace B. 99					
Bohn, Dorothy A. 98		27/5	66-10002	6.40	3.00
Bolton, Ina A. 40					
Bond, Frederick W. 97					
Bond, Horace M. 71					
Bond, J. Max 88					
Boney, Jew D. 52		25/10	65-4283	7.40	3.00

	Page	DA	Order No.	Xerographic Copy	Microfilm Copy
Bonner, Leon W.	40	17/2	19963	6.00	3.00
Boom, Kathleen W.	71				
Boose, Sidney S.	53	14/10	8925	12.60	3.60
Borinski, Ernst.	90	14/9	8880	14.85	4.25
Borlick, Martha M.	5	27/4	66-9275	10.60	3.05
Bottosto, Samuel S.	36	20/3	59-3538	10.15	3.00
Boucher, Morris R.	76				
Bouquet, Susana	7	22/11	62-2037	8.20	3.00
Bowen, Harry W.	92	23/12	63-2419	5.60	3.00
Bowen, Hilliard A.	40				
Bowen, Irwin W., Jr.	36				
Bowman, Robert L.	88	26/3	65-8994	15.10	4.30
Boyd, Laurence E.	53				
Boyd, Willis	83				
Boynton, John O.	12				
Bozeman, Herman H.	92	16/8	17417	14.65	4.20
Bracey, Isaac C.	60	22/7	61-2862	5.00	3.00
Bradbury, William C., Jr.	33	13/1	4557	23.85	6.70
Bradford, Joseph	38	22/10	62-1955	8.60	3.00
Bradley, Nolén E. Jr.	40	27/6	66-12606	9.70	3.00
Braithwaite, Coleridge	99				
Brazeal, Brailsford R.	33				
Breen, Michael D.	23	27/5	65-14413	9.25	3.00
Brewer, David L.	12	27/6	66-13548	8.60	3.00
Brewer, James H.	76				
Brewer, June H.	23	24/7	64-45	6.40	3.00
Brice, Edward W.	40				
Brigham, Robert I.	71	9/2	1274	12.85	3.70
Briney, Martha M.	93	27/6	21049	27.70	7.75
Brisbane, Robert H., Jr.	92				
Brittain, David J.	68	20-9	59-6215	14.20	4.05
Brittain, Joseph M.	88	19/3	58-2902	11.05	3.20
Broderick, Francis L.	73				
Brodhead, John H.	53				
Brooks, John W.W.	53	21/3	60-2995	9.45	3.00
Brooks, Lyman B.	36				
Brooks, Maxwell R.	98				
Brooks, Thomas E.	40	15/12	13213	9.90	3.00
Brown, Aaron	53				
Brown, Donald N.	83	21/7	60-5185	13.05	3.70
Brown, Donald V.	65	17/2	19399	3.00	3.00
Brown, Jessie L.	41				
Brown, Jonel L.	41				
Brown, Letitia W.	76				
Brown, Louis P.	58	14/4	7615	18.45	5.25
Brown, Paula M.	18	17/3	17637	8.60	3.00
Brown, Theresa K.	41	20/2	59-1044	11.95	3.40
Brown, Warren	98				
Brown, William Crawford	41	21/10	61-357	6.00	3.00
Brown, William Crews	41	21/10	61-358	23.65	6.65

	Page	DA	Order No.	Xerographic Copy	Microfilm Copy
Brown, William H. 53					
Brozovich, Richard W. 20		27/5	66-11238	6.40	3.00
Bruce, Myrtle H. 21					
Brunson, Rose T. 9		23/5	62-4424	7.80	3.00
Bryan, Laurence L. 24		17/2	19458	9.00	3.00
Bryant, Ira B. 53					
Bryson, Ralph J. 64		18/3	58-676	18.25	5.15
Bryson, Winfred O., Jr. 31					
Buck, James R., Jr. 41		25/9	65-344	7.60	3.00
Buckland, Roscoe L. 83		15/9	12883	10.60	3.00
Buckman, Gabe 38		18/7	58-2268	5.00	3.00
Bugansky, Alex 18		19/12	59-1012	11.70	3.35
Buni, Andrew 83		26/10	66-3147	14.65	4.15
Burgess, Margaret E. 7		21/9	60-6977	13.30	3.80
Burrows, Robert N. 93		20/7	59-4601	21.15	5.95
Butcher, Charles P. 93		16/7	16892	13.50	3.85
Butler, Loretta M. 71		24/9	63-7975	8.80	3.00
Byrd, James W. 93		15/10	13304	17.80	5.00
Byrd, Laurie L. 56		27/6	66-12723	11.95	3.45
Byuarm, Samuel W. 7		23/8	62-6113	17.80	5.00
Cahill, Edward E. 33		26/8	66-313	6.20	3.00
Caine, Augustus F. 92		26/2	65-6055	20.50	5.75
Caldwell, Marion M. 41		20/10	60-1171	11.25	3.25
Caldwell, Martha B. 83		10/1	1543	6.40	3.00
Caldwell, Wallace F. 90		26/3	65-8509	16.00	4.55
Caliman, Alvis W. 24		13/5	5914	5.60	3.00
Cameron, Mary B. 18		14/1	6434	11.50	3.30
Campbell, Ernest Q. 68		17/6	20489	21.40	6.05
Campion, Donald R. 24		21/5	60-3568	15.30	4.35
Caplan, Eleanor K. 7					
Cappelluzzo, Emma M. 61		26/3	65-9844	7.00	3.00
Capps, Marian P. 71					
Carlsen, George R. 64					
Carlson, Robert O. 29		12/5	4164	16.45	4.65
Carnathan, Wiley J. 76					
Carpenter, Henry D., Jr. 41					
Carpenter, Marie E. 65					
Carper, Noel G. 83		26/12	65-5569	19.35	5.50
Carroll, James W. 12					
Carroll, Joseph C. 76					
Carter, Luther C., Jr. 1					
Carter, Wilmoth 7					
Cartwright, Walter J. 7					
Cash, Eugene Jr. 5		16/5	16371	5.60	3.00
Cavanagh, Helen M. 76					
Champagne, Joseph E. 33		27/4	66-7400	10.35	3.00
Chapman, Oscar J. 41		3/2	325	20.05	5.65
Chappat, Janine S.A. 56					
Charles, Norman 99		19/4	58-3313	11.25	3.25

	Page	DA	Order No.	Xerographic Copy	Microfilm Copy
Charlton, Huey E. 5		19/7	58-1976	8.00	3.00
Chasteen, Edgar R. 92		27/4	66-8970	15.10	4.30
Cheaney, Henry E. 83					
Cheek, William F., III 73		22/5	61-4534	18.25	5.20
Cherry, Frank T. 9					
Christensen, Janice E. 90		13/2	4849	30.85	8.65
Christian, Edwin C. 99					
Christophe, LeRoy M., Sr. . . .41		14/12	8016	9.25	3.00
Christopher, Nehemiah M. . . .71					
Claiborne, Montraville I. 61		10/3	1814	10.35	3.00
Clark, Geraldine L. 41					
Clark, Joseph E. 93		19/4	58-3598	26.10	7.35
Clarke, Jacquelyne M.J. 92		21/8	60-6355	8.60	3.00
Clary, George E. 41		26/5	65-10286	7.20	3.00
Claster, Daniel S. 7		22/1	61-2202	10.35	3.00
Claye, Clifton M. 24		19/3	58-2751	6.40	3.00
Clayton, Bruce L. 93		27/6	66-12726	15.10	4.30
Clem, William W. 41					
Clift, Virgil A. 41					
Coan, Josephus R. 1		22/6	61-5212	23.65	6.65
Cobb, Henry E. 83					
Cobb, Willie L. 58					
Cochrane, William G. 83		18/1	23928	20.95	5.90
Codwell, John E. 29					
Cohen, Arthur M. 42		25/4	64-10584	6.40	3.00
Cohen, Leon S. 88		26/7	65-14324	8.00	3.00
Cohen, Melvin 24		27/1	66-5652	7.20	3.00
Coker, Donald R. 56		27/5	66-11605	5.20	3.00
Cole, Charles C., Jr. 76		12/1	3329	19.35	5.50
Cole, Earl L. 42					
Coleman, John W. 1					
Collins, Ernest M. 88		20/10	60-643	10.80	3.05
Collins, Gladys B. 61		14/2	7128	9.70	3.00
Collins, John D. 97		24/2	63-4727	20.25	5.75
Collins, William M. 42		18/3	23127	22.30	6.25
Colson, Cortlandt M. 42		18/1	24096	16.00	4.55
Colson, Edna M. 65					
Colson, Elsie C. 42		21/7	60-5423	9.45	3.00
Colston, James A. 42		11/1	2177	10.60	3.05
Combs, Willie E. 61		25/8	65-387	10.80	3.05
Connor, Miles W. 42					
Connors, Sister Maureen 58		26/11	65-10366	4.40	3.00
Constantine, James R. 76		14/1	6436	17.55	4.95
Conyers, Charline F.H. 42		21/10	60-3767	17.55	5.00
Conyers, James E. 42		23/12	63-3027	7.20	3.00
Cook, Culbreth B., Jr. 33					

	Page	DA	Order No.	Xerographic Copy	Microfilm Copy
Cook, Lester H.	76				
Cook, Raymond A.	93	19/11	58-5125	11.25	3.20
Cooke, Jacob E.	74				
Cooper, Alice A.	74				
Cooper, Charles L.	58				
Cooper, Matthew N.	42	16/3	13600	10.60	3.05
Cooper, Theodore B.	42				
Cope, Robert S.	76				
Cope, William Jr.	42	19/12	59-71	6.60	3.00
Copeland, Lewis C.	24				
Cordery, Sara B.	42				
Corke, Patricia P.	24	22/8	61-5780	5.60	3.00
Corlew, Robert E.	83				
Cornish, Dudley T.	76				
Cosman, Bernard	88	22/8	62-71	13.75	3.90
Cothran, Tilman C.	24				
Cotton, George R.	42				
Cottrell, Ted B.	24	25/9	65-312	3.00	3.00
Cox, LaWanda F.	83				
Cox, Oliver C.	5				
Coyner, Martin B., Jr.	74	22/5	61-4536	27.90	7.85
Craine, James F.	58				
Cram, Leo L.	38	25/12	65-6199	9.90	3.00
Cramer, Miles R.	68				
Crawford, Evans E., Jr.	1	17/8	21938	8.20	3.00
Crawford, Harold W.	42	21/6	60-2318	7.60	3.00
Crump, Cecille E.	31	20/4	59-4275	13.30	3.80
Crump, William L.	33				
Culbertson, Francis J.M.	12	15/8	12561	6.00	3.00
Culver, Dwight W.	1				
Curry, Marion M.	29	20/12	60-2004	8.20	3.00
Cuthbert, Marion V.	43				
Dabney, Lillian G.	71				
Dallmayr, Winfried R.	90	21/8	60-6026	24.30	6.85
Dalomba, Roland F.	68	18/6	20279	12.40	3.50
Daniel, Mariel M.	21				
Daniel, Vattel E.	2				
Daniel, Walter G.	43				
Daniels, Roland H.	68	20/7	59-5321	8.40	3.00
Daniels, Virginia R.M.	34				
Dauterive, Berna B.	37	27/6	66-10538	18.00	5.05
Davids, Robert B.	36				
Davidson, Alene J.	24	14/2	7092	10.35	3.00
Davidson, Frank C.	97	13/2	4515	12.60	3.55
Davis, Alonzo J.	24				
Davis, Charles S.	76				
Davis, Henderson S.	99				
Davis, Jerry B.	12				
Davis, Lawrence A.	43	21/3	60-2763	20.95	5.95
Davis, Malcolm A.	43	15/2	7129	11.50	3.25

	Page	DA	Order No.	Xerographic Copy	Microfilm Copy
Davis, N.F.	34	21/9	60-6285	10.80	3.10
Davis, William R.	71				
Davitz, Lois J.	11	20/3	59-3095	5.60	3.00
Dawson, Carrie B.	56	17/5	20857	8.00	3.00
Dean, Elmer J.	53				
DeLevie, Ari	12	27/5	66-10286	6.80	3.00
Del Porto, Joseph A.	76	14/2	6850	13.95	3.95
Dellefield, Ca.vin J.	39	26/7	66-216	8.80	3.00
Denison, Ronald H.	100	22/7	61-6528	7.00	3.00
Derbyshire, Robert L.	43	25/5	64-11098	15.10	4.30
DesChamps, Margaret B.	76	19/11	58-5132	11.05	3.15
Dew, Lee A.	90	22/2	60-5906	17.10	4.85
Dexter, Erwin B.	100	22/3	61-3324	9.00	3.00
Diamonstein, Barbara L.D.	43	25/2	64-6528	9.90	3.00
Dickinson, Donald C.	93	25/11	65-5891	13.75	3.90
Diggs, Mary H.	18	7/1	814	6.80	3.00
Dillard, James A.	2				
Dillon, Merton L.	76	11/4	2582	18.25	5.15
Dixon, Frank J.	98				
Doherty, Joseph F.	5				
Dohlstrom, Arthur H.	61	15/10	13602	13.30	3.80
Dorey, Frank D.	2				
Dorne, William P., Sr.	100	20/8	59-6094	6.40	3.00
Doster, William C.	93	20/3	59-3557	8.80	3.00
Douglass, Joseph H.	7				
Dove, Pearlie C.	43	20/10	60-1064	10.80	3.05
Dowdy, George T.	31	18/4	58-783	8.20	3.00
Dowdy, Lewis C.	43	27/2	66-3112	9.90	3.00
Downing, Gertrude L.	66	27/4	66-9495	4.20	3.00
Drake, E. Maylon	61	26/10	64-2572	12.15	3.45
Drake, Joseph F.	43				
Drake, Richard B.	83	19/10	58-5136	13.95	3.95
Draper, Dorothy W.	61	19/11	58-5608	9.00	3.00
Dreer, Herman	89				
Drew, Jesse M.	43				
Driscoll, Willis C.	24	19/5	58-3489	3.00	3.00
Drumright, Russel G.	24	17/1	19488	7.20	3.00
Drusine, Leon	24	16/8	16588	7.80	3.00
Duncan, Catherine W.	43				
Dungee, Grant A., III	53	26/3	65-420	9.00	3.00
Dunn, Frederick L., Jr.	68	20/8	59-6845	11.70	3.30
Dunn, Theodore F.	12	19/10	58-2809	7.80	3.00
Dunston, Beverly N.	29	22/10	62-1393	9.00	3.00
Durham, Elizabeth	29				
Durham, Francis M.	74	14/1	6608	20.50	5.80
Dusinberre, William W.	76	22/1	61-2209	16.00	4.50
DuValle, Sylvester H.	43				
Dwyer, Robert J.	68	17/10	22767	15.55	4.40

	Page	DA	Order No.	Xerographic Copy	Microfilm Copy
Eagleson, Oran W.	25				
Eberhart, E.K.	34				
Eby, Cecil D., Jr.	74	19/4	58-3320	23.85	6.70
Echols, Jack W.	43				
Eckhardt, Rudolph A.	30	27/2	66-7091	3.00	3.00
Eckley, Wilton E.	94	26/11	66-3028	12.40	3.55
Eddy, Edward D., Jr.	43	16/11	18272	30.40	8.50
Eddy, Elizabeth M.	69	21/12	61-2210	8.80	3.00
Edmonds, Helen G.	83				
Edwards, Gilbert F.	34				
Edwards, Otis B.	10	15/12	14354	9.90	3.00
Eichorn, Robert L.	89	15/1	10577	13.50	3.85
Einstein, Florence	66	21/10	60-3741	8.20	3.00
Ellen, John C., Jr.	98	19/10	59-668	16.65	4.75
Elliott, Theodore B.	61	25/10	65-1522	4.00	3.00
Ellis, Frankie N. Golden	71	26/6	65-10698	8.60	3.00
Ellsworth, Clayton S.	77	5/2	618	9.70	3.00
Emanuel, James A.	94	27/2	65-7484	20.70	5.85
Engelder, Conrad J.	77	25/6	64-12589	14.85	4.25
England, James M.	77				
English, Walter H.	58				
Epley, Dean G.	12	14/3	7160	9.90	3.00
Epps, Edgar G.	18	21/5	60-1513	5.00	3.00
Erickson, Leonard E.	71	20/9	60-735	21.40	6.05
Erno, Richard B.	94	22/11	62-1776	23.40	6.60
Ervin, John B.	69				
Espy, James A.	44	25/7	64-4061	17.35	4.90
Essien Udom, Essien	84				
Eubanks, John B.	2				
Everett, Donald E.	77				
Everhart, Rodney W.	100	13/3	5033	6.00	3.00
Facen, Geneva Z.	12	20/3	59-3039	6.60	3.00
Fahey, Frank J.	2				
Farley, Reynolds	5				
Farrell, Harold A.	94				
Farrell, James E.	61	24/6	64-231	5.40	3.00
Farris, Charles D.	89				
Farrison, William E.	100				
Favor, Homer E.	32	21/8	60-6178	8.60	3.00
Fenderson, Lewis H.	98				
Fendrich, James M.	25	26/8	66-375	11.25	3.20
Fensch, Edwin A.	53				
Ferguson, Ira L.	30	10/2	1647	11.70	3.35
Fichett, Elijah H.	77				
Fields, Marvin A.	53	15/6	12023	11.25	3.20
Fife, Robert O.	77	21/9	60-6289	14.85	4.20
Finley, Jarvis M.	5	19/4	58-3272	6.80	3.00
Finnie, Gordon E.	77	24/1	63-3585	27.25	7.65
Fischer, Stephen J.	44				
Fishbein, Annette	32				
Fishel, Leslie H., Jr.	84				
Fisher, John	58	23/2	62-3238	6.80	3.00

	Page	DA	Order No.	Xerographic Copy	Microfilm Copy
Fisher, Miles M.	99				
Fitts, Howard M., Jr.	30				
Fladeland, Betty L.	74	12/4	3746	21.15	6.00
Floan, Howard R.	77	14/9	8657	17.35	4.90
Floyd, Raymond B.	39				
Fodor, Eugene M.	56	27/4	66-10261	6.40	3.00
Foley, Albert S.	2				
Foner, Philip S.	77				
Forbes, Frank L.	44	15/3	6293	9.90	3.00
Ford, Leon I.	12	16/12	18847	4.20	3.00
Ford, Nick A.	94				
Ford, Robert N.	12				
Forslund, Morris A.	18				
Fort, Edward B.	69	25/11	65-2985	19.35	5.50
Fortenberry, James H.	66	20/7	59-5492	6.80	3.00
Fortune, Hilda O.	5	24/10	63-6689	7.40	3.00
Fowler, William L.	21	17/1	18603	9.90	3.00
Fox, Grace I.	11				
Fraley, Lester M.	30				
Franklin, Charles L.	34				
Franklin, George W.	58	15/11	13922	5.40	3.00
Franklin, John H.	77				
Franklin, Laline O.	61	18/6	20281	8.20	3.00
Franzblau, Rose N.	21,30				
Frazier, Gordon E.	36	26/10	66-1071	6.80	3.00
Freedman, Philip I.	12	24/5	63-7419	6.40	3.00
Freeman, Felton D.	12				
Freeman, James N.	39				
Fulbright, Steward B., Jr.	32	19/7	58-7202	7.20	3.00
Fuller, Luther M.	84				
Fulton, Robert L.	32	21/1	60-2322	9.00	3.00
Funches, De Lars	61	22/5	61-5019	4.20	3.00
Gallagher, Buel G.	44				
Gallagher, Rev. Eugene F.	9	25/1	64-4246	15.55	4.45
Galvin, Emma C.B.	94				
Gamberg, Herbert B.	32	25/6	64-12123	10.60	3.00
Gamblin, Hance	61	22/10	62-1752	4.40	3.00
Gardner, Burleigh B.	7				
Gardner, Mary E.B.	7	23/2	62-1397	9.00	3.00
Garfinkel, Herbert	92				
Garman, Harold W.	2	26/5	65-11244	12.60	3.55
Garrett, Romeo B.	20	26/2	64-247	7.80	3.00
Gasser, Edith S.	25	22/12	62-1464	5.20	3.00
Gast, David K.	94	27/2	66-6902	9.45	3.00
Gaston, Edward A., Jr.	34	19/10	58-5143	24.55	6.90
Gates, Robbins L.	69	23/5	62-4230	13.75	3.90
Gatlin, F. Nathaniel	99				
Gay, Cleveland J.	25	27/1	66-6409	6.20	3.00
Gayles, Anne R.	44	22/4	61-3207	11.50	3.30

	Page	DA	Order No.	Xerographic Copy	Microfilm Copy
Geisel, Paul N.	66	23/9	63-1838	15.10	4.25
Geller, Max	66				
Gelman, Martin	2	26/12	66-4614	13.30	3.80
Genovese, Eugene D.	77	20/10	60-1139	11.25	3.20
George, Arthur A.	44	15/2	10661	16.00	4.50
George, Zelma W.	99	14/5	8021	13.75	3.90
Gerner, Henry L.	92	25/2	64-8258	14.40	4.05
Gershenfeld, Walter J.	34	25/12	65-5762	9.25	3.00
Gerson, Walter M.	11	24/11	64-4504	11.70	3.35
Gilbert, Jean P.	59	23/8	62-5219	7.40	3.00
Gilbert, Robert B.	94	13/5	5508	13.95	4.00
Gillette, Thomas L.	5	22/11	61-6108	13.50	3.85
Gilmore, Henry F.	62				
Ginott, Haim G.	25				
Gist, Annie L.	30	18/6	17645	6.00	3.00
Glass, Victor T.	2				
Glenn, Norval D.	20	23/1	62-2544	18.25	5.20
Gloster, Hugh M.	94				
Gloster, Jesse E.	32	15/12	13865	16.65	4.70
Goff, Regina M.	25				
Goines, Leonard	99	24/8	64-1476	13.30	3.75
Going, Allen J.	84				
Goins, William F.	44				
Goldaber, Irving	71	26/7	65-7293	12.60	3.60
Goldberg, Albert L.	97	17/2	17769	6.80	3.00
Golden, Joseph	5				
Golden, Loretta	65	25/7	64-13549	16.00	4.50
Goldenberg, Herbert	25				
Goldman, Hanna S.	94	15/5	11453	13.75	3.90
Goldman, Morris M.	94				
Goldstein, Naomi	12				
Goldstone, Richard H.	94	21/4	60-3073	10.60	3.05
Golovensky, David I.	12	18/6	22,949	14.65	4.15
Gomillion, Charles G.	7	20/9	60-741	11.50	3.30
Good, Warren	36	25/7	64-13687	12.85	3.65
Gooden, John E.	89				
Goodwin, Louis	44	17/3	19989	14.85	4.20
Gordon, Edmund W.	25				
Gordon, Joan L.	5	15/5	11409	10.15	3.00
Gordon, John E., Jr.	13	27/2	66-5778	8.00	3.00
Gordon, Robert A.	25				
Gore, George W., Jr.	62				
Gossett, Thomas F.	84	13/6	6381	18.90	5.30
Gottfried, Alex	74				
Graham, Hugh D.	98	26/1	65-6296	20.05	5.65
Graham, William L.	44	15/7	12215	11.70	3.35
Grant, Ernest A.	62				
Grantham, James W.	62	22/5	61-4437	13.05	3.70

	Page	DA	Order No.	Xerographic Copy	Microfilm Copy
Graves, Lawrence E.	62	17/4	20283	13.95	4.00
Graves, Linwood D.	44				
Gray, William H., Jr.	44				
Green, Jerome	25				
Green, Meredith W.	13	14/10	8670	4.80	3.00
Green, Robert L.	25	24/5	63-6152	4.20	3.00
Greenberg, Harold I.	25	26/8	65-10037	5.60	3.00
Greenberg, Herbert M.	36	15/10	13609	10.15	3.00
Greene, Lorenzo J.	77				
Greenfield, Robert W.	69	20/9	60-745	6.00	3.00
Gregg, Howard D.	53				
Grier, Boyce M.	37				
Griffin, John A.	36	16/5	16168	12.40	3.55
Grimshaw, Allen D.	18	20/6	59-4624	18.45	5.25
Gross, James A.	92	22/11	62-2242	9.90	3.00
Gross, Theodore L.	94	21/4	60-3075	12.60	3.60
Grossley, Richard S.	44				
Guines, James T.	44	22/9	61-6727	7.80	3.00
Gulley, William H.	7	22/10	61-6111	8.60	3.00
Gunter, Pearl K.	62	24/11	64-4878	9.90	3.00
Gunthorpe, Muriel B.	53	25/2	64-8477	9.00	3.00
Gustafson, Lucile	65	18/3	21703	5.80	3.00
Haggstrom, Warren C.	25	23/8	63-359	11.50	3.30
Haigwood, Thomas J.	69	20/2	59-2886	11.25	3.20
Hair, William I.	84	23/3	62-3648	19.80	5.60
Hale, William H.	34				
Hall, Clyde W.	71	13/6	6494	12.85	3.65
Hall, Egerton E.	34				
Hall, John E.	53	23/4	62-3310	7.20	3.00
Hall, Mary A.	56	27/1	66-3080	9.45	3.00
Hall, Wade H.	94	22/10	62-616	32.00	9.00
Hamilton, Charles V.	90				
Hamilton, David A.	39	20/8	59-6780	8.40	3.00
Hamilton, Howard D.	90	10/4	2070	13.05	3.75
Handorf, William G.	72	23/5	62-4187	18.45	5.25
Haney, Eleanor H.	13	26/8	65-15051	16.20	4.60
Hansen, Burrell F.	13	13/5	5535	24.55	6.90
Hansen, Chadwick C.	100	20/6	59-6054	9.70	3.00
Hardman, Dale G.	7	25/8	65-828	20.50	5.75
Hardy, Blanch B.	44	21/5	60-3413	6.00	3.00
Hardy, John G.	18				
Hare, Nathaniel	34				
Harkness, Donald R.	77	16/4	15928	19.80	5.60
Harlan, Louis R.	72				

	Page	DA	Order No.	Xerographic Copy	Microfilm Copy
Harlow, Harold C., Jr. 2		22/6	61-4570	15.75	4.45
Harper, Laura J. 30		19/7	58-5712	6.80	3.00
Harr, Wilber C. 2					
Harrell, David E., Jr. 77		23/4	62-4508	26.10	7.35
Harrell, Kenneth E. 84		27/5	66-10903	17.55	4.95
Harris, Albert T. 39		8/2	1054	10.80	3.10
Harris, Alfred G. 77					
Harris, Nelson H. 53					
Harris, Ruth M. 62					
Harrison, Elton C. 54					
Harrison, General L. 45					
Harrison, Walter R. 2					
Hart, Charles R.D. 77		26/8	65-15384	13.50	3.85
Hart, Thomas A. 13		19/11	59-1045	12.40	3.55
Harte, Thomas J. 2					
Hartshorn, Herbert H. 34					
Harvey, John A. 11					
Harwood, Thomas F. 77		20/6	59-4720	38.15	10.70
Hast, Eugene E. 57					
Hatch, Robert H. 62		25/11	65-4772	5.60	3.00
Hatton, John M. 25		26/7	65-12792	3.60	3.00
Haynes, Leonard L., Jr. 2					
Haynes, Roland E. 45		22/4	61-3403	12.15	3.50
Hazel, David W. 90		18/4	58-1411	13.95	3.95
Hazel, Joseph A. 78		24/9	64-2755	14.65	4.15
Headd, Pearl W. 45		21/9	60-6056	8.40	3.00
Hearn, Edell M. 37		20/11	59-6283	17.80	5.05
Hedrick, James A. 45		15/2	10816	16.00	4.55
Heller, Herbert L. 72					
Helper, Rose 32					
Henderson, George 26		26/9	66-1235	11.95	3.40
Henderson, Romeo C. 45					
Henderson, Thomas H. 36					
Henderson, Vivian W. 32		12/5	4068	14.20	4.05
Hendricks, George L. 78		14/12	10265	12.15	3.45
Hendricks, Harry G. 62		21/10	61-830	15.10	4.30
Hennessey, Sister Mary A. 13		19/11	59-898	10.60	3.05
Hertz, Hilda 13					
Hesslink, George K. 8					
Hibler, Madge B. 100		21/6	60-5479	5.60	3.00
Hickerson, Nathaniel 54		24/6	63-6179	6.20	3.00
Hicklin, Fannie E.F. 97		25/11	65-6217	25.00	7.05
Hiestand, Dale L. 34		26/1	64-2759	16.45	4.65
Higbee, Jay A. 91		15/12	15052	12.85	3.65
Hildebrandt, Charles A. 13		23/9	63-2503	6.20	3.00
Hill, Adelaide C. 20					
Hill, Mozell C. 8					
Hill, William B. 39		20/3	59-3196	9.25	3.00

	Page	DA	Order No.	Xerographic Copy	Microfilm Copy
Hillger, Martin E. 94		20/7	59-4011	14.85	4.25
Himes, Joseph S., Jr. 19					
Hindman, Baker M. 54		14/2	7101	8.20	3.00
Hinton, William H. 45					
Hirsch, Charles B. 78		14/4	7532	17.55	5.00
Hirshson, Stanley P. 84		22/12	62-1919	15.55	4.40
Hobson, Abigail K. 54		24/2	63-3719	10.35	3.00
Hodges, Louis W. 13		21/8	60-6032	13.75	3.90
Hodges, Ruth H. 2		27/4	66-9480	16.65	4.75
Hogen, Mildred E. 98					
Holland, Ira H. 13					
Holland, Jerome H. 34		13/6	6317	7.60	3.00
Holland, John B. 10		11/1	2206	15.30	4.35
Holland, Timothy J. 78					
Holley, James M. 45		19/2	58-2630	10.80	3.10
Holmes, Dwight O.W. 45					
Holmes, William F., III 74		25/4	64-10174	10.80	3.10
Holtzclaw, Thelbert E. 59		15/3	8151	12.15	3.45
Hong, Sung C. 13		20/12	60-858	9.90	3.00
Hooker, Emile N. 10					
Hooper, Robert E. 74		27/5	66-10702	11.70	3.35
Hoot, John W. 89					
Hopson, James O. 94					
Hopson, Raymond W. 45					
Hornseth, Richard A. 13					
Horowitz, Eugene L. 13					
Horowitz, Murray M. 74		16/2	15631	15.30	4.35
Houser, Leah S. 13		18/3	24250	12.15	3.45
Houser, Paul M. 30		9/1	1151	19.35	5.50
Howard, David H. 26		25/2	64-5458	13.30	3.80
Howard, John R. 2		26/11	66-2569	10.80	3.10
Howard, Victor B. 78		22/10	62-778	17.10	4.85
Howard, Warren S. 78					
Howell, Hazel W. 3		27/4	66-10295	15.30	4.30
Howell, William H. 26		18/6	58-2078	5.20	3.00
Hubert, Gadus J. 100					
Humes, Dollena J. 74		17/6	18019	19.15	5.45
Humiston, Thomas F. 45		20/8	59-3665	7.00	3.00
Hunter, Robert W. 45					
Hurd, Merrill F. 36		21/9	61-511	17.55	4.95
Hurst, Robert L. 31		15/1	9181	10.80	3.05
Hutson, Darlene L. 54		25/9	65-1437	10.80	3.10
Hypps, Irene C. 32					
Ilardi, Robert L. 21		27/6	66-12609	3.80	3.00
Ingram, Sam H. 69		20/4	59-4257	8.60	3.00
Isler, Stanley M. 26		25/1	64-5684	6.80	3.00
Itzkoff, Seymour W. 14		26/2	65-8845	11.50	3.25
Ives, Chauncey B. 95					

	Page	DA	Order No.	Xerographic Copy	Microfilm Copy
Jackson, Earl C.	65				
Jackson, Ervin, Jr.	59	24/3	63-6705	4.80	3.00
Jackson, George B.	95	13/3	5049	10.60	3.05
Jackson, Julia	45				
Jackson, Kenneth T.	84				
Jackson, Luther P.	78				
Jackson, Margaret Y.	78				
Jackson, Reid E.	45				
Jackson, Thomas A.	34	23/9	63-2175	9.90	3.00
Jackson, William S.	66	15/2	10634	9.00	3.00
Jacobs, Mary G.	45	18/5	25494	11.05	3.15
Jacobson, Paul H.	5	12/4	3894	8.60	3.00
Jaffe, Bernard D.	66	27/6	66-10112	6.00	3.00
Jahn, Julius A.	1				
James, Stuart B.	95	21/6	60-4288	8.60	3.00
Jans, Ralph T.	91				
Jay, Florence E.	8	16/12	18239	10.15	3.00
Jenkins, Clara B.	45	26/7	65-12946	7.20	3.00
Jenkins, John J.	3				
Jenkins, Martin D.	26				
Jenkins, Shirley	14	18/3	58-633	12.60	3.60
Jerrems, Raymond L.	36				
Johnson, Autrey B.	59	23/9	62-6564	5.00	3.00
Johnson, Beulah V.	95	16/3	15566	25.20	7.05
Johnson, Clifton H.	78	20/7	59-5561	26.80	7.55
Johnson, Everett O.	74	18/6	58-1420	12.60	3.60
Johnson, George L.	26	16/12	18098	8.20	3.00
Johnson, Harry A.	45				
Johnson, Henry M.	72				
Johnson, Howard M.	69				
Johnson, Keith W.	34				
Johnson, Kenneth L.	30	20/6	59-5537	15.30	4.35
Johnson, Lulu M.	78				
Johnson, Mayme E.L.	57				
Johnson, Norman C.	69	14/4	7906	8.40	3.00
Johnson, Norman J.	46	21/12	61-1753	17.80	5.00
Johnson, Robert B.	8	15/12	15018	23.20	6.50
Johnson, Ruth B.	46				
Johnston, Andrew V.	62	25/3	64-7971	8.60	3.00
Johnston, James H.	78				
Johnston, William E., Jr.	46				
Johnstone, Ronald L.	3	25/3	64-8178	9.25	3.00
Jones, Arlynne L.	66	21/10	61-800	6.20	3.00
Jones, Bobby F.	78	26/7	65-14357	12.40	3.55
Jones, Butler A.	37	18/6	24441	26.80	7.55
Jones, Clifton R.	20				
Jones, Douglas R.	69	19/11	59-1106	13.50	3.85
Jones, Katherine L.S.	57	27/5	66-11609	4.40	3.00
Jones, Richard M.	26				

	Page	DA	Order No.	Xerographic Copy	Microfilm Copy
Jones, Roy J.	14	22/5	61-3714	7.20	3.00
Jones, Samuel O.	59	25/2	64-5965	8.00	3.00
Jones, Thomas B.	14				
Jones, Tom M.	66	16/8	16959	5.80	3.00
Jones, Wendell P.	98				
Jordan, Winthrop D.	78	23/5	62-5752	17.35	4.90
Jowers, Joseph B.	3				
Jung, Raymond K.	11	24/12	64-5327	9.90	3.00
Justice, David B.	19	27/6	66-10352	12.85	3.65
Kafka, Francis J.	46	27/4	66-10298	10.35	3.00
Kahn, Lessing A.	14	10/3	1730	5.60	3.00
Kaiser, Louis H.	54	21/11	61-1343	5.20	3.00
Kamii, Constance K.	6	26/12	66-5089	7.40	3.00
Kaplan, Harold	89	22/5	61-3442	20.25	5.75
Kapos, Andrew	14	13/3	5053	9.25	3.00
Karashkevych, Boris	6	26/9	65-6639	7.60	3.00
Karon, Bertram P.	26	19/11	58-7852	9.45	3.00
Katzenmeyer, William G.	21	24/5	63-2227	4.40	3.00
Kaufman, Mae E.	62	21/9	60-6059	7.40	3.00
Kean, George G.	6	26/4	65-8827	11.95	3.40
Kearney, Kevin E.	84	20/12	60-1904	13.95	3.95
Keeler, Kathleen F.R.	54	25/2	64-4194	4.60	3.00
Kegley, Tracy M.	72				
Kelley, Glen E.	62	22/12	62-2278	4.40	3.00
Kelley, Joseph B.	32	24/10	64-2763	13.95	4.00
Kelsey, George D.	84	27/6	65-2492	12.85	3.65
Kennedy, James S.	100	23/2	62-1470	7.80	3.00
Kennedy, Joseph C.	46	19/2	58-2690	5.80	3.00
*Kephart, John E.	98	21/2	60-2543		3.15
Kettig, Thomas H.	62	17/6	21481	5.40	3.00
Khoshboo, Yousef D.	14	25/5	64-7355	16.65	4.70
Kiah, Calvin L.	54				
Kidd, Richard D.	46	20/4	59-4278	10.15	3.00
Kiehl, Robert E.	34	18/5	225/1	11.25	3.25
Kifer, Allan F.	84	22/3	61-3124	13.75	3.90
King, Charles E.	6				
King, Karl B., Jr.	6	25/4	64-10587	5.40	3.00
King, Louis E.	11	26/6	65-4575	7.60	3.00
Kirk, James H.	8				
Kirkhart, Robert O.	26	20/10	60-1190	7.20	3.00
Kittles, Emma L.	31	22/11	62-2145	9.45	3.00
Kittrell, Flemmie P.	6				
Kleiman, Bert M.	57				
Knight, Charles L.	46				
Knuth, Helen E.	84	19/6	58-5763	15.75	4.45
Koepper, Robert C.	63	27/5	66-11231	7.80	3.00
Konietzko, Kurt O.	19	20/2	59-2657	10.80	3.10

* Although the microfilm copy is satis-
factory, the xerographic copy is not
considered legible enough for distribution.

	Page	DA	Order No.	Xerographic Copy	Microfilm Copy
Kooker, Arthur R.	78				
Koontz, Miriam E.	26	16/1	15468	5.40	3.00
Koponen, Niilo E.	69				
Korn, Shirley	6	25/3	64-10009	7.20	3.00
Kostiuk, Nick	57	24/12	64-5373	6.20	3.00
Kramer, Alfred S.	3	15/10	13621	14.20	4.05
Kramer, Samuel A.	19	22/7	61-5097	7.40	3.00
Kraus, Sidney	14	20/6	59-5720	6.20	3.00
Krueger, Thomas A.	84	26/7	65-15202	17.80	5.00
Kupferer, Harriet J.	54	15/2	10672	6.20	3.00
Ladd, Everett C., Jr.	89	25/7	64-13810	18.90	5.35
Lamanna, Richard A.	63				
Landa, Bjarne E.	95	12/2	3949	14.40	4.10
Landau, Claire	14	17/9	21800	15.10	4.25
Lanier, Raphael O.	46	18/6	58-634	15.10	4.25
Lash, John S.	65,95				
Lashley, Leonard C.	74				
Lawner, Rhoda L.	14	16/8	16597	20.25	5.70
Lawrence, Charles R.	84	13/1	4577	18.00	5.10
Lawson, Hilda J.	97				
Lawton, Samuel M.	3				
LeBeau, Oscar R.	46				
Lee, Carleton L.	8				
Lee, Lurline M.	46	15/6	12151	13.30	3.80
Lefcourt, Herbert M.	26	24/11	64-6926	4.40	3.00
Lent, Richard A.	14				
Leonard, Rev. Joseph T.	3	24/4	63-7566	19.80	5.60
Leonard, Neil Jr.	100				
Lepper, Robert E.	57	26/8	65-15475	5.40	3.00
Leslie, william R.	78				
Levin, Hannah A.	26	25/12	64-10931	4.80	3.00
Lewis, Dorothy G.	14	23/1	62-1109	11.05	3.15
Lewis, Edward S.	8	22/2	61-2556	15.10	4.30
Lewis, Elmer C.	72	17/10	22853	9.70	3.00
Lewis, Ruth B.	74	23/8	63-65	6.40	3.00
Lewis, William J.	72	15/12	14319	16.65	4.75
Liedel, Donald E.	95	22/6	61-6385	12.60	3.60
Lightfoote, William E.	46	22/3	61-3214	5.60	3.00
Lincoln, Charles E.	3	21/5	60-3466	18.45	5.25
Lindenfeld, Frank	89	22/12	62-1923	10.60	3.00
Lindner, Ronald S.	21	23/2	62-3512	5.20	3.00
Lindsay, Crawford B.	78				
Lindsay, Inabel B.	84				
Lines, Stiles B.	79	21/4	60-3107	14.65	4.15
Linnehan, Edward G.	97	13/3	3967	11.05	3.15
Linneman, William R.	95	21/6	60-3947	14.85	4.20
Lipscomb, Patrick C., III	79	20/12	60-1984	28.15	7.90
Litwack, Leon F.	79				

	Page	DA	Order No.	Xerographic Copy	Microfilm Copy
Lively, Edwin L.	19	20/10	60-1198	4.20	3.00
Livingston, Omeda F.	32	25/10	65-973	7.60	3.00
Lloyd, Arthur V.	79				
Lloyd, Kent M.	35	25/2	64-7665	14.40	4.10
Loescher, Frank S.	3				
Lofton, Williston H.	72				
Logan, Frenise A.	85				
Lombard, Lee R.	95				
Lombardi, Donald N.	14	23/4	62-3769	7.20	3.00
Long, Herman H.	15	9/3	1349	10.35	3.00
Long, John C.	72	21/3	60-2779	13.30	3.75
Loop, Anne S.	35				
Loper, Doris J.	57	26/10	66-659	5.80	3.00
Lopez, Juan F.	63	27/2	66-7106	12.85	3.65
Lord, Francis A.	79	9/1	1162	25.65	7.25
Lorenzini, August P.	8	23/8	63-1168	20.05	5.65
Louie, James W.	26				
Lowe, Robert A.	85	26/11	66-1988	9.70	3.00
Lowry, Carmen E.	46	17/11	23016	8.60	3.00
Ludlum, Robert P.	74				
Luke, Orral S.	27				
Lumpkins, Josephine	79				
Lusienski, Dean R.	22	25/5	64-11936	6.20	3.00
Lyles, Joseph H.	36	19/6	58-5956	12.15	3.50
Lynn, Sister Annella	6				
Mabry, William A.	85				
Machover, Solomon	22				
MacKenzie, Barbara K.	15				
Macklin, Arnett G.	59				
Madden, Samuel A.	46				
Maddocks, Lewis I.	74	20/6	59-5918	14.20	4.05
Mahaffey, Theodore	54				
Mahar, Pauline M.	27	15/7	12370	19.35	5.45
Major, Anthony J.	63				
Maliver, Bruce L.	15	25/4	64-10006	8.00	3.00
Malone, Erwin L.	1	17/5	20587	17.35	4.90
Mandel, Bernard	79				
Mann, George L.	72				
Mann, Harold W.	74	23/12	63-3600	20.05	5.65
Mann, John H.	15	16/7	16905	3.80	3.00
Manners, George E., Sr.	32	20/8	60-133	23.65	6.70
Margolies, Edward L.	95	27/6	66-9543	19.60	5.50
Marion, Claud C.	46				
Marshall, David C.	46	17/12	17447	10.15	3.00
Martin, James G.	15	17/12	22697	9.25	3.00
Martin, Ralph H.	35	22/3	61-2874	6.00	3.00
Martin, Robert E.	89				
Martin, Walter T., Jr.	47	27/6	66-12743	9.25	3.00
Martin, William H.	63				

	Page	DA	Order No.	Xerographic Copy	Microfilm Copy
Mason, Julian D., Jr.	95	23/12	63-3505	13.75	3.90
Matthew, Eunice S.	63				
Mathews, Donald G.	3	25/6	64-13179	18.45	5.20
Matzen, Stanley P.	66	26/11	66-2518	7.00	3.00
Mauney, Jack E.	19				
Mawhinney, Eugene A.	91	16/2	15239	14.20	4.05
May, Clifford B.	69	25/1	64-5105	13.30	3.75
Mayhew, Bruce H., Jr.	1				
Mayhew, Leon H.	91				
Mayo, George E.	15				
Mays, Benjamin E.	95				
McBee, Susanna B.	92				
McCarrick, Earlean M.	69	25/12	65-4551	11.70	3.30
McClellan, James F.	47				
McConnell, Roland C.	85				
McCown, George W.	54	21/9	60-4928	8.20	3.00
McCuistion, Fred	47				
McCulloch, Samuel C.	75				
McDaniel-Teabeau, Hazel	101	20/11	59-6387	17.35	4.90
McDaniel, Vernon	47	23/3	62-3301	8.40	3.00
McDonald, Franklin R.	15				
McGinnis, Frederick A.	47				
McGuinn, Henry J.	91				
McGurk, Frank C.	66				
McIntyre, Jennie J.	6	27/4	66-9075	5.20	3.00
McKee, James W., Jr.	75	27/6	66-12773	14.65	4.15
McKee, Jay W.	38				
McKinney, Frederick J.D.	59	14/2	7011	9.90	3.00
McKinney, Richard I.	47				
McManus, Edgar J.	79	20/4	59-4077	14.20	4.00
McMillan, Naman M.	47	26/7	65-6605	9.70	3.00
McMillan, William A.	47	18/5	58-956	8.80	3.00
McPhail, James H.	63	24/11	64-4046	12.60	3.60
McPheeters, Alphonso A.	47				
McPherson, Phillip E.	70				
McQueen, Albert J.	10	20/5	59-4953	9.70	3.00
McQueen, Finley T.	47	18/6	58-2086	14.85	4.20
Meador, Bruce S.	37	20/5	59-4729	16.90	4.80
Meeks, Donald E.	20	27/6	66-907	6.00	3.00
Meese, Billie G.	19	22/9	61-6868	5.80	3.00
Meier, August	85	17/8	22058	44.50	12.50
Meldrum, George W.	79				
Mellette, Peter	85				
Menchan, William M.	47				
Merbaum, Ann D.	27	23/2	62-3140	7.40	3.00
Merkel, Benjamin	79				
Mermelstein, Egon	57	26/2	65-8396	4.20	3.00
Merrill, Pierce K.	67	13/1	4505	7.60	3.00
Meyer, Alan S.	70	23/9	63-1504	19.15	5.40

	Page	DA	Order No.	Xerographic Copy	Microfilm Copy
Meyers, Alfred V.	37	25/9	65-1840	9.00	3.00
Milam, Albert T.	8	20/7	59-5496	4.60	3.00
Miller, George R., Jr.	54				
Miller, James E.	89				
Miller, James O.	67	24/12	64-5086	4.60	3.00
Miller, Kenneth C.	47	19/7	58-7188	12.15	3.45
Miller, Robert M.	85	15/11	13115	35.75	10.05
Miller, Ruth V.	65	12/4	3906	21.60	6.05
Miner, John B.	67	15/11	13713	7.40	3.00
Minor, Edward O.	47	14/10	8934	14.85	4.20
Minor, Richard C.	10				
Misra, Bhaskar D.	6				
Mitchell, Chloe H.	22	24/6	64-213	4.80	3.00
Mitchell, Frank J.	85	23/9	63-1407	20.95	5.90
Mitchell, Howard E.	20	11/2	2370	6.00	3.00
Mock, Wayne L.	31	26/5	65-11001	8.60	3.00
Mondlane, Eduardo C.	27	21/6	60-4780	6.60	3.00
Montell, William L.	95	25/11	65-3502	27.70	7.80
Mooney, Chase C.	79				
Mooney, Horace W.	31	13/3	5075	10.60	3.05
Moore, Bradley G., Jr.	63	20/10	60-1203	14.65	4.15
Moore, Parlett L.	55				
Moore, Ross H.	85				
Moore, Wilbert E.	79				
Moore, William Jr.	57	25/8	64-13475	10.80	3.10
Moore, William F., Jr.	10	19/8	58-729	5.60	3.00
Moore, William L.	95				
Moreland, Agnes L.	95	21/5	60-3118	11.25	3.25
Morello, Michael	19	19/8	58-1980	6.40	3.00
Morgan, John W.	47				
Morrison, Alexander H.	35	20/4	59-4240	17.80	5.05
Morrison, Marshall L., Jr.	8	23/10	63-2180	10.15	3.00
Morrison, Richard D.	35	14/8	8506	11.25	3.25
Morrow, Ralph E.	3	14/4	7535	16.45	4.65
Morrow, Robert O.	59	22/5	61-4556	9.70	3.00
Morse, Carlton H.	59	20/7	59-5497	6.80	3.00
Morsell, John A.	89	11/4	2842	10.15	3.00
Mosby, Reba S.	91	21/10	61-761	10.35	3.00
Mose, Ashriel I.	67	18/6	25498	6.80	3.00
Moseley, Thomas R.	79	26/4	65-1691	17.35	4.90
Moses, Earl R.	10	10/4	2055	13.75	3.90
Moss, James A.	63	18/2	25148	14.65	4.15
Mudd, Sister Rita	65	22/9	61-6480	18.70	5.30
Mugge, Robert H.	10				
Mugrauer, Bertha M.M.	8				
Muhyi, Ibrahim A.	15	12/4	3908	4.40	3.00
Mundy, Paul W.	35				
Murphy, Ella L.	47	21/11	61-341	16.90	4.75
Murray, Alexander L.	79	21/4	60-3674	27.25	7.65
Murray, Constance C.	79	21/4	60-3472	20.70	5.85

	Page	DA	Order No.	Xerographic Copy	Microfilm Copy
Murray, Thelma T.	48				
Murray, Thomas J.	101	21/11	61-1770	7.20	3.00
Murray, Walter I.	22				
Muse, Charles S.	59	25/6	64-13353	5.00	3.00
Mussen, Paul H.	15				
Myers, James G.	100	26/6	65-8852	5.80	3.00
Myers, John L.	79	21/11	61-1895	33.75	9.50
Needham, Walter E.	27	27/5	66-11849	7.80	3.00
Neilson, Herman N.	48	16/6	16618	17.55	4.95
Nelson, Bernard H.	91				
Nelson, John H.	95		OP 41753	5.95	3.00
Nelum, Junior N.	63				
Neumann, Holm W.	30	23/6	62-5066	5.60	3.00
Newbold, Catharine	79	23/6	63-1920	22.30	6.30
Newborn, Captolia D.	3				
Newsom, Lionel H.	91	16/6	16629	6.40	3.00
Neyland, Leedell W.	85	20/2	59-2450	9.90	3.00
Nicholas, James F.	48				
Nichols, Charles H., Jr.	95				
Nicholson, Elsie M.	57	27/3	66-8020	13.30	3.75
Nicholson, Lawrence E.	59				
Nielson, Alfred M.	15	16/4	16091	5.40	3.00
Nilon, Charles H.	96		S214		
Noble, Jeanne L.	48				
Noel, Donald L.	15	22/11	62-956	17.35	4.90
Nolen, Claude H.	85	24/6	64-101	17.55	4.95
Norris, Clarence W.	27				
Northrup, Herbert R.	35				
Norton, L. Wesley	98	20/8	60-222	14.20	4.05
Nyabongo, Virginia S.	48				
Oak, Vishnu V.	48				
Oaks, Harold R.	98	25/9	65-139	8.40	3.00
O'Brien, Kenneth B., Jr.	38	16/10	17732	14.85	4.25
O'Brien, William J.	19	24/12	64-5330	6.20	3.00
O'Dell, Richard F.	80	8/2	1069	19.60	5.50
Ohsberg, Harry O.	3	26/1	65-7939	7.60	3.00
Oliver, Clinton F., Jr.	96				
Oliver, Leavy W.	35	16/12	17972	11.70	3.35
Olson, Edwin	80				
Omari, Thompson P.	10				
Onwuachi, Patrick C.	3	25/1	64-4264	8.80	3.00
Oppenheimer, Martin	92	24/6	63-7075	14.20	4.00
Orbell, John M.	92	27/1	66-4724	8.60	3.00
O'Reilly, Charles T.	15	16/5	15676	10.80	3.05
Orr, Charles W.	48				
Orr, Clyde L.	48	26/8	65-15160	10.60	3.00
Orr, Oliver H., Jr.	75	19/9	59-55	24.55	6.90

	Page	DA	Order No.	Xerographic Copy	Microfilm Copy
Osborne, William A.	4	14/12	10273	11.25	3.20
Osofsky, Gilbert	85	27/6	65-7467	12.40	3.55
Owens, Robert L. III	48	13/6	6548	10.35	3.00
Pace, Walter T.	27	22/10	62-915	7.00	3.00
Paige, Joseph C.	48	26/4	65-9937	11.05	3.15
Palmer, Edward N.	35				
Pardoe, T. Earl	101				
Park, Lawrence	15	11/1	2194	10.15	3.00
Parker, Marjorie H.	72				
Parmee, Leila K.	27	27/1	66-6897	9.25	3.00
Parrish, Charles H., Jr.	8				
Partridge, Gaines R.	27	22/9	62-136	6.80	3.00
Patterson, Cecil L.	100	22/4	61-3577	12.15	3.45
Patterson, Joseph N.	48	17/4	20423	15.75	4.45
Payne, Joseph A.	48	18/3	24836	10.80	3.10
Payne, William V.	48	26/11	66-1814	12.40	3.55
Pearson, Colbert H.	4	8/2	983	6.00	3.00
Pecilunas, Leonard P.	19	26/10	66-2098	5.60	3.00
Peck, Richard C.	72				
Pemberton, Zelda C.	59	7/1	821	5.80	3.00
Pembrook, Carrie D.	97				
Pender, William M.	55	21/6	60-4574	12.85	3.65
Pendleton, Lawson A.	80	25/3	65-9047	17.55	5.00
Pendleton, Othniel A.	80				
Penetar, Michael P.	4				
Perez, Joseph A.	4	25/5	64-11646	9.90	3.00
Perpener, John O., Jr.	38				
Perry, Benjamin L., Jr.	39	15/1	10601	17.35	4.90
Perry, James O.	48	23/5	62-4807	11.05	3.15
Pettigrew, Thomas F.	15				
Pettit, Paul B.	96				
Pfanner, Daniel J.	72				
Phansomboom, Somsak	30	14/2	7059	3.00	3.00
Phelps, Ralph A., Jr.	48				
Phillips, Augustus C.	48				
Phillips, Ernest C., Jr.	63	17/2	20011	10.80	3.10
Phillips, Paul D.	85	26/1	65-1813	16.20	4.60
Phillips, William M., Jr.	35				
Picher, Oliver L.	16	27/2	66-7367	6.40	3.00
Pierce, Juanita G.	49	MA 7/1	803	10.15	3.00
Pierro, Armstead A.	49	23/9	63-429	16.20	4.60
Pierro, Earl H.	59	15/6	12119	5.40	3.00
Pinkney, Alphonso	16	22/8	61-6758	13.05	3.70
Pinnock, Theodore J.	39	26/6	65-9257	6.00	3.00
Pirkle, William B.	49	16/11	19394	9.45	3.00
Pisani, Lawrence F.	16				
Piscopo, John	30	21/10	60-6430	11.70	3.35
Pitkin, Victor E.	63	11/1	2195	19.60	5.50
Pitman, Dorothy E.	27	21/7	60-4855	11.05	3.15

	Page	DA	Order No.	Xerographic Copy	Microfilm Copy
Pitts, Nathan A.	8				
Pitts, Willis N., Jr.	101	12/4	3790	14.20	4.05
Platter, Allen A.	20	22/7	61-5678	11.95	3.40
Player, Raleigh P., Jr.	96	27/2	66-6678	6.40	3.00
Pogue, Betty C.	27	26/6	64-10468	6.00	3.00
Pool, Frank K.	4				
Porch, Marvin E.	20				
Poulos, Nicholis	55	27/2	66-6680	10.15	3.00
Powe, Alphonso S.	92	15/6	11948	8.80	3.00
Powell, Alice M.	16	20/1	59-2535	7.60	3.00
Powell, Christus N.	60	24/12	64-5382	6.20	3.00
Powell, Edward C.	27				
Powell, Ingeborg B.	92	26/7	65-13566	16.90	4.80
Powell, Milton B.	80	24/11	64-3415	11.25	3.20
Powers, Thomas J.	75	27/3	66-6161	6.00	3.00
Prestwood, Charles M., Jr.	4	21/5	60-3477	20.05	5.65
Price, Arthur C.	27	15/12	14338	5.40	3.00
Pride, Armistead S.	98		S-272		
Psaltis, Betty	16	24/7	64-1495	8.80	3.00
Puckett, John R.	49	20/11	59-6287	7.80	3.00
Purifoy, Lewis M., Jr.	80	26/10	66-4728	10.80	3.10
Qualls, Youra T.	80				
Quarles, Benjamin A.	75				
Quinn, Alfred T.	70	25/1	64-7312	6.40	3.00
Rabassa, Gregory	96	14/11	10182	13.50	3.85
Rachiele, Leo D.	22				
Rackley, Larney G.	49	23/12	63-3795	4.60	3.00
Ragan, Roger L.	16	24/6	63-7237	10.60	3.05
Rall, Clifford L.	63				
Rand, Earl W.	49				
Rasmussen, Donald E.	16	12/3	3597	16.00	4.55
Rast, Robert	16	24/11	64-2851	3.00	3.00
Ratner, Lorman A.	80	22/5	61-4888	11.95	3.40
Rawick, George P.	85	20/12	60-1883	18.90	5.30
Raymond, Richard D.	35	24/9	64-1996	9.70	3.00
Rea, Katharine	49	19/9	59-418	10.60	3.05
Record, Cy W.	85				
Redcay, Edward E.	55				
Reddick, Lawrence D.	98				
Redekop, Calvin	16				
Reed, William T.	49				
Reeves, Earl Y.	19	23/12	63-4169	6.60	3.00
Reeves, Elizabeth W.	101				
Reeves, Walter P., Jr.	96	24/10	64-2838	22.30	6.30
Refsell, Oliver M.	80	20/5	59-4735	60.50	16.90
Reid, Ira DeA.	1				
Reid, Robert D.	80				

	Page	DA	Order No.	Xerographic Copy	Microfilm Copy
Reilley, Edward C.	80				
Reimers, David M.	85	22/3	61-2975	15.75	4.45
Reinders, Robert C.	80	18/2	25174	39.65	11.15
Reuben, Anna M.D.	55	27/1	66-2664	14.85	4.25
Reuter, Frederick W.P.	70	23/3	62-1448	11.70	3.30
Reynolds, Jack Q.	72	17/8	21955	8.60	3.00
Rice, Jessie P.	72				
Rice, Pamela H.	38				
Richards, Eugene S.	1				
Richards, Violet K.	49				
Richardson, Harry Van B.	4				
Richardson, Joe M.	85	24/11	64-3611	18.25	5.15
Richardson, John F., III	49	24/7	64-265	8.80	3.00
Ricks, George R.	100	21/5	60-4788	19.35	5.45
Ridley, Walter N.	49	14/7	7984	11.05	3.15
Riggs, Sidney N.	37				
Risen, Maurice L.	38				
Rivers, Marie D.	63	20/4	59-3954	13.75	3.90
Robert, Edward B.	72				
Roberts, John L.	55	22/12	62-2409	12.60	3.60
Roberts, Rev. Richard J.	32	22/9	61-6488	20.05	5.65
Roberts, Shearley O.	27				
Roberts, Tommy L.	39	26/2	65-9137	11.50	3.30
Robinson, Andrew A., Jr.	57	24/8	64-1499	10.15	3.00
Robinson, Donald L.	80	27/6	66-11043	26.10	7.35
Robinson, James H.	86				
Robinson, Leonard H.	10				
Robinson, William H.	49	15/2	10646	21.15	5.95
Roche, Richard J.	49				
Rochelle, Charles E.	49				
Rodgers, E. George	67	17/5	21716	6.20	3.00
Roebuck, Julian B.	19	20/9	59-2798	20.05	5.65
Roethler, Michael D.	80	25/6	64-13229	12.85	3.70
Rogers, Oscar A., Jr.	55	21/3	60-2772	5.00	3.00
Romanoli, Peter J.	38	26/6	65-8314	7.80	3.00
Roseman, Tena M.	28	23/3	62-3287	5.00	3.00
Rosenblum, Abraham L.	21	20/12	59-4399	12.60	3.55
Rosengarten, Leonard	19	20/1	59-2344	6.40	3.00
Rosner, Joseph	16	14/12	8010	11.05	3.15
Ross, Bernard	16	19/4	58-3727	9.25	3.00
Rousseve, Ronald J.	28	19/3	58-3082	13.05	3.70
Rowland, Monroe K.	55	21/8	60-6924	8.40	3.00
Ruchames, Louis	35	11/3	2856	22.05	6.20
Rudwick, Elliott M.	75	16/9	17269	31.80	8.95
Ryder, Jack M.	64	23/12	63-3740	11.25	3.25
Rydman, Edward J., Jr.	6	26/7	65-13277	8.00	3.00
St. Clair, Sadie D.	75	8/1	938	15.10	4.25
St. John, Nancy H.	67				

	Page	DA	Order No.	Xerographic Copy	Microfilm Copy
Sain, Leonard F.	60	27/4	66-10119	10.15	3.00
Samelson, Babette F.	16				
Samples, Ralph E.	72	27/3	66-8205	14.40	4.10
Sanders, Charles D.	49	24/9	64-2380	12.60	3.60
Sandford, Paul L.	50	26/10	66-4451	8.40	3.00
Sandle, Floyd L.	97	20/7	59-5527	13.95	4.00
Sandmeier, Thelma L.	57	25/12	65-6566	7.20	3.00
Samuels, Ivan G.	67	19/6	58-2934	5.80	3.00
Sartain, James A.	70	27/5	66-10999	7.60	3.00
Satterwhite, Mildred M.	60				
Satneck, Walter J.	50	24/4	63-5380	13.05	3.75
Saunders, Mauderie H.	22	22/2	61-2905	8.00	3.00
Saunders, Socrates W.	37				
Savage, William S.	80				
Savoca, Anthony F.	67	26/4	65-11405	3.00	3.00
Sawyer, Robert M.	50	27/4	66-9000	17.10	4.80
Sawyers, Emanuel C.G.	65	24/5	63-8086	6.60	3.00
Sayler, Edward	8				
Scarborough, William K.	80	23/12	63-3516	13.75	3.90
Schaefer, Dorothy F.	22	26/8	65-14987	6.00	3.00
Scharf, Richard K.	70				
Scheiner, Seth M.	86	24/5	63-7231	11.25	3.20
Schietinger, Egberg F.	33				
Schnell, Kempes Y.	81	15/9	12643	16.20	4.60
Schnitzer, Maxine M.	101	23/6	62-4460	12.85	3.65
Schrader, Donald R.	67	25/5	64-8710	10.60	3.05
Schoen, Harold	81				
Scott, John I.E.	64				
Scott, Will B.	50	26/10	65-14068	5.00	3.00
Scott, Woodrow W.	16	20/9	59-6400	13.05	3.75
Scroggs, Jack B.	86				
Scruggs, Sherman D.	22				
Seagull, Arthur A.	21	26/3	65-3437	6.00	3.00
Seasholes, Bradbury	89	23/12	63-3518	13.95	3.95
Seifman, Eli	81	27/4	66-9519	9.45	3.00
Senior, Robert C.	81				
Seshachari, Candadai	86	25/4	64-8259	13.75	3.90
Shannon, Irwin V.	72				
Shapiro, Deborah	28	27/6	66-12592	23.65	6.70
Shapiro, Elliott S.	28	20/11	59-6252	8.40	3.00
Sharp, Evelyn W.	17	20/6	59-1021	11.70	3.35
Shaw, Van B.	86	11/4	2901	19.80	5.60
Shaw, Warren C.	81				
Shaw, William H.	64	24/8	64-1540	9.70	3.00
Sheeler, John R.	86				
Shelley, Herman W.	37	17/7	20779	14.65	4.20
Shenfeld, Nathan	17	18/6	58-1950	4.60	3.00
Shepard, Loraine V.	17	14/4	7723	12.40	3.50
Sherman, Alfonso	97	26/9	65-3518	11.95	3.40
Sherman, Sam	101	15/12	14081	16.90	4.80

	Page	DA	Order No.	Xerographic Copy	Microfilm Copy
Shipman, F. George	50	22/8	61-5828	11.05	3.15
Shockley, Grant S.	4				
Shootes, Queen Esther	50	25/12	65-6242	7.40	3.00
Sicha, Mary H.	28				
Sills, Joe F.	55	25/9	64-12530	15.55	4.40
Silver, Reuben	97	22/10	62-811	25.20	7.10
Silverman, Pincus	50	35/9	65-1151	5.80	3.00
Silvestro, Clement M.	86	21/11	60-4645	20.25	5.75
Simon, Walter A.	75	22/3	61-2570	9.70	3.00
Simpson, Albert F.	81				
Simpson, George E.	99				
Simpson, Hazel D.	64	24/6	63-7465	12.40	3.50
Simpson, William B.	37				
Sinclair, George H., Jr.	4	25/12	65-2679	13.95	4.00
Singer, Benjamin D.	28	26/12	66-4651	10.60	3.05
Singer, Lester C.	17	19/2	58-2603	13.95	4.00
Singletary, Otis A.	86				
Sio, Arnold A.	81	19/10	59-577	11.70	3.35
Sisk, Glenn N.	86				
Smart, Alice M.	37				
Smith, Benjamin F.	60	12/2	3452	6.80	3.00
Smith, Bettie M.S.	55	23/6	62-5352	14.40	4.05
Smith, Charles V.	8				
Smith, Donald H.	101	25/6	64-12753	17.35	4.90
Smith, Elizabeth C.	37	25/4	62-1454	16.00	4.50
Smith, Fred T.	17				
Smith, Helena M.	96	20/8	59-6799	18.90	5.35
Smith, James D.	86	21/8	60-4621	22.30	6.30
Smith, Paul M., Jr.	28	19/5	58-5216	10.35	3.00
Smith, Richard W.	75	20/6	59-5870	17.35	4.90
Smith, Robert G.	17				
Smith, Robert Gordon	81	24/2	63-5043	13.50	3.85
Smith, Wilfred R.	70	20/5	59-4706	12.60	3.60
Smith, William N.	67				
Smith, William P., Jr.	50	20/7	59-5329	9.25	3.00
Smolka, Richard G.	89	27/6	66-12815	17.80	5.05
Smothers, Robert L.	8	25/4	64-11047	9.00	3.00
Solomon, Thomas R.	89				
Spain, Rufus B.	86	22/4	61-3604	18.00	5.10
Spangler, Earl	86	22/3	61-2722	10.80	3.10
Spann, Annabelle E.	50	18/6	58-1931	7.60	3.00
Spear, Allan H.	86	26/4	65-9716	17.80	5.05
Speigner, Theodore R.	50	21/12	61-1793	14.85	4.25
Spellman, Cecil L.	55				
Spiaggia, Martin	28	19/12	59-1039	6.20	3.00
Spraggins, Tinsley L.	81	17/11	21968	11.50	3.30
Spruill, Albert W.	70	19/11	59-1518	7.80	3.00

	Page	DA	Order No.	Xerographic Copy	Microfilm Copy
Spurling, John J.	17	23/6	62-5353	6.20	3.00
Stamler, Rose S.	30				
Stanbury, Harry D.	39	27/6	66-8492	7.00	3.00
Stanton, William R.	81	16/12	19545	15.30	4.35
Star, Shirley A.	17				
Starlard, Victor D.	89	21/4	61-1350	6.80	3.00
Starling, Marion W.	96				
Starke, Catherine J.	96	24/1	63-5730	13.95	4.00
Staudenraus, Philip J.	81	21/9	60-6792	18.90	5.35
Stavisky, Leonard P.	81	18/7	58-2246	13.30	3.80
Steckler, George A.	28				
Steely, Will F.	81				
Stegall, Alma L.	55				
Steinberg, Aaron	96	27/5	66-9531	18.00	5.10
Stephens, Louise C.	9	17/12	24427	11.05	3.15
Stephenson, Chester M.	64				
Stewart, Richard H.	67	25/9	64-7602	12.40	3.50
Stewart, William W.	64				
Stinson, Harold N.	28	24/12	64-5089	5.60	3.00
Stirton, Thomas	81				
Stocking, George W., Jr.	86	21/5	60-3698	32.30	9.10
Stodolsky, Susan B.S.	6				
Stoff, Sheldon	70	26/1	65-6975	8.80	3.00
Stoker, Winfred M.	64	19/6	58-2654	7.00	3.00
Stone, Edith V.	9	21/7	60-4871	13.05	3.75
Stone, Olive M.	86				
Stone, Raymond P.	91	25/6	64-12140	18.25	5.15
Stone, William J.	30	27/3	66-8253	3.60	3.00
Stosberg, William K.	64	18/7	58-668	11.25	3.20
Stout, Charles O.	60				
Stowe, William M.	81				
Strickland, Arvarh E.	9	23/8	62-6236	12.60	3.60
Strickland, Shirley W.	87				
Strider, Rutherford H.	50	15/7	12241	9.70	3.00
Strong, Evelyn R.	73	22/5	61-5206	13.95	3.95
Strong, Samuel M.	9				
Strong, Willa A.	9	17/12	24429	11.25	3.20
Strother, David B.	38	19/11	59-587	9.00	3.00
Stump, William D.	81	23/2	62-3345	13.95	4.00
Sudnow, David N.	9	27/3	66-8405	12.85	3.65
Sullivan, Donald F.	91	26/5	65-4953	20.05	5.70
Sullivan, Floyd W.	55	25/4	64-6543	9.45	3.00
Sullivan, Troy G.	67	26/3	65-10074	5.60	3.00
Svoboda, William S.	55	26/1	65-7673	6.40	3.00
Sweat, Edward F.	82	17/10	22709	12.60	3.60
Swint, Henry L.	73				
Swinton, Sylvia P.	67	16/10	17781	5.80	3.00
Tabachnick, Benjamin R.	28	19/11	59-1430	4.20	3.00

	Page	DA	Order No.	Xerographic Copy	Microfilm Copy
Taeuber, Alma F.A. 33					
Taeuber, Karl E. 33					
Tate, Ernest C. 75		20/4	59-2092	8.00	3.00
Taylor, Alrutheus A. 87					
Taylor, Cyrus B. 50		16/5	15964	21.60	6.10
Taylor, Grady W. 11		19/2	58-2579	12.85	3.65
Taylor, Henry L. 56					
Taylor, Hubert V. 82		25/11	65-3316	13.05	3.70
Taylor, Joe G. 82					
Taylor, Joseph T. 51		14/4	7427	12.60	3.60
Taylor, Lloyd C., Jr. 75		16/12	19367	15.75	4.45
Taylor, Orville W. 82					
Taylor, Paul L. 51		19/9	58-5219	9.00	3.00
Taylor, Prince A., Jr.........51		9/1	1155	7.80	3.00
Taylor, Walter F., Jr.........96		25/5	64-11221	13.05	3.70
Ten Houten, Warren D. 56		26/9	66-444	22.75	6.40
Tewell, Fred 9		16/9	17454	11.50	3.25
Theman, Viola 68					
Thomas, Charles H., Jr. 17		20/7	59-5500	5.40	3.00
Thomas, Dominic R. 101		23/3	62-3918	18.45	5.25
Thomas, James S. 4					
Thomas, Leland C. 73		21/9	60-5867	9.00	3.00
Thomas, Paula J. 6		26/11	66-3046	11.05	3.20
Thomas, Ruth M. 65		7/1	820	13.75	3.90
Thomasson, Maurice E. 11					
Thompkins, Robert E. 73					
Thompson, Cleopatra D. 51		21/12	61-1111	8.60	3.00
Thompson, Daniel C. 64		16/8	17084	10.15	3.00
Thompson, Herbert W. 73		26/2	65-6769	9.70	3.00
Thompson, Ray 51		13/5	5937	9.45	3.00
Thornbrough, Emma L. 82					
Thornton, Peter B. 51		24/3	63-5901	6.80	3.00
Thorpe, Earlie E............87					
Threatt, Robert 68		24/2	63-5785	7.00	3.00
Tiber, Norman 22		24/3	63-6366	3.00	3.00
Tiedemann, John G. 17		22/4	61-3725	12.15	3.50
Tillman, Nathaniel P. 75		22/6	61-6003	13.95	4.00
Timmons, F. Alan 96					
Tindall, George B. 87					
Tingley, Donald F. 87					
Titus, Walter F. 28		27/6	66-12690	5.40	3.00
Todd, Hollis B. 101		26/8	66-753	13.30	3.75
Todd, Willie G. 82		26/3	65-9067	16.90	4.80
Toles, Caesar F..............51		13/5	5749	9.70	3.00
Tolleson, Sherwell K. 28		25/12	65-4070	8.40	3.00
Tolson, Arthur L. 87		27/6	66-11792	9.00	3.00
Tomasson, Richard F.........31		21/5	60-3618	18.00	5.10
Tomlinson, Helen 22					

	Page	DA	Order No.	Xerographic Copy	Microfilm Copy
Touchstone, Frank V.	29	17/7	21317	5.60	3.00
Towner, Lawrence W.	82	15/11	13145	21.60	6.10
Townes, Ross E.	51				
Traber, Michael	99	21/5	60-3762	15.10	4.25
Trent, Richard D.	29				
Troesch, Helen DeR.	97				
Troup, Cornelius V.	51				
Tullis, David S.	68	26/2	65-1464	6.40	3.00
Turner, Bridges A.	51				
Turner, Harold E.	70	17/3	19765	16.20	4.60
Turner, Howard	73				
Turner, James D.	89	17/1	17983	8.00	3.00
Tuttle, Lester E., Jr.	22	25/12	65-6012	5.40	3.00
Twersky, Atarah S.	82				
Tyer, Harold L.	38	26/9	66-92	11.95	3.40
Tyrrell, Frank E.	57	26/2	65-8925	11.95	3.40
Ulrich, William J.	87	20/9	60-802	18.00	5.05
Uzzell, Odell	60	19/10	59-432	6.60	3.00
Vader, Anthony J.	17				
Valdes, Donald M.	17	19/4	58-3468	4.80	3.00
Valentine, Foy D.	87				
Valien, Preston	1				
Van De Riet, Vernon	22	23/10	63-1832	4.40	3.00
Vander Zanden, James W.	87	19/6	58-5972	20.25	5.70
Van Wright, Aaron, Jr.	51	26/3	65-9758	5.20	3.00
Vardeman, Martha H.	56	20/12	60-1729	21.60	6.10
Vaughan, William P.	73	22/7	61-5130	14.20	4.05
Vega, Manuel	22	26/2	64-10590	3.00	3.00
Venable, Tom C.	73				
Vittenson, Lillian K.	29	26/6	65-12175	13.75	3.90
Voegeli, Victor J. III	82	27/2	66-1586	11.05	3.20
Walker, George H.	51	10/2	1569	7.40	3.00
Walker, Harry J.	9				
Walker, Jack L., Jr.	9	24/6	63-8045	9.70	3.00
Walker, John E.	37	24/6	64-730	7.60	3.00
Walker, Lewis	19	25/3	64-9596	5.00	3.00
Walker, Paul	38	21/11	61-406	17.10	4.80
Wallace, David A.	33				
Wallace, Elsie H.	58				
Walls, Jean H.	51				
Walton, Donald F.	29	26/5	65-4757	9.90	3.00
Walz, Robert B.	87	18/6	58-1675	27.25	7.65
Ward, John H.	51	15/12	12246	13.95	4.00
Ward, Judson C.	87				
Ware, Gilbert	91	23/9	63-572	9.90	3.00
Wargny, Frank O.	65	24/4	63-5656	13.75	3.90
Warnock, Henry Y.	87	24/9	64-2539	14.65	4.15

	Page	DA	Order No.	Xerographic Copy	Microfilm Copy
Washington, Justine W.	29	26/5	65-11694	8.20	3.00
Waskow, Arthur I.	20	24/6	64-621	14.20	4.00
Waters, E. Worthington	60				
Watkins, Elizabeth L.	31				
Watson, Ora V.R.	1	17/3	17456	15.75	4.45
Watson, William H.	60	10/1	1498	8.60	3.00
Watts, Frederick P.	20				
Watts, Lewis G.	10	25/8	64-12876	10.60	3.00
Wax, Darold D.	82	24/1	63-3147	18.90	5.35
Wayson, William W.	64				
Weatherford, Allen E. II	51				
Webb, Allie B.W.	87	23/3	62-3674	12.85	3.65
Webber, Irving L.	31	18/2	17457	16.45	4.70
Webster, Elizabeth J.	29	22/8	61-5486	5.60	3.00
Webster, Sherman N.	39	21/3	60-3017	15.10	4.30
Weddington, Rachel T.	21				
Welch, Lucille S.	52				
Wendel, Egon E.	17	22/12	62-1458	8.80	3.00
West, Earle H.	73	22/10	61-5832	29.95	8.40
West, Gordon L.	52	20/8	59-6590	10.60	3.05
Weston, Rev. M. Moran	87	14/10	8860	31.50	8.85
Wharton, Vernon L.	87				
Wheeler, Raymond H.	33	23/1	62-2805	9.45	3.00
Whitaker, Hugh S.	90	26/10	66-2102	10.15	3.00
White, Frank H.	87	21/11	61-705	12.15	3.45
White, Howard A.	87	20/3	59-1082	13.75	3.90
White, James C., Jr.	23	23/10	63-1834	5.00	3.00
White, Robert M.	92	25/9	65-339	12.60	3.55
Whitehead, Matthew J.	53	6/1	677	6.20	3.00
Whiting, Albert N.	4				
Whitmore, Paul G.	70	17/4	20501	4.00	3.00
Wight, Willard E.	82	19/10	58-5190	11.05	3.15
Wiley, Alfred D.	70	22/10	62-203	13.75	3.90
Wiley, Bell I.	88				
Wiley, Electa C.	96	25/10	65-1521	7.20	3.00
Wiley, Walter E.	38				
Wilhoit, Francis M.	90				
Wilkerson, Doxey A.	37	19/12	59-1026	17.80	5.05
Wilkinson, Rachel E.D.	52	13/1	4539	10.60	3.05
William, Joshua L.	52				
Williams, Cornelius A.	39	23/6	62-5838	8.80	3.00
Williams, Dorothy S.	1	22/1	61-2541	9.00	3.00
Williams, Frank B., Jr.	90	12/6	4411	15.75	4.50
Williams, Hazel B.	101	13/4	5429	15.75	4.50
Williams, Jayme C.	101	20/6	59-5949	14.85	4.25
Williams, Johnetta K.	58	13/1	4553	14.65	4.20
Williams, Percy V.	58	16/3	15555	10.60	3.05
Williams, Robert E.	17				

	Page	DA	Order No.	Xerographic Copy	Microfilm Copy
Williams, Thomas T. 31		15/11	14505	6.80	3.00
Williams, William J. 10		27/5	66-11597	12.85	3.65
Williams, Wyman L., Jr. 70		16/3	15802	5.40	3.00
Williamson, Edward C. 88		14/9	8593	17.10	4.80
Williamson, Joel R. 88		25/3	64-9108	27.45	7.70
Williamson, Juanita V. 101		21/12	61-1811	6.60	3.00
Willie, Charles V. 1		18/1	24139	14.85	4.20
Willis, Larry J. 68					
Wilson, Alan B. 68					
Wilson, Herbert A. 52					
Wilson, James Q. 9					
Wilson, John L. 23		17/10	22993	7.20	3.00
Wilson, John M. 20		26/9	65-4480	11.50	3.30
Wilson, Norman 31		21/8	60-6828	8.40	3.00
Wilson, Raleigh A. 88					
Wilson, Robert L. 4		19/6	58-5794	7.60	3.00
Winder, Alvin E. 17					
Winder, Thelma V. 52		18/3	58-501	13.95	4.00
Wingeier, Douglas E. 4		23/4	62-4559	35.00	9.85
Winslow, Samuel W. 6		24/7	64-1120	9.70	3.00
Winstead, Elton D. 38		27/6	66-13693	13.05	3.75
Wirth, Janina W. 64		27/5	66-11144	5.20	3.00
Wishart, Claire K. 58		26/2	65-2008	12.40	3.55
Wogaman, John P. 4		21/4	60-3493	15.30	4.35
Wolf, Eleanor P. 10		22/6	60-2334	13.95	3.95
Wood, Forrest G. 88		26/2	65-8284	19.15	5.40
Wooden, Ralph L. 56		17/5	20735	9.00	3.00
Woodmansee, John J., Jr. 18		26/11	66-3299	5.60	3.00
Woodson, Grace I. 52					
Woolridge, Nancy B. 96					
Works, Ernest 18		20/1	59-2068	7.20	3.00
Wormley, Margaret J. 96					
Wright, Howard E. 96					
Wright, Marion T. 73					
Wright, Stephen J. 73					
Wynes, Charles E. 88		21/8	60-4627	11.25	3.20
Yancey, Maude J. 64		12/4	3680	11.25	3.25
Yancey, Sadie M. 60					
Yanuck, Julius 82		13/3	5218	12.15	3.45
Yarbrough, Dean S. 11					
Yokley, Ratha L. 29					
Young, Kenneth E. 52		13/5	5822	9.70	3.00
Young, Marechal-Neil E. 11					
Young, Percy 52					
Young, Ulysses S. 29		26/8	66-1370	6.60	3.00
Young, William L. 18					
Zangrando, Robert L. 93		24/10	64-3516	22.75	6.40
Zilversmit, Arthur 82		24/6	63-5469	17.35	4.90
Zimbleman, Ernest A. 23		26/8	65-12253	9.90	3.00
Zion, Carol L. 71		26/12	66-5462	7.40	3.00